101 of the
Greatest Ideas in Management

101 of the Greatest Ideas in Management

Auren Uris

John Wiley & Sons

New York • Chichester • Brisbane • Toronto • Singapore

Library of Congress Cataloging in Publication Data:

Uris, Auren.
    101 of the greatest ideas in management.

    Includes index.
    1. Management. I. Title. II. Title: One hundred
one of the greatest ideas in management.
III. Title: One hundred and one of the
greatest ideas in management.
HD31.U658   1986   658   86-15663

    ISBN 0-471-01202-5
    ISBN 0-471-84278-8 (pbk)

Printed in the United States of America

10 9 8 7 6

Preface

This book offers you the management wisdom of scores of great minds, from the fifteenth century thinker Niccolò Machiavelli, to today's investigators, including Peter Drucker, B. F. Skinner, and Kurt Lewin. These contents contribute a resource to jog the memory and supply the means to solve current problems.

Brilliant scientists and practitioners have built a huge edifice of management wisdom. But entrance to the treasure house is blocked by guard dragons, whose collars bear the legends Time Waste, Where to Begin, and How Can I Tell the Good Ideas from the Bad. Obviously, the author had to play St. George to these challenges, and, having penetrated the treasure house, to decide what to take and what to set aside.

To become one of the 101, an Idea had to pass what I came to call the RPS test, that is, it had to have the following qualities:

- Relevance. Is the Idea of interest and use to today's hard-pressed executive?
- Practicality. Does it lend itself to a recommendation for use, as explicit as a recipe or the directions on a medicine bottle?
- Suitability. Is it flexible enough to fit into the repertory of the executive who is in pursuit of excellence, whether he or she works in a plant or office, in government or the private sector, in an organization large or small?

The emphasis on relevance was crucial. Countless ideas have flared on the management horizon, made their contribution, and disappeared into well-earned oblivion. I wanted to avoid a collection that reeked either of the cemetery or the museum.

As a result of the selection process, you will find in the pages ahead a galaxy of Ideas, some large in scope, others sharply focused. You will find the concept of Corporate Culture, with all its subtleties, along with The "Why Not?" Rejoinder, a simple phrase capable of communicating a potent motivational impulse.

Concepts have been included that, despite neglect, retain their usefulness for today's managers. Brainstorming (seemingly a fad, still produces worthwhile answers) and Participative Management (refined in Japan in Quality Circles), are examples of born-again seeds for action.

For some inclusions I ask your special acceptance. As the author of many books on management, I felt that two or three of my own ideas deserved a place, not as a self-indulgence, but because of their objective value. For example, Selective Leadership is the distillation of my book *Techniques of Leadership*. And Executive Dissent offers the core idea of my book of the same title.

The challenge of idea selection was followed by that of organizing the material for ready availability. I divided the material into four activity areas, or Parts, as follows: One, Dealing with People; Two, Procedures; Three, Lore and Insights; and Four, Self-Help. Another helpful detail is the triple listing of all 101 Ideas: They are listed in the Contents, under the headings of the four Parts, and finally, in a comprehensive alphabetical Index.

Any one of these Ideas, applied to your own situation, could pay for the reading time invested. Apply two Ideas and you are well ahead of the game. And the book provides a panorama of management thought and action that gives a useful framework of the field.

I am aware that many worthy ideas are not included, and make the traditional disclaimer that I alone am responsible for the final choices. In the end it was the limitation of space that forced decisions as between Idea A and B, the loser in each case being the one that failed the RPS test in some degree.

In doing the research I was struck by the brilliance of the people from whose minds sprang the insights that have helped transform management from a seat-of-the-pants activity to a profession on which progress, and indeed our civilization, depends. Just mentioning some of the names, Machiavelli, Pareto, Taylor, Mayo, Lewin, McGregor, Herzberg, Maslow, Skinner, Drucker, Follett, Strauss, and Sayles, builds a seminal c.eativity of impressive dimensions.

AUREN URIS

Lomala, Hopewell Junction, New York
August 1986

Acknowledgments

Credit is due the immensely capable individuals whose assistance made what at times seemed a back-breaking task, doable. Most have been thanked in person, but some deserve special mention:

For help with the production of the manuscript, Margaret Arthur, whose calm and continuing efforts kept the march of the manuscript on track, page by page.

Evelyn Mertens, who worked with me on the formative stages of structuring and writing the first Ideas.

Mike Holoszyc, who not only sold me my word processor, but helped me grope toward mastering it.

Marty Edelston and Marty Greenberg, president and director, respectively, of *Boardroom Reports,* with whom an early version of the book's concept was contemplated.

Mike Hamilton, an old friend and editor at John Wiley & Sons, who was quick to perceive and enthuse over the concept of the book, first mentioned casually over lunch in a Mexican restaurant in New York City.

And, saving the best for last, eternal gratitude to my wife, Doris Reichbart Uris, who fed me and read me, making corrections and suggestions along the way, so that the final product was rid of some poor thinking and writing, and achieved a higher level of excellence than it otherwise would have had.

A.U.

Contents

THREE. Lore and Insights 181

FOUR. Self-Help 245

101 of the
Greatest Ideas in Management
and How to Use Them

PART ONE

DEALING WITH PEOPLE

Managers work side by side with individuals and groups, striking sparks that can brighten or burn. The ideas in this Part can maximize your interactions with others for your mutual benefit and for the benefit of your organization.

Mentoring, Counseling, and extending Emotional First Aid to fellow human beings are signs of caring. Motivational Ideas from the Great Jackass Fallacy to Skinner's Behavior Modification can help you guide people to higher goals and performance. The following Ideas appear in this Part:

*   *   *

◁ **1**

Buddy System

CONCEPT

The Buddy System is a traditional and effective procedure for helping new employees adjust. First days on the job can be an ordeal, a needless handicap to the newcomer in becoming a contributor, mastering his or her duties, and satisfactorily integrating into the workgroup. The buddy approach provides a manager-appointed guide and mentor, chosen because of his or her familiarity with the company and the new employee's job. A friendly manner and the ability to smooth contacts between the rookie and coworkers further helps the newcomer feel welcome.

The value of the "Buddy" becomes clear when the newcomer's problems are listed:

- The boss is too busy to spend time with the beginner.
- Even groups without malice may not bother to make the person feel at home.
- Everything from the location of the restrooms to the best way to get around the office can be bewildering.
- Questions about the job can be answered immediately.
- The new employee has the security of a friend and an information source close at hand.

ACTION OPPORTUNITIES

Any time a new employee is brought in through hiring, transfer, or even on a temporary basis, the buddy procedure can serve the important function of easing and shortening the indoctrination period, and can get the individual off to the best possible start.

EXAMPLE

Department head Ted Wald has been so involved in discussing expansion plans for his area that when Jess Brown shows up to start his new job, the arrival is unexpected and has not been prepared for. Fortunately, Helen Graves, whose desk is next to Brown's, is an old-timer and a warm person. Instructions to Graves, explaining what Brown's indoctrination requires and an introduction between them suffice. Wald can go on to other things knowing that the newcomer is in good hands.

HOW TO USE

Consider using the Buddy System in any of the situations suggested in the previous Action Opportunities section. To make it work most advantageously:

1. Be sure the physical arrangements for the new employee are made in advance. Nothing that happens afterward can quite erase the putdown of a last-minute scramble to clean out a desk, provide necessary supplies, and so on.

2. Select the most appropriate person for the buddy role. Some of the qualifications suit all cases: friendliness, familiarity with the work, the department, the company, and the respect of the group. But other qualities, such as age, sex, willingness to take on the assignment of indoctrination, ability to accept the interruption of one's own work, will vary with your particular situation.

3. Explain what you want done. If the employee is an experienced buddy, all you may have to say is, "Go." If the buddy is not experienced, tell him or her in as much detail as necessary what the assignment consists of: Job training? Tour of the premises, the whole company, or just the department? Personal contact points, such as washrooms, coffee source, cafeteria, recreation or rest area? Any other departments, particularly those with which the newcomer will be working? Any people outside the department to be introduced, perhaps your boss, heads of adjoining areas, and so forth? Take the person to lunch?

4. If you can, check back once or twice to see how things are going, and to let the new employee know you're interested.

5. Try to see the buddy and his or her charge at the end of the day, to give the latter a chance to voice any questions or opinions, and to get the former's "report" as to how things are going.

This procedure has an important side benefit: It can also be a sign of favor and prestige, a reward for the buddy.

▷ **2**

Counseling

CONCEPT

Counseling consists of a one-to-one conversation in which managers try to help subordinates cope with problems that upset them. Call it an interview, talk, or meeting, it is the special tone of confidentiality and openness, the absence of judgmental statements by the interviewer, and the sharp focus on the employee's problem or situation that makes counseling work.

The procedure was developed at an electrical plant in Hawthorne, Illinois, where executives of the Western Electric Company and management experts from Harvard University joined in a study that came to be known as the Hawthorne Experiments (see page 200) designed to study the human factor in work. In the course of their investigations into motivation and productivity, it was found that employees upset by personal problems could have their peace of mind and their ability to perform restored by counseling from their immediate superiors or staff professionals.

ACTION OPPORTUNITIES

Counseling can help when an employee's will to work is marred by emotional upset created by problems on or off the job. According to Ray A. Killian, vice-president of Belk Stores of Charlotte, North Carolina, "There is a need for counseling when there are changes in an employee's attitude, behavior or job performance." Situations like these may suggest a need for counseling:

- *Mood change.* The employee is not his or her usual self.
- *Performance sag.* A good worker's output, for no obvious reason, becomes unsatisfactory.
- *Quarrelsomeness/irritability.* An ordinarily cooperative person becomes a behavior problem.
- *Fatigue.* An employee tires easily, without obvious physical cause.
- *Accident-proneness.* A careful worker has a series of mishaps.
- *Touchiness.* A cooperative employee suddenly resents criticism or suggestions.

- **Troublemaking.** An employee tosses monkey wrenches into the department's operation or interferes with the work of others.

EXAMPLES

1. *Manager Cy Miller realizes that his assistant has been stretching his lunch period. Occasionally he has returned from lunch smelling of alcohol, and is slow or erratic in the performance of his work.*

Miller asks the subordinate to see him at the end of the day. He picks the time because routine demands and interruptions are out of the way, and he wants a relaxed atmosphere. It takes two meetings before the assistant admits that he has a drinking problem, and another before it is agreed that he will seek help at an alcoholism treatment center affiliated with a local hospital.

The National Alcohol Council reports that 6 percent of the nation's workforce suffers some form of alcohol or drug abuse. The figures suggest that the average company probably includes a number of drug-troubled employees. Substantial dollar losses result from time lost, errors committed, need for replacement of absentees, to say nothing of the personal suffering.

In addition to those that are drug-related, problems like the following may benefit from counseling:

Conflict with other employees

Health

Finances

Family difficulties

2. *Senior accountant Mae Ford is over an hour late. Treasurer Phil Taylor is wondering why he hasn't heard from her when she comes into his office, obviously distraught. "Sorry, Phil. I had some trouble at home."*

Taylor closes the door. "Sit down, Mae. Perhaps you'd better tell me about it."

"I hate to burden you, but I don't know what to do . . ."

Taylor nods encouragingly and the woman continues, "Al and I have been having problems for several months. Last night he packed up and left, to live with a girl friend. And our kids are only six and eight . . ."

Taylor says, "I can understand that you're upset, and the company and I will do everything we can to help."

Mae Ford says that the first thing she wants is a modified work schedule to make arrangements for care of the kids. Her boss helps her plan new starting and quitting hours, and adds, "Our personnel office has lists of all kinds, from baby sitters to agencies that specialize in marital difficulties. I'm sure you will come out all right, just don't let it get you down. And call on me if there is anything else I can do to help."

HOW TO USE

Some executives like to counsel, while others try to avoid it. But usually managers must counsel—not necessarily at length—but enough to show concern and render assistance where possible. Most managers see it as an obligation of the superior/subordinate relationship. Here are the basic steps:

1. Be aware of the need. Counseling is usually triggered by what some observers call the "Counseling Chain," a cause-and-effect relationship among four factors. Here is how the Chain might look in the Taylor-Ford situation:

The Counseling Chain

Problem →	Personal Symptoms →	Job Symptoms →	Company Losses
Marital difficulties.	Emotional upset. Distraction from work. Lessened job interest.	Attendance difficulty. Interference with work.	Increased cost. More supervision needed. Possible quit.

2. Trigger. Watch for a signal suggesting that counseling may be required. Sometimes the employee will ask for help. At other times you may have to take the initiative.

3. Distinguish between the two counseling approaches:

■ *Informal (also called nondirected).* This is a free-flowing conversation between executive and subordinate, to seek causes of and remedies to the problem. In some cases, the cause may not be identifiable, or even matter. The employee participates in moving the conversation towards its goals. The interviewer may ask, to expedite a lagging exchange, "Why do you think Chris behaved that way?" Questions like this can be the manager's chief tool to keep the other actively adding input.

■ *Formal (also called directed).* Here the counseling is a company-sponsored and taught procedure. Managers may counsel, but specialists may also be available, either from Personnel or from the outside. The formal approach has the advantage of setting limits and setting a clear conversational path. But it is less flexible and may not elicit the openness that a no-holds-barred talk can.

4. Sharpen your technique. Consider these guidelines:

■ Show courtesy, attention, patience and sincerity to the other person.

■ Promise confidentiality and maintain it absolutely.

■ Let the employee set the pace but ask questions necessary for clarification.

■ Try to pinpoint the real problem. It may be hidden by the employee's reticence, or even ignorance of what is really wrong. Probe tactfully, stopping if the resistance is too strong. But your ace, if it needs playing, is to point out the consequences of the problem for the employee—sagging performance, and any other symptoms causing discomfort. These, in most cases, will win cooperation.

■ Get acceptance. If there are moves you must make—for example, "I will have to give you another assignment, at least temporarily,"—let the employee know what you intend to do, why, and when you intend to do it. Also, get agreement on moves required by the employee, for instance, "All right, I promise to report to the clinic every Wednesday."

■ Are other managers involved? For example, a financial problem such as a garnishee of earnings may require action by a member of Personnel, but *you* may have to bring manager and employee together.

5. Don't take on the employee's burden. Here are three temptations managers must resist:

■ Don't give advice, especially in professional areas. Legal, medical, or financial guidance, if required, should be given by lawyers, doctors, or financial experts.

■ Avoid specific recommendations. For example, "See Dr. Smith, he's a very good dermatologist," sounds innocent enough. But Dr. Smith is your doctor, and if anything goes wrong, you are open to blame. If professional help is needed, have the subordinate check with Personnel, or recommend general sources, such as local banks or a medical association, to suggest specific services or individuals. You may say, however, "Here are the names of three lawyers (or dentists, or real estate agents) you can consider. Talk to them and see if any suit you." Then it's their choice, not yours.

■ Don't offer opinions or make judgments on your subordinate's ethics, morals, values, or even his or her actions. Your aim is not to render justice or judgment, but assistance.

Finally, don't overcounsel. It can be wearing, and is certainly time-consuming. A minimum of counseling can provide important help to individuals and show your group that you care. Too much can ruin your schedules and your reputation as a manager.

▷ 3
Critiquing

CONCEPT

Critiquing is controlled criticism. Criticism has a bad name in some management circles because it is seen as a putdown, a discouragement, and a killer of enthusiasm. While this may be true, criticism often must precede improvement. "You can't make something better until you know what's wrong with it," says one executive. Critiquing is a systematic approach to spotting weakpoints, flaws, errors, mistakes, or simply things that are not good enough. As a group process, it benefits from the dynamics of group activity.

ACTION OPPORTUNITIES

Critiquing is useful in situations that can benefit from remedy, preferably those that are continuing or repetitive, across the entire range of management action.

EXAMPLE

A publisher puts out a weekly management periodical and has built critiquing into its regular editorial procedure. Staff members, who both write and edit copy, convene every Tuesday to critique the first drafts of items that will go into the publication. A typical session:

Editor-in-Chief Barbara Vance has circulated all the copy to each of the six editors. She starts the meeting: "Let's take Ed's piece on the security system at the ABC Company. Rex, what's your reaction?"

"I always like these field reports, they seem so solid. And I think Ed did a good job as far as he went. But the piece focuses too much on the security

director. I'd like the department heads' and employees' views on how the program is working."

Bob Blake speaks up. "I think Ed gives us a good picture of a well-thought-out security setup. Do we want to go beyond that?"

Sally Henning says, "I agree with Rex. We get a clear and favorable picture of the program, but how do the people who live with it feel? As it reads now, it's got a public relations flavor."

Vance says, "What do you think, Ed?"

"I guess it would be a better piece with more nuts and bolts coverage. But can we run that long? It will take a full page as is."

One of the other conferees says, "Security's hot now. I think we could run two pages."

Vance says, "I go along. Our mail shows a lot of interest in security. Ed, how long to beef it up?"

"I could get the rewrite to you by tomorrow. I've got some notes and could pick up the rest by phone. I know the people I want to interview."

Vance asks for any other comments, minor points are mentioned, and the spotlight swings to the next item.

HOW TO USE

Especially noteworthy in the case above is the matter-of-fact tone of the discussion, an essential for successful critiquing. Additional guidelines:

1. Pinpoint the subject. In the publishing case, the physical copy makes it easy to get everyone in the group on the same track, but sometimes the subject area may be less clear. The meeting format helps, since the leader may start by stating the subject, and asking for any questions that will prevent misunderstanding or misperceptions. For example:

"Our subject is Lynn's suggested procedure for handling customer complaints. . . ." followed by the data, background information, and present situation. Then, "Any questions?" The critique then proceeds.

2. Equal exposure. To make the evaluations consistent, each conferee must have the same information. In the case of the editorial group, imagine the complications that would arise if different versions of Ed's copy circulated.

3. Follow regular meeting procedures. A leader should make sure that:

- Everyone has a chance to speak up.
- Comments are kept impersonal and objective.

- Comments are specific. "I don't like it," isn't as helpful as, "I feel the new package is overdecorated and tawdry."
- Destructive comments are stopped cold. Backbiting, feuding, and fault-finding that is patently hostile are out of order.
- The standard practice of protecting a "victim" is especially important. The person whose work is criticized must be permitted to respond to the comments, point by point, after the others have had their say. The leader must exercise control so as to avoid acrimonious argument.

4. Review format. Critiquing, like any other repeated type of session, can become boring. Use the critiquing approach itself to freshen up the meetings: "How can we liven up our critiquing sessions?" The group is sure to have suggestions.

▷ **4**
Emotional First Aid

CONCEPT

First aid is an accepted concept for physical well-being. Most people get some knowledge or training in staunching a wound, setting a broken limb, or assisting a person with a heart seizure. Emotional problems may also reach a crisis stage, and on the workscene, you may be expected to apply emotional first aid. To do nothing, or to have someone else step in, may tarnish your leadership status.

People capable of applying a tourniquet or giving mouth-to-mouth resuscitation may be at a loss when dealing with an individual suffering from a storm of anger, tears, or despondency. For home-related or job-related reasons, an employee may lose self-control. You should be prepared to act.

ACTION OPPORTUNITIES

Emotional upset is often readily identifiable, for instance: A call comes in for a subordinate, reporting serious injury to a family member. The subordinate may faint, weep, and/or become helpless, or the signs may be more subtle, and you still may have to act. In general, any upset that interferes with an employee's ability to function requires emotional first aid until professional help is available.

EXAMPLE

1. At 9 A.M. Grace Miller's assistant is sitting at her desk in a funk. Another subordinate comes over and tells Miller that Clara is having serious trouble at home. Miller realizes that action is needed.

She asks Clara to come into her office and closes the door. The assistant immediately collapses on the sofa and begins to weep. Miller sits beside her, takes her hand and makes comforting sounds. After a minute or two Clara becomes calmer, and her boss says, "Let me help you. Tell me what's wrong." Eventually the story comes out. Clara's young brother was arrested that morning for delivering drugs to a user. "It's the first time. What's going to happen to him now?"

Miller expresses her sympathy and asks, "Would you like to go home?" To her surprise, Clara says she'd rather keep busy. The manager promises complete confidentiality. Clara works until noon, then asks for permission to leave for the day. When Clara comes in next morning, Miller makes a point of checking with her. "We got a lawyer," Clara says. "He doesn't think it will be too bad. And thanks."

2. Loud voices in the corridor attract Manager Ray Olds, and when he finds their source, two young men from the mailroom are taking wild swings at one another. Olds rushes forward, and with the help of an onlooker, separates the fighting pair. The argument returns to the shouting level, a crowd gathers.

"He stole five dollars from my locker," asserts one, aquiver with rage.

"He's crazy," is the reply.

Olds realizes there are two problems. One is to cool things down, the other is to settle the question of the five dollars. He decides the second one should be handled by the head of the mailroom. He turns his attention to the enraged employee.

"Come with me," he says, and leads him into his office. The employee goes into a tirade against the suspect, and Olds lets him unburden himself. Then he points out that there is no proof, only a suspicion of wrongdoing, and says the problem of the missing five dollars will be looked into later. "Right now," he points out, "understand that company premises isn't a prize ring. If you have a case, take it up with your boss." He then phones and gets the supervisor to join them. On his arrival he explains what's happening and concludes, "It's up to you now, Greg," and the supervisor escorts the calmed-down employee out the door.

HOW TO USE

The major hazard in dealing with emotion-laden situations is to avoid playing psychiatrist. If the behavior is extreme, seek immediate medical assistance. However, if the emotional storm is within normal limits, such as justifiable anger or depression for a logical cause, you can probably help. In the average case, you are simply staging a holding action. When the immediate crisis is over, what happens next, such as seeking professional care, depends on the seriousness of the upset. In all cases, confidentiality should be observed.

The following approaches are based on suggestions made by Dr. Mortimer Feinberg and his professional staff at BFS Psychological Associates of New York City.

Crying, or Related Behavior

1. Show your concern. Make clear your desire to help.
2. Take the employee to your office or another private place.
3. Give the employee time to regain composure. Don't exert pressure. Use a quiet, sympathetic tone of voice.
4. Ask, "What's wrong?" Don't insist on an answer.
5. Ask, "How can I help?" If the response is a shake of the head, or, "You can't," say, "Try me." If reluctance persists, let matters rest. Offer water or a soft drink.
6. If the employee explains the cause of the tears, listen, and offer sympathy and understanding. Don't make judgments or prescribe. If it's serious, suggest the possibility of professional help.
7. When calm returns, give the employee the choice of going back to work or leaving early.
8. Check back after a while to show your interest and to learn how the employee is doing.

Anger, or Related Behavior

1. Face the individual firmly and assert your authority.
2. Be firm without responding in anger. Make clear your intention to cool things down before any action is taken.
3. Isolate the employee in a corner or a separate room.
4. Ask the reason for the upset. Discourage tirades. Seek, "Just the facts," as TV personality Sergeant Friday used to say.

5. Listen to the complaint. This will further quiet matters.
6. There may be a reverse of feelings if the employee regrets the outburst. Be ready to deal with shame or sheepishness. Alleviate this feeling by assuring him or her, "It's just one of those things."
7. If professional counseling seems advisable, suggest it but avoid the phrase, "See a psychiatrist," or anything similar. This suggests a diagnosis of abnormal behavior, which will probably be resented. Make the suggestion tentative. It's up to the employee.

Despondency

1. Talk to the employee in private.
2. Don't make a judgment as to the individual's condition. Say, "You seem down in the mouth. Anything wrong?" You may get a reply in the negative. But stay with it a while longer. In a friendly way suggest that the present mood "isn't like you. I'd like to help."
3. Don't stop tears. Weeping is usually a desirable alleviant.
4. If your familiarity with the employee suggests a serious cause for the despondency, suggest that "You might want to talk things over with a professional." If your company has a medical department or outside medical service, suggest a visit and leave it to the nurse or doctor to refer the employee to a source of help.

As in the mailroom example, the employee's own boss should be brought in early. It's his or her responsibility. Where there is a reaction from others, discourage gossip. Your main objective is to offer help quickly, as needed. Any follow-up is best made off the premises by qualified people.

(Also, see Counseling, page 4.)

▷ 5
Expectancy Theory

CONCEPT

Some scientists have attempted to lay down a baseline against which theories of motivation can be analyzed. One such effort is the following

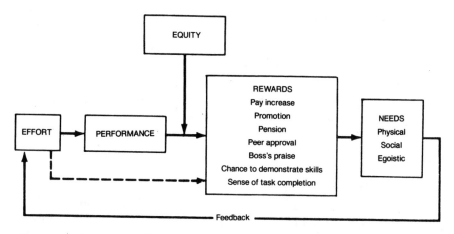

Figure 1. A simplified expectancy model; George Strauss, Leonard R. Sayles, *STRAUSS AND SAYLES'S BEHAVIORAL STRATEGIES FOR MANAGERS,* ©1980, p.42. Reprinted by permission of Prentice-Hall, Inc., Englewood Cliffs, NJ.

chart that shows the sequence of goals and actions in the motivation process. It depicts the expectations of reward and satisfaction that stimulate the work effort and shape performance.

In *Behavioral Strategies for Managers,** professors George Strauss and Leonard R. Sayles comment on the Expectancy Theory:

> It suggests that employees will be motivated to produce only if they expect that productivity will lead to (or is a path toward) a goal they value. More explicitly, increased effort will lead to increased performance (productivity) and increased performance will lead in turn to rewards that provide satisfaction of important employee needs. A final requirement is that the satisfaction resulting from this initial effort be sufficiently great (equitable) to make the effort worthwhile.

ACTION OPPORTUNITIES

Managers will find the chart useful for analyzing motivation hypotheses. Strauss and Sayles also say that Expectancy Theory may be used to assess

* Strauss, George, and Sayles, Leonard R. (1980) *Behavioral Strategies for Managers.* Englewood Cliffs, NJ: Prentice Hall.

job redesign, management by objectives, salary administration, and fringe benefits as sources of reward and satisfaction of needs.

EXAMPLE

Esther Loy and Ben Riley are discussing motivation of managers. Riley says, "The trouble with our work is that it's so abstract. Sometimes you spend weeks on a study and end up with a dozen typed sheets of paper which nobody reads. When you can't expect a payoff (reward) there's no incentive to perform."

"Are you saying your work is less rewarding than a bricklayer's?"

"I'm saying that if it weren't for future prospects, and my own feeling of achievement, I'd quit tomorrow."

Manager Ben Riley's feelings about his work show the interplay of effort, performance, reward, and needs. Also illustrated is the element of equity, as shown in the chart. This is the point at which effort must yield sufficient satisfaction for it to be continued.

HOW TO USE

In addition to clarifying the relationship among the basic work factors, the chart can help you evaluate the practicality of motivational concepts. For example, in Herzberg's motivator/hygiene hypothesis, working conditions, a hygiene factor, is considered less motivating than challenging work. With specific people in mind, not excluding yourself, insert "improved working conditions" at the "Rewards" point in the formula. What effect would there be on effort? Next, using the same person, use "promise of promotion." Would the latter reward spark greater effort from the individual? Chances are you will get an answer that helps assess Herzberg's approach, as well as demonstrates the usefulness of the expectancy chart.

The performance-reward interaction is usually the key link in the chain. Superior effort is likely to be sustained if it is recognized by rewards suited to the individual's value system. Superior effort that is not rewarded draws from the employee the classic: "Why should I knock myself out if no one gives a damn?" It is the employee's perception of reward rather than the reward itself that matters. For some, a pat on the back is highly satisfying, while to others it is a patronizing and inadequate gesture. Employees generally have a sense of equity, a personal measure of how and how much they should be rewarded for what they do.

The broken line between "Effort" and "Reward" on the chart suggests that effort in itself may be rewarding. For example, just doing research may be satisfying for a scientist.

Finally, the chart demonstrates the importance of feedback. It is the final link that loops the chain, and tells the individual not only how he or she is doing, but how the performance is regarded by those whose judgments determine the rewards and satisfactions for effort expended, and who influence future effort.

▷ 6
Followership

CONCEPT

Studies of leadership sometimes neglect a key aspect, that of "Follower-ship," or the attitudes of those to be led. This is an unfortunate oversight, since one key to a leader's achievement is the behavior of his or her followers.

In the leadership canon, subordinates are often assumed to be pas-sive, a group automatically responding to the boss's initiatives. But ob-servations of followers, individually and in groups, show that they play a major part in leadership dynamics. Using the categories described in the Selective Leadership approach (see page 83), followers are shown to have a preference among the three basic methods of autocratic, demo-cratic, or "free-rein" leaders. Listen in:

> *Alice:* "I liked Mr. Smith the first day he took over the department. He is so self-confident, so positive. He doesn't leave you hanging. He tells you exactly what he wants and how he wants it." (autocratic leadership)

> *Fay:* "That's exactly what I don't like about him. He acts as though he has all the answers, and doesn't let you work out your own way of doing things. I feel like an idiot who can't be trusted to deal with problems on my own." (free-rein leadership)

Studies undertaken for *Techniques of Leadership** by Auren Uris came up with some useful findings:

* Uris, Auren (1964). *Techniques for Leadership*. New York: McGraw Hill.

- Followers can be categorized according to their preference for the autocratic, democratic, or free-rein leadership approaches.
- People work best with leadership that corresponds with their followership type. For example, a subordinate who has an affinity for the autocratic approach responds favorably to the autocratic leadership technique.
- The lack of a match between leadership style and followership preference may account for friction and poor employee performance.

ACTION OPPORTUNITIES

Insight into the followership role may clarify working relationships with your subordinates and to your own boss. Many factors determine the nature of these relationships, and examining them from the followership perspective may reveal an area for improved effectiveness.

EXAMPLE

An anecdote from another era puts the followership role in a new light. This exchange was reported of an outstanding executive interviewing a job candidate:

John D. Rockefeller: *"Are you a leader?"*

Applicant: *"I can't really say, but I can tell you this, I'm a good follower."*

Rockefeller: *"I'm full up on leaders already. I sure can use one good follower. You're hired."*

HOW TO USE

Thinking about followers as part of your human resources may turn up some useful insights. Consider these points:

1. Be aware of followership styles, that is, how people respond to orders or to the opportunity for independent action, whether they cooperate and participate in appropriate work situations, and so on. Their behavior may suggest changes in your leadership approach.

2. Consider a followership solution to work problems with subordinates, or with your boss. Frictions or feelings of isolation on the part of

the manager may be explained by poor interaction with his or her followers, or poor execution of the follower's role.

3. Realize that you can vary your leadership methods to better suit an individual's followership needs. For instance, if you get poor performance from someone capable of better things who doesn't take advantage of the independence you provide, see whether closer supervision will cater to unexpressed followership needs and reinforce shaky self-confidence.

4. As a follower, is it possible that you could work more productively with your boss if you could get him to go along with your preference for freer rein and greater independence of action? Or is democratic followership your style and do you prefer fewer one-to-one situations and more contacts, meetings, and action teams with your peers? If the answer is affirmative, your boss's use of democratic techniques might improve your working relations and results. Try to restyle your working relationship along those lines.

▷ 7
Friendship

CONCEPT

Friendship is a great enricher of the work experience. Corporate companions bring to wage earning the pleasures of camaraderie, humor, and warmth that may be the greatest unmentioned factor in job satisfaction.

Cases differ. Some managers avoid having work-connected friends, while others have no other kind. Some treat business and social friends pretty much the same, others draw a heavy dividing line. For example, Executive A leaves his business friends at the office, along with his desk and in-box, while B tries to mingle the two groups. Despite the pluses, friendship for the manager requires special precautions.

ACTION OPPORTUNITIES

Conditions at work create strains and ethical conflicts that can burden a relationship, not only for you, but for the other person. Also, managers in their counseling role may be expected to advise a subordinate whose friendships cause a major tangle. Knowing how to handle this problem area can protect mental well-being and careers.

EXAMPLES

1. Office manager Pearl Ketchum and Florence Greene were old friends and continued to be after Pearl became manager of the office in which they had started together. But one day the treasurer told Ketchum that the word processing equipment they had been considering was on its way. After the group had been informed, Florence protested to Pearl. "I want to use my old machine. I was never any good with fancy equipment."

Ketchum also had doubts about the other's ability to perform. Florence asked her to get permission to continue with her present typewriter and the manager said she would try.

"The answer," the treasurer said, "is no. Once we start making exceptions, we're licked. Besides, we want to get rid of some of the dead wood. We'll be bringing in young people who have trained on the new equipment."

Told of the refusal, Florence said, "I guess I'll have to look for a new job. Luckily for me, I take shorthand." And that was the outcome. Pearl felt guilty, not being able to help, and Florence thought her friend hadn't tried hard enough. The friendship ended.

2. The meeting broke up and his boss said to Henry, "When are you going to tell Bob?"

"Friday afternoon, the weekend will cushion it a bit." And that Friday Henry Ball told Bob Pritchard, his golf buddy, a friend and colleague of fifteen years, that he was fired. After it sank in, Bob asked if he couldn't stay on for another year or two, after which he could consider early retirement.

"You've got to do that at least, Hank."

"God, Bob, I can't. I've already talked to T.R., but it's just not in the cards. He says he's got to cut to the bone. I tried everything. . . ." It was the hardest day's work Henry Ball had ever done. He never forgot the pain in Bob's eyes.

HOW TO USE

The examples suggest the stresses corporate strictures may impose on friendship. The two cases illustrate crisis situations. Fortunately, there is a brighter side. Here are some points that put the matter into perspective:

1. Friendship incubator. The work setting fosters friendship. You and your colleagues share interests, experiences, and may even team up on projects. "Talking shop" may be a pejorative term among spouses, but for the principals, being able to recount, analyze, discuss, argue about, and exult over job life is a unique luxury.

2. Friendship versus friendliness. Here is a helpful distinction which is sometimes overlooked. For people in authority, understanding the difference between friendliness and friendship can help avoid the hazards of favoritism:

- Friendship involves special feelings toward a select few.
- Friendliness implies a warm and sympathetic attitude that may be shown to all.

3. Compensate for friendship. As a manager, your close bonds to a few suggests a potential for unfairness, so:

- Be prepared to offset resentment by friendliness to others.
- If appropriate, tell friends that they, like yourself, may have to pay a price. In some cases you may have to bend over backwards to avoid the appearance of favoritism, so that a friend may lose out, thus making a necessary sacrifice.

4. Come to terms with the confidentiality factor. As an executive you are privy to information not intended for a third person's ears. Decide when you can and when you shouldn't let friends in on privileged matters.

5. Friendship versus promotion. Advancement needn't destroy past associations, but it sometimes does. For example, Roger X moves up to the presidency from his job as division head. Overnight his perspective, power, and personal freedom change. Past associations wither and new patterns—lunch companions, expensive restaurants, joining an exclusive club, and relationships—grow.

Some bonds may withstand even these pressures. But for the most part, friends expect things to change when one or the other moves up.

6. Decisions may become tests of conscience. Choosing between two candidates for a promotion may be easy, ordinarily. But when one is a friend, the selection involves new factors: If the candidates are nearly equal, do you favor your friend? Even Solomon might have difficulty with this one. The wisest course is to make the best fit of candidate and job, in terms of its consequences for the company, the two people involved, and your conscience.

7. When boy meets girl. Friendships between the sexes can be explosive. They needn't be, of course. Custom has come a long way from the 1850s, when department store employees of the opposite sex seen together off the premises were fired on the spot. Today the two sexes mingle freely, within reason. On the other hand, many a manager has been denounced for favoritism based on a romantic interest.

Here's a revealing case. In a company employing two couples, one was rent asunder by management for "setting a bad example," and the other, after their marriage, revealed gleefully to friends that they had been sharing an apartment for three years, undetected. The difference: discretion, and the willingness to take the trouble to veil their togetherness.

8. A pang to avoid? "I recently retired," the letter to a columnist read, "after a happy and successful career. At a farewell dinner everyone from the president to the elevator starter asked me to come back to visit. Six months later I did. What a catastrophe! It wasn't just the unfamiliar faces. Even ex-buddies were too rushed to spend more than a few minutes with me. The president, with whom I had been friendly, was 'in conference.' I was finally able to persuade an old acquaintance to have lunch with me. The food and conversation were third rate. I guess you can't go home again. Or can you?"

The columnist spelled out her suggestions:

- Don't expect to revive the "good old days."
- Don't just drop in. It's likely that ex-pals would be happy to have lunch with you if arranged in advance.
- Friendships have to be nurtured. A six-month hiatus is too long. Occasional contacts can help keep the channels open.

Friendship on the job is different from other kinds of friendship, but it also has its similarities. Those capable of sustaining good relationships off the job should be able to reap the rewards of business friendships— to the point where the word "business" can be removed as an unnecessary qualifier.

▷ 8
The Great Jackass Fallacy

CONCEPT

This is a cautionary idea about motivation from a well-known business psychologist. Dr. Harry Levinson, after starting and heading up the Division of Industrial Mental Health of the Menninger Foundation, went on to an affiliation with Harvard, and then became president of the Levinson

Institute. On the way, he authored numerous works including *The Great Jackass Fallacy.* Here is how he described the origin of the phrase:

> *Executives fall into the trap that I have called the Great Jackass Fallacy.* While conducting executive seminars I frequently ask participants what the dominant philosophy of motivation in American management is. They almost invariably say that it is the carrot-and-stick: reward and punishment. Asked to close their eyes and form a picture that has a carrot at one end and a stick at the other, and asked what they see in between, the most frequent image they report is that of a jackass. Obviously, the unconscious assumption behind reward and punishment is that one is dealing with a jackass.*

Dr. Levinson is pointing an accusing finger at the abuse of the punishment-reward system of motivation. Disciplinary measures for unacceptable behavior and rewards for outstanding performance can be logical and effective responses. But when a human being is seen as an automaton to be motivated by pushbutton techniques, the human potential of creativity, ingenuity, team play, and dedication will not be tapped.

ACTION OPPORTUNITIES

Use Dr. Levinson's concept as background in reading, thinking, and actions centering on motivation, considering your own efforts or those of subordinate managers. The jackass image is one against which to measure other approaches. One executive says, "It is an excellent idea for an organization's discussion and evaluation of its motivational system."

EXAMPLE
Doug Leeds is considered a good manager who runs a tight ship. "He's firm but fair," his proponents say. His detractors feel there is something wrong with Leeds as a boss, but they can't be specific. Perhaps a woman who took a job as his secretary and left after three months put her finger on it: "He said good morning to me every working day, and never meant it once." His boss has another view that strangely, he feels is complimentary: "That Doug, he's a great manipulator." Jackasses, Dr. Levinson points out, are to be manipulated and controlled.

HOW TO USE

To avoid the Great Jackass Fallacy trap and derive other benefits from the idea:

---

* *The Great Jackass Fallacy,* (1973). Cambridge, MA: Harvard Grodvale School of Business Administration.

1. Be clear on Dr. Levinson's point. It is not meant to preclude punishment and reward as motivational strategies. Used properly, they can be the core of an effective approach. (See Sl ner's Behavior Modification, page 87.)

2. Understand the context. The psychologist's criticism is essentially against treating employees as dependent beings dominated by a management which is alone responsible for making decisions and solving problems. Says Levinson, "They are merely told what to do and are paid for doing it. They are exhorted to be responsible and to invest themselves in their work, but they are often not allowed to assume any real or important responsibility for what they do."

3. In discussions of motivation, inject the Levinson idea into the discussion, and do it early. Because of its clarity and practicality, it can get the talk off to a good start in a subject area that can be foggy.

The ingenuity of Levinson's Great Jackass Fallacy is implicit in the words: If people are treated like jackasses, it should not come as a surprise when they behave that way.

▷ **9**
Group Dynamics

CONCEPT

Kurt Lewin, one of the outstanding theorists in modern management, is credited with the early development of Group Dynamics. He said of it, "In Group Dynamics more than in any other psychological field are theory and practice linked in a way which could provide answers to theoretical problems and at the same time strengthen . . . an approach to practical ones."

At the heart of Group Dynamics is the observation that special forces come into play among people in groups. Heightened susceptibilities and emotional levels make group situations differ from individual behavior. Managers were quick to see the aptness of Group Dynamics insights for management meetings. (See Management Meetings, page 141.)

ACTION OPPORTUNITIES

In addition to the management meeting, usually limited to three to twelve members, Group Dynamics findings apply to larger groups, such as "all production personnel," "sales staff," and that key aggregation, "all employees." With groups like these, some typical functions lend themselves to the reinforcements of Group Dynamics:

- Fighting a rumor (See Rumor Handling, page 80.)
- Building group spirit
- Acceptance of new policies or rules
- Announcement of changes in routines and procedures

When the dynamics are triggered by an effective leader, favorable group reactions can be aroused—to persuade, reassure, create enthusiasm, and so on.

EXAMPLES

Company President Eliot Plant was told by his Vice-President, Personnel, that a rumor was going around that the firm was going to be acquired by the XYZ Company and closed down. Anxiety spread, morale sagged.

Plant recalled, "We did have a contact with XYZ last month. Their executive in charge of real estate was in here trying to get a price on that land we own down by the railroad station. I told him we weren't selling. . . ."

The head of Personnel said, "He's a neighbor of our receptionist, Minna Garrick. She may have told one of her friends of the visit, and they put two and two together and got twenty-two. You know how rumors grow. We'd better get the folks together. . . ."

Next day the company cafeteria was packed with the entire employee group, most expecting confirmation of the bad news. After a half an hour's talk by Eliot Plant, ending with a bright picture of the company's present performance and future prospects, the meeting broke up with the group transformed from its worried stance to one of enthusiastic optimism. The points made in the president's speech are covered in the section below.

HOW TO USE

Group Dynamics is a communications factor that can create audience responses that favor company goals. Some guidelines:

1. Build employee cohesiveness and trust. These elements are not goals in themselves so much as results of effective employee relations policies and practices. The predisposition of your group is a major factor in the benefits you can derive from a group dynamics policy. If your company has a history of square dealing, the employee group will be more responsive.

2. Look for opportunities to harness the group dynamics effect. You can communicate a message, for example, and get instant feedback, flush out objections, and get additional ideas. (See Brainstorming, page 111.) Here is how President Eliot Plant, described in the previous example, presented his case to employees:

- He opened the meeting, beginning with a few ice-breaking pleasantries to minimize the group's sense of foreboding.
- He got right to the destructive sellout rumor to show that there was to be no pussyfooting.
- He provided the facts that explained how the misinformation had originated. He made no mention of Minna Garrick's role, however, but simply stated that a representative of the XYZ firm had been on the premises to make an offer on company-owned property that was not for sale.

He used the situation to reassure the group: "Let me take this opportunity to give you a favorable report on our company's performance for the last quarter. . . ." The feelings of the group surged from doubt to optimism. As a result of the interactions of the group, as emotions tend to be infectious, employees emerged from the meeting in a more positive state of mind. It would be difficult to obtain the same result with the printed word, without the benefit of the dynamics effect.

3. Use the leverage of group dynamics knowingly. The dynamics are always present unless a group is bored to death or asleep. But to have them work favorably, you must have a setting, leader, and agenda that will trigger the reactions you are after. If you are gathering key people to announce an important finding by the Research and Development group that will lead to a whole new line of promising products, you will maximize the reaction by (1) creating excitement and suspense in advance, (2) providing comfortable surroundings, (3) using speakers who are both capable and of impressive status (for some subjects only the presence of the chairman of the board, the president, or other top people will signal the importance of the subject), and (4) an agenda geared to dramatizing, impressing, and selling your ideas to the assemblage.

◊ **10** ⚜

Herzberg's Motivator/Hygiene Concept

CONCEPT

Dr. Frederick Herzberg of the University of Utah developed a theory that helps clarify what makes an employee satisfied or dissatisfied in a job. In doing so he clarified two mysteries that plague executives:

- Money is supposed to be the ultimate incentive on the workscene, yet, when you give an employee a raise, a week later the elation fades, and work attitudes return to where they were before the cash injection.
- Prospective employees have been known to walk out when shown working surroundings that weren't sufficiently attractive, yet, as one executive moaned, "We spent thousands of dollars putting first-rate original paintings in our corridors and cafeteria, and after a flurry of interest, none of us can see an iota of change in attitude, and certainly none in performance." (Many will accuse the executive of unrealistic expectations.)

Herzberg defined two sets of conditions which affect an employee at work. He calls one *motivators,* and the other, *hygiene factors.* The first group has the power to *satisfy* an employee. The second group can *dissatisfy* or demotivate when present in unsatisfactory form. The five most important motivators are achievement, recognition, the work itself, responsibility, and advancement. The five major hygiene factors are company policy and administration, supervision, salary, interpersonal relations, and working conditions.

As Herzberg says, the motivators "describe man's relationship to what he does . . ." The hygiene factors describe the employee's "relationship to the context or environment in which he does his job." They "serve primarily to prevent job dissatisfaction while having little effect on positive job attitudes."

As Ernest Dale notes in *Management: Theory and Practice,* * "Just as good medical hygiene may prevent disease but will not cure it, so good pay, considerate supervisors, and good working conditions may prevent active dissatisfaction, but will not motivate employees to do better

* Dale, Ernest (1973). *Management: Theory and Practice.* New York: McGraw-Hill.

work." What does motivate is the challenge and pleasure of the work itself, the sense of achievement, recognition of a job well done, a feeling of responsibility, and the desire for advancement.

ACTION OPPORTUNITIES

Use Herzberg's concept to:

1. Rethink your own ideas about why people work and how to encourage them to improve their effort and performance.
2. Interview job candidates. Try to pinpoint what factors were important or unimportant in former jobs.
3. Review employees' performance. Focus on individuals' possible reasons for satisfaction and dissatisfaction.
4. Think about your own job, and how you relate to the motivator/hygiene factors.

EXAMPLE

James Green, president of a small company, notices that Tim Mayer, the vice-president of marketing, is losing enthusiasm and drive. Green, worried that Mayer might quit, gives him a large corner office and new furniture. Nevertheless, Mayer resigns and joins the competition. On Mayer's last day, Green asks him into his office for a friendly chat (exit interview). As they talk, Mayer reveals his reason for choosing his new employer. "They plan to groom me for a higher-level job," he says. Green then realizes the problem: Mayer felt stuck in a dead-end job, and no amount of fine furniture could cure that.

HOW TO USE

In applying the Herzberg approach, familiarize yourself with specific examples of his two categories. The following two lists will be helpful to that end:

Motivators

1. Job with an important purpose
2. Achievement opportunities
3. Recognition of good work
4. Chances for promotion

5. Job that requires decision making
6. Responsibility
7. Job that encourages growth

Hygiene Factors

1. Considerate supervision
2. Good pension plan
3. High pay (Since Herzberg first proposed his ideas, there has been considerable argument for placing this under motivators.)
4. Clear company policy
5. Agreeable working conditions
6. Job security
7. Good relationships with coworkers

You can expand or amend both lists.

Assess the satisfactions of your own job. If you want to go into the details—the results can be surprising and helpful in clarifying your own motivations—rate the factors listed above in your own job on a scale of 1 to 10 to see how needs are being met in each category. This may point to ways in which your own job could be improved.

Estimate ratings for subordinates in the same manner. Of course, different people have different needs (Kim may care more about pleasant working conditions than Ted, for example), these ratings could help you to pinpoint sources of dissatisfaction that could be cured before you lose a valuable employee. They may also help you spot areas of satisfaction you can use to reward individual employees (for example, Eric gets a low rating for achievement opportunities, so you consider some assignments that could challenge him).

▷ 11
The Integrated Solution

CONCEPT

In the 1920s Mary Parker Follett, an American management expert, came up with a unique method for resolving conflict. She called it the "integrated solution," because it integrated—that is, sought to combine—the desires of both parties. In certain cases the approach settles disputes better than the best compromise, because in compromise each party gets only part of what is wanted. Follett's idea can wholly satisfy both parties.

In presenting her idea, Follett pointed out that there are three ways to settle disputes:

- **Domination.** Disagreement is resolved by one side triumphing over another. Although this is the simplest way of dealing with conflict, it may fail in the long run because resentments can fester and the issues may rise again.
- **Compromise.** Perhaps the most common approach, each party gives up part of its objective for the sake of a settlement.
- **Integrated solution.** An end to disagreement is sought that gives both parties full satisfaction.

ACTION OPPORTUNITIES

The Follett approach may be considered in almost any disagreement for which a settlement is sought. For the best results, those involved must reveal what their real interests and objectives are. Mary Parker Follett often used her idea to resolve arguments and conflicting demands between management and labor groups, but the scheme can work in any situation where the disputants are flexible and willing to join in seeking answers.

EXAMPLES

1. Here is a simple case to demonstrate the principle in action:

Harry Lyons, head of an accounting firm, is called on to settle an argument between two accountants who share an office. One accountant wants the window open to get more fresh air, the other demands that it be shut to prevent drafts.

Lyons doesn't even consider settling the squabble by the domination principle, because neither accountant has a strong case. He says, "How about a compromise? Let's leave the window half open." Both men protest.

Then Lyons has an inspiration that embodies the integrated solution idea. "The adjoining room is empty," he says. "Let's open the window in there and keep the connecting door open as well." Both men are satisfied.

The one who wanted the window shut won't be bothered by the wind blowing on his back. The other, who wanted more air, will get it.

2. *A labor/management committee is to hold a meeting, but where should it take place? Management favors holding the meeting on company premises to cut down on travel time and expenses. The employees are against the idea because they fear company influence.*

The integrated solution: Hold the meeting in the employees' club building on factory grounds. The meeting will thus be held on company premises, but the workers will feel at ease on what they see as their "turf." The aims of both sides have therefore been satisfied.

HOW TO USE

Integration requires imagination and a willingness to do some original thinking. Another key ingredient is the ability to make the distinction between what the parties want and what they ask for. Finding an acceptable solution becomes considerably easier when intentions of both sides are known. Here are key guidelines:

1. ***Forget domination.*** Both sides must abandon the desire to "win." As long as the disagreement is viewed as a contest, obfuscation and evasions will interfere.

2. ***Clarify real intentions.*** The parties must avoid camouflage, and must pinpoint the real demands. Both sides must try to understand their actual motivations.

3. ***Openness.*** Real issues, the areas of actual disagreement, must be clear to both parties.

4. ***Reevaluate goals.*** Intentions or perspective may change during the course of the discussion. When both sides reconsider, there can be a spontaneous understanding and agreement.

5. ***Analyze demands.*** One or both of the parties' demands may seem indivisible, but if they are broken down into basic elements, the settlement becomes easier.

6. ***Unite the elements of the demands.*** This is the reverse of the previous point. In some cases, you can be confused because the real demand is obscured by murky statements, or by a spate of minor demands. You can then achieve clarity and acceptance by eliminating the extraneous and getting to the heart of the matter.

▷ 12
Job Redesign

CONCEPT

Job redesign is the altering of structure and content to make a job more meaningful and satisfying. Behind it lies the belief that job satisfaction requires more than good pay, working conditions, and supervision. The work itself must provide stimulus for interest and effort. This may require reshaping jobs to bring tasks more into line with jobholders' skills and abilities. When this is successful, both the employees and the company benefit. (See Job Satisfaction, page 34.)

ACTION OPPORTUNITIES

In companies with sophisticated management, job design incorporates features aimed to give employees and the company the benefits of increased job satisfaction and higher productivity. Problems such as absenteeism, turnover, tardiness, and poor job performance may push management to consider the job redesign solution. Cases reported reveal that while productivity benefits may be uncertain, increased job satisfaction can usually be achieved.

EXAMPLE

In Sweden, where management innovation is often pursued, an automobile assembly operation group performed poorly. Not only was quality and quantity of output unsatisfactory, but one eight-person group showed other symptoms of employee dissatisfaction such as irregular attendance and insubordination.

Management decided that the division-of-labor principle had been applied to tasks to the point where the work was overly limited and monotonous. The eight workers were reorganized as a team to do the entire assembly. The new method afforded greater job interest, the satisfaction of completing a task, and a chance for the group to chat as they worked. The negative behavior, absenteeism, and so on, diminished, and output was slightly higher.

HOW TO USE

Job redesign is usually a procedure undertaken by the Personnel Department. It has been applied successfully at the department level, however, where there is unified management, and functional lines need not be crossed. Guidelines for implementation follow:

1. **Techniques.** Know the techniques available to the job redesigner—or designer, for that matter:

- **Job rotation.** Switching jobs to end monotony and broaden skills and horizons.
- **Job enlargement.** So-called "horizontal" change, in which employees perform a larger operation, such as a complete task, rather than a limited one high in monotony and low in interest.
- **Job enrichment.** So-called "vertical" change, in which employees plan, procure tools and materials, and inspect their own output. In nonfactory jobs, elements may include work planning, decisions as to procedure, goal and standard setting, or, in creative occupations, chance for innovation. Self-supervision and contact with other echelons may be included.

2. **Scope.** Conceivably, a department head might undertake a modest experiment in redesigning jobs, with a superior's approval. But a program may create organizational waves among other managers, a union (if one is involved), and employees themselves. These must be anticipated and dealt with for the outcome to be successful.

3. **Backing.** Complications are best prevented when the program is accepted by groups affected, including all levels of management, top to bottom. Not to be underestimated is the uneasiness of supervisors as their habits, authority, and status seem threatened by the greater latitude given to subordinates.

4. **Participation.** Change as basic as job redesign is likely to cause resistance. Successful redesign usually features discussions with interested parties as to:

- Explanation to all concerned as to the reasons for the program
- Questions by employees whose jobs are to be altered
- Ideas for implementing the program

5. **Limitations.** While the management-wise will readily anticipate the potential complications of a broad redesign effort, it should be noted that even a small experimental plan faces some hazards. For example, the program should be introduced into a department with unified supervision

and management. And, as would be true for any innovation, morale must be high enough to assure a needed level of cooperation. Also, the employees whose jobs are redesigned should not, if possible, include recalcitrant individuals whose attitudes are likely to be a handicap.

6. Startup. A newly designed job may be undertaken either piecemeal or in its entirety at a specific time. Supervisors should be prepared and indoctrinated so that they help advance the project. Done with the right balance of support and latitude for each employee, the results can be advantageous. Oversupervision can interfere with the sense of freedom and autonomy that the new job is supposed to afford.

7. Feedback. Continued monitoring to assess progress and spot problems requires open communication from the job front to those managing the program. Since facts can become distorted, both from misperception and intentional or unintended misrepresentations, firsthand observation from time to time may be desirable. And the flow should go both ways: Employees will want to know how they are doing, or discuss one or another aspect of the new job design.

8. Evaluate. A formal or informal evaluation session will do justice to your original planning, give you the opportunity to compare results with objectives, and decide whether progress is satisfactory or adjustments, minor or major, are necessary.

9. Final judgments. They should include:

- *Underpinnings.* As promising as job redesign may seem, managements should not chop off the top of the iceberg and think they have the whole thing. Redesign is unlikely to succeed unless it grows from a company philosophy that assumes that people prefer to work at a job in which they are interested, that employee participation is acceptable, and that financial gains, if any, are to be shared with employees.

- *Disenchantment.* Even favorable results may not match expectations, from employees right up to top management. Early indoctrination should strive to keep hopes realistic.

- *Unexpected hurdle.* Success does not always bring its own reward. *Business Week* reported in an article on General Foods' Topeka dogfood plant, "Some management and staff personnel saw their own positions threatened because the workers" whose jobs had been redesigned "performed too well." Apparently, managers must be indoctrinated and motivated so that benefits are not watered down by their resentment and resistance.

- *Transplants.* If others intend to duplicate favorable results, the difficulties of exact repeats should be anticipated. In human procedures like job design, the number of variables involved is large, and different people, climates, and management, may be obstacles to replication. On the other hand, there is no reason why managers who are sensitive to their own milieus cannot match or exceed benefits won by others.

▷ 13
Job Satisfaction

CONCEPT

To some extent the label defines the subject: Job satisfaction concerns employees' sense of satisfaction with their jobs. The reality is more complicated, however. The factors that influence satisfaction are well established. Here is a typical list:

- Recognition as a person
- Friendly colleagues
- Equitable pay—compared to levels inside and outside the company
- Sense of belonging, acceptance by others
- Fair treatment
- Job security
- Benefits—medical insurance, retirement plan, pension, and so on
- Good boss relations
- Suitable working conditions—facilities, schedules, safety
- A chance to be heard
- Learning, a sense of growth
- Challenge, a chance to stretch and demonstrate abilities
- Interest and pride in work

This is the complex network of factors with which management must deal in its consideration of how to satisfy employees' practical and psychic job needs.

Although management has been interested in job satisfaction for decades—in the continued pursuit of increased productivity, among other reasons—basic answers get lost in a stalemate of differing views:

- Some people say employee satisfaction doesn't matter as long as the work gets done.
- Some believe job satisfaction is the key both to employee well-being, considered a social good in itself, and increased productivity.

■ Others take the half-way position, typically, that when people are content in their jobs, they perform them better. If they are dissatisfied, the negative consequences, ranging from absenteeism to sabotage, can be costly.

ACTION OPPORTUNITIES

This subject is important for managers concerned with the well-being and performance of subordinates. A study of job satisfaction can: (1) clarify and explain employee behavior that might otherwise remain a mystery; (2) hold out the promise of being able to improve morale and possibly productivity; and (3) give some insight into executive job satisfaction, including their own.

EXAMPLES

1. *Gertrude Neely says to Mr. Harris, head of a video post-production house: "I'll be glad to work for a minimum salary. I want to learn the business." Harris likes the ambition of the young woman, and the directness of her proposal. He hires her.*

She stays on for a year, and as Harris says, "She was the best employee I ever had, loved her work, nothing was ever too much, no hours too long, and everything she tackled was done well."

Moral: If you want a job done well, assign it to a subordinate who is interested in doing it.

2. *"Some of these new people," department head Art Lewis tells his boss, "are not to be believed. It's impossible to motivate them. They perform at a minimum level, are annoyed if you criticize their work, and come back from lunch half an hour late. They are getting a fair day's pay for half a day's work. I think we'd better start recruiting on Mars."*

Moral: Companies suffering from Art Lewis's type of complaint had better tackle the problem of worker alienation—an opposite of work satisfaction—or else. How? Anything from setting recruiting sights higher, toward better-oriented workers, to reviewing job-satisfaction factors to improve employee attitudes.

HOW TO USE

Managers who want to develop their expertise in this important human relations and productivity subject will find food for thought in the following points:

1. Understand the two reasons for corporate interest in job satisfaction: (1) it is better—pleasanter and easier on the nerves—to have contented people on the roster than to have disgruntled ones; (2) job-satisfied people may not necessarily perform better, but they will respond better to motivational techniques—everything from rewards to challenge—than dissatisfied ones.

2. Don't automatically buy the idea that job satisfaction results in higher productivity. Like morale, it is a good in itself, but may or may not result in better performance.

3. There is a mix of material and psychic rewards that influence job satisfaction. For example, in the list at the start of this Idea, only two rewards—pay and benefits—are monetary. Frederick Herzberg maintains that money is a hygiene factor and not a motivator. However, while a person's salary may be taken for granted, raises aren't, and serve at least as a temporary spur to increased effort. The current belief is that only the last item on the list, the work itself, provides real job satisfaction.

But even here there is a variable. Some experts believe that challenging work may not be important. Certain individuals may find dull work attractive because it is easy to do, or because they have interests off the job and expect no more from work than a paycheck.

4. Don't overlook the salutary effect of supervision. A study at the University of Tennessee found that job satisfaction increased when supervisors provided: (1) participation in goal setting; (2) goal clarity and planning; (3) freedom for the subordinate to perform on his own; and (4) feedback and evaluation of results. To some people, close supervision can be supportive.

5. There are a number of circumstances that lessen satisfaction, and act as demotivators:

- **Contactlessness.** A feeling of being isolated from the boss, or from other employees
- **Sadistic criticism.** Comment to punish rather than correct
- **Floundering.** Little guidance, one doesn't know what is expected
- **Leadership by whim.** An inconsistent, unpredictable boss
- **Overexpectation.** Goals set too high
- **Lack of challenge.** Goals set too low
- **Unsatisfactory equipment.** Inferior tools, facilities
- **Insufficient recognition.** No rewards when deserved

6. If you agree with Herzberg (see Herzberg's Motivator/Hygiene Concept, page 26) that the work itself is the ultimate motivator, make this the keystone of your approach to increasing job satisfaction, as well as improved performance.

7. Use the points presented previously to review your own professional satisfactions. However, a *Nation's Business* survey showed that executives' expectations differ from those of lower-echelon employees. For example, executives find satisfaction in:

- Being an important part of the organization
- Leading a group toward a common goal
- Solving challenging problems
- The opportunity for exercising creativity

Not mentioned in the survey, but clearly a key factor, is the status and sense of power that accrues to the executive group.

▷ 14
Law of the Situation

CONCEPT

Mary Parker Follett, a leading business philosopher of the 1920s and 1930s, pioneered in helping management clarify its approach to resolving industrial conflict. Her "law of the situation," like her "integrated solution" (see page 28), analyzes basic aspects of confrontation and negotiation.

Follett said that rarely is real-life conflict simple. Outcomes result from the interaction between people, who seldom behave in uncomplicated ways. She compared the conflict situation to a tennis match in which players respond not simply to each other, but to factors they themselves help create. An action is at least partially influenced by a previous response, and so on.

ACTION OPPORTUNITIES

Follett's law of the situation offers managers a fresh view of disputes, such as:

- Disagreement between two managers

- An argument between supplier and customer over terms, performance, nature of a verbal understanding, and so on
- Management and labor differences during contract talks

EXAMPLE

Mary Parker Follett was deeply involved in labor relations, and so her law of the situation has particular application to contract confrontations. The concept aims to create a more constructive perspective in disputes in general. See how it works between an executive and subordinate manager:

Executive Joe Brown learns that department head Frank Eden has been missing production goals. Efforts to nudge Eden toward improved performance fail. In a one-to-one meeting, Brown broaches the performance problem and Eden comes out fighting.

"Things haven't been going smoothly, mostly because maintenance has been doing a rotten job and the warehouse is late in delivering materials . . ."

Brown asks, "What would it take to improve matters?"

"Authorize me to discuss with maintenance and the warehouse ways and means of cooperating so as to improve services."

Brown realizes he may have made a misjudgment. He had assumed that the manager was getting lazy, or didn't care. The other's view seems reasonable, and he feels progress is being made.

Eden's resentment is softening. He adds, "And another thing . . ." The "other thing" turns out to be Eden's feeling that his efforts are not appreciated. For example, "I hear that Ritchie got a merit increase, and aside from the recent sag, my department has been doing as well as his."

Brown sees another cause of the problem, Eden's anger over what he sees as mistreatment. He is now in a better position to understand and deal with the situation.

HOW TO USE

Be aware of how past and present incidents and interactions influence attitudes. Also, keep in mind possible changes as well as those that have already taken place. For example, in a labor-management negotiation, the company representative found the other side making a big issue of a recent accident. He accepted the need to maintain safety measures at high levels, but suggested that since the company's safety record was excellent, the mishap in question was isolated and didn't represent, as charged, a lapse in management's safety-mindedness. Here the representative acted out Follett's recommendation on understanding as fully as possible the actions and reactions in negotiation.

Discussion must be forthright so that neither party need sacrifice interest, values, or objectives. An arbiter may help keep discussion balanced. This may or may not require a third party. A disputant who is fair-minded, as was executive Joe Brown, may be able to guide the conversation productively.

Most helpfully, the arbiter should spot intentions and goals as they are clarified, and use them to set guidelines for discussion. The objectives of each new element of the situation should be kept up front. It is the perception of the new elements that makes the difference between failure and success in the outcome.

Follett admitted that satisfactory conclusions are not always possible. Prejudice, ignorance, and communications barriers can interfere. Covering up feelings may make them explosive, or lead to a stand-off in which parties are frozen into hostile positions.

Leveling between parties is a key element for success. Progress is difficult unless there is mutual understanding. The real objectives of the parties must be known to each other. If objectives are in conflict, this must be recognized and there must be analysis and a final consensus in order to reach an acceptable solution.

⇨ **15**
Managerial Grid

CONCEPT

Dr. Robert R. Blake and Dr. Jane S. Mouton, industrial psychologists from the University of Texas and associates in the consulting firm of Scientific Methods of Austin, developed a tool for representing the dichotomy of two related but opposed leadership tendencies of managers. (The grid may also be used for rating managements, but the emphasis here is on individuals.) The two factors, a *concern for people* and a *concern for production,* may be plotted on a grid, the former on the ordinate, and the latter on the abscissa. Each are divided into nine assessment points. A manager's leadership style may be evaluated by rating his or her tendency in each of the two qualities from 1 to 9.

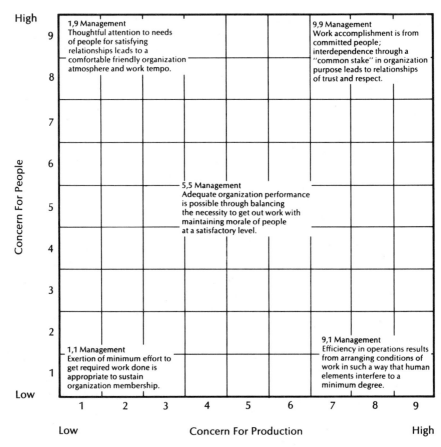

Figure 2. Managerial grid; Robert R. Blake and Jane S. Mouton, "Managerial Facades," Advanced Management Journal, July, 1966, p.31.

The intersection at five strategic points, as shown on the grid, provides a convenient way of characterizing five management styles. These have been labeled as follows by Mouton, Blake, and others:

1,1. The "Hope-nobody's-looking" leader, operating at a minimum level

1,9. The "Unrealist," who favors people to the point where output needs are neglected

9,1 The "Driver," who is all out for production, and lets the human chips fall where they may

5,5. Mr. or Ms. "Medium," who balances the two tendencies by compromising one or the other from time to time

9,9 "Superstar." This is the top leader who performs well in both areas. Blake and Mouton believe that the 9,9 rating usually comes from a team approach, with subordinate participation.

ACTION OPPORTUNITIES

The Blake-Mouton chart is a tool with which managers can analyze their leadership. The grid's five designations offer recognizable types for comparison. And the chart can also serve as a goal-setting device for managers who wish to modify their leadership style.

EXAMPLE

Grace Henry, two years into management, is concerned with her leadership results. Her boss has given her some vague idea of his evaluation: "You don't do well with the people part of your job," and suggests she look over the Blake-Mouton chart. She sits down with it and after some thought, rates herself on the "Concern for production" scale at 8, and on the "Concern for people" scale at 5. While there seems to be nothing earthshaking about the assessment, her self-evaluation is now down on paper. In addition, she sees that she does indeed have a greater concern for getting the work out than for her subordinates. The rating puts her near the "adequate" 5,5 leader, except that she is a bit stronger on the production side. Seeing herself located on the grid gives her a picture of where she stands, and she feels that increased attention to the human factor might improve results.

HOW TO USE

Here's how to get a payoff from the Managerial Grid:

1. **Input.** Place yourself on the grid, making the double rating and seeing where they intersect.
2. **Insight.** Remember that the grid rating is based on your leadership emphasis, not methods, but one thing leads to another. Now you may have a clearer idea of the kind of leader you are.
3. **Improvement.** If you are not satisfied with your performance, and the grid confirms strong or weak tendencies, what action should you take? Use the following guides for possible actions:

   ■ Remember that the two grid factors represent tendencies. It is the way they show up in your behavior that determines the kind of leader you actually are.

■ Before planning any change, think through its implications: Expect the transformation to be slow. No change as basic as your leadership style can take place overnight.

■ Think of the behavior that each tendency represents. For instance, a concern for people may mean holding on to a marginal employee because of a dire family situation, or spending time thinking about the future of a promising subordinate. A concern for production means focusing on output, and bearing down on the easygoing employees who are operating at a get-by level, even though they may label you a slavedriver.

4. Identification. Work out the actions that will constitute a change in your leadership tactics. If it is to increase your concern for production, list the tightening up of assignments, scheduling, and monitoring you may want to do. If it is the people factor you want to reinforce, list the moves that will bring you closer to your subordinates, help understand them, and work more closely with them.

Monitor your leadership over a period of time. Use the Managerial Grid after some time has passed (preferably four to six months), to evaluate progress.

▷ 16
Maslow's Hierarchy of Needs

CONCEPT

Psychologist Abraham H. Maslow's contribution to motivation theory focuses on the human being's basic needs and the order of importance into which they fall. His idea helps clear up seeming contradictions, for instance, why a talented and capable individual obviously destined for executive heights turns down a promotion, explaining, "I like my present job too much." According to Maslow, he "likes" his present job because he feels secure in it, and that counts more to him than status and respect of others that would come with the advancement. Maslow's hierarchy of needs, listed below, shows that the "safety" incentive comes before, and is more important than, the "esteem" factor which includes prestige and admiration of others.

The Needs Hierarchy

Physiological. These are the needs for basics such as food, shelter, and sexual gratification
Safety. Protection against danger and threats from the environment or people
Social. Need for love, affection, and sense of belonging
Esteem. Wish for self-respect and the good opinion of others
Self-fulfillment. The need to derive satisfaction from one's work; the sense that it is of some value in the world

Maslow's insights include the belief that people seek their satisfactions in the sequence above, that is physiological needs are satisfied first, and then, when those are achieved, the next level becomes primary, and so on through the hierarchy.

Maslow himself insisted on more flexibility for his scheme than some of his proponents did. For example, in his *Personality and Motivation** he discusses individuals whose need for self-esteem may take priority over social needs, which precede it in the hierarchy, because their desire for the good opinion of others is stronger than the desire for belonging or affection.

From management's standpoint, the hypothesis has a major weakness, namely, the place of money—salary, wages, bonuses—as an incentive. Maslow's statements failed to specify adequately which category money belonged in. The fault for this seems less the psychologist's than that of the ambiguity of what money represents in human needs. The imprecision reflects differences among individuals. For some people, money is considered essential to satisfying the most basic, physiological requirements for food, shelter, and so on. For others, money may be related to the final need, that of self-fulfillment. For example, a person whose greatest wish is to live in luxury needs funds to satisfy that desire.

ACTION OPPORTUNITIES

Maslow's insights can help executives in two areas, increased understanding of the tortuous subject of motivation, and the understanding of attitudes of individuals at all echelons; their ambitions, drives, and the kinds of things that incite them to greater effort to achieve.

* Maslow, Abraham H. (1954). *Personality and Motivation.* New York: Harper & Row.

EXAMPLES

1. Executive Frank Prince says, "Peter is one of my more money-minded subordinates. He let me know his salary was important to him, and that he would work hard to win increases. The trouble was, he always demanded raises six months before I felt they were deserved, and he became quite heated in his arguments when I suggested that his requests were premature. Once he got a raise, quiet descended, and his performance slacked off until he started getting up a head of steam for his next raise."

Frank Prince's experience validates Maslow's contention that a need, when gratified, loses its ability to motivate. Note how Peter goes through a "quiet" period after getting a raise, which represents his satisfaction with his earnings. It's only when he feels he's ready for another salary boost — the money incentive has regained its strength — that he makes the effort to deserve, or at least to get his boss to O.K., the increase.

2. Charles Brent was known in the real estate business as a hard-driving, cut-corners operator, willing to come close to unethical, even illegal practices to put over a deal or finish a project profitably. However, his sixtieth birthday was like a curtain, revealing an Act II in which Brent changed character. No one knew what instructions he had given his PR staff, but suddenly he emerged as a philanthropist, a patron of the arts, a contributor to worthy causes. Eventually it had to happen: He published an "as-told-to" book entitled Dream Builder, in which, in a combination of personal history and imaginative fiction, Brent was depicted as a poet/builder, driven to erect his commercial structures for the same reason the ancients built Stonehenge and Aaron Copland wrote his music.

Maslow would say Brent had achieved the first three needs, physiological, safety, and social, and his book was an effort to satisfy the last two, esteem and self-fulfillment. His gratification probably came not from the PR campaign that launched the poet/builder image, but from his believing in it himself. Self-delusion is a traditional path to self-satisfaction.

HOW TO USE

Maslow's thinking can help your own when questions of your personal goals or drive, or those of subordinates and colleagues, arise. Pondering the motivation of individuals in relation to their advancement and careers may be assisted by considerations like these:

1. Keep the Hierarchy of Needs in mind when speculating as to what makes people tick.

2. In thinking through the strivings and goals of a particular individual, ask yourself:

- Which level of needs has he or she reached? Your familiarity with the person, as well as their current behavior, will help answer the question.
- What behavior cues shall I look for? For example, individuals who seek to strengthen their security and hesitate to take career chances, are likely to be hung up on the second set of needs, the safety level. One who shows a strong desire for approval and wants to be "on the team," would fit in at the third, social set of needs.

3. Remember the corollary of Maslow's hypothesis, that an achieved need loses its power to motivate, and that the employee then moves on to the next level. This insight can help you decide the kinds of incentive need to spur individuals to increased effort. For instance, an employee can be reminded that developing a plan for an improved house organ can get her considerable recognition. Her focus on the esteem needs will make her especially responsive.

In general, savvy managers feel that no one concept of the many extant today of itself explains all motivation phenomena. Each of the major contributors, of whom Maslow is one, can add to your understanding. You can fill out the picture further by consulting the Index under "Motivation."

▷ 17
McGregor's Theory X Theory Y

CONCEPT

Toward the end of the 1950s, management experts began to focus on the emotional climate of work as a motivating factor. Observations at the time suggested that neither cash, working conditions nor punishment served as a continuing incentive. Professor Douglas McGregor, then at the Massachusetts Institute of Technology, proposed that attitudes toward employees, and the treatment that derived from them, could influence performance. His ideas, developed at MIT and described in his book, *The Human Side of Enterprise,** held that two different philosophies of management emerge from assumptions about people. He labeled these assumptions Theory X and Theory Y:

Theory X	Theory Y
1. Human beings are inherently lazy and will shun work if they can.	1. For most people, physical and mental effort expended at work is as natural as that expended for play or rest.
2. People must be directed, controlled, and motivated by fear of punishment or deprivation to be impelled to work as the company requires.	2. People will exercise self-control in the service of objectives which they accept.
3. The average human being prefers to be directed, wishes to avoid responsibility, has relatively little ambition, and above all, wants security.	3. Under proper conditions, the average person learns to accept and even to seek responsibility.
	4. The capacity for exercising imagination, ingenuity, and creativity exists generally among people.

Though McGregor presented the two sets of assumptions impartially, his allegiance and hope for greater employee fulfillment as well as managerial satisfaction lay with Theory Y.

ACTION OPPORTUNITIES

In addition to the X and Y approach enlarging your understanding of motivation, these areas may also benefit from the MIT scientist's idea:

- Your personal and/or your company's employee relations philosophy and policies
- The level of trust adopted in dealing with your department's or company's employees
- Policies and practices relating to employee procedures, such as the amount of supervision needed, internal security measures, and so on
- Your personal leadership practices

* McGregor, Douglas (1960). *The Human Side of Enterprise.* New York: McGraw-Hill.

EXAMPLES

1. Jack Hale, Tom Brennan's manager, believes that Tom is basically lazy and will do just enough work to get by. He keeps a tight rein on Tom, sets rigid work schedules, and supervises him closely. Some typical instructions he gives are: "Turn in this report by Friday at the latest," or, "Go to the Atlanta plant on Monday, return on Wednesday, and have the results of your assessment on my desk by Thursday at 9 A.M." Continuing checks on progress and performance are made to make sure that Tom doesn't slack off. The trouble is, Tom scores zero in initiative, and when Hale needs ideas, Tom doesn't produce them. Jack has frozen his subordinate's ability to think or act for himself.

2. Department Head Eileen Doyle supervises with a light hand. She will tell her assistant Jim Crane that new markets are needed for a particular product, and then will leave it to him to come up with possibilities. On key decisions she asks Jim to examine the options and submit his recommendations. Jim is growing under Eileen's leadership and qualifies for increasing responsibilities.

HOW TO USE

Management experts have debated the pros and cons of both approaches since McGregor first proposed them. The practical question for managers is not which theory of human nature is "correct," but which produces better results in their particular situation.

Dr. Robert N. McMurry, management consultant, argues for Theory X in an article in *Business Management* as follows: "There appears to be little awareness that . . . the so-called victims of Theory X might relish their bondage; that rigid structure is not fettering but reassuring . . ." Others assert that Theory Y fits best in today's world, among them Peter Drucker, in his *Management: Tasks, Responsibilities, Practices.** He writes, "The traditional Theory X approach to managing, that is, the carrot-and-stick way, no longer works."

In your own case you may see advantages and drawbacks to each approach, and it is possible to develop an effective management style by borrowing from both theories. Here are some tests you can try if you are not satisfied with your present practices:

1. Spend less time in close and direct supervision and see how your people fare.

* Drucker, Peter (1974). *Management: Tasks, Responsibilities, Practices.* New York: Harper & Row.

2. Give an open-ended assignment to a mediocre and uninspired performer. Present it in an involving and exciting manner. (It is possible to make a silk purse out of a sow's ear, but not overnight.) Judge the result carefully, taking into account the unfamiliarity of a first-time autonomous task.

3. Increase the amount of responsibility you give subordinates, and encourage them to make their own decisions. Some executives who have followed such a course confirm a conclusion made by one management consultant: "When people are afraid to make decisions, company productivity can be hurt." Presumably, the opposite tack has a beneficial effect.

4. Foster creativity and idea production by setting your subordinates challenging goals, assign lingering or unsolved problems to creative individuals. Some executives find this practice an effective way to build job interest in general.

5. Think about your Theory X people, those who, because of insecurity or past experience, shy away from independent action. Provide the support they need. It can be tough to be a Theory X person in a Theory Y world. Their job satisfaction and performance may improve as a result of your understanding.

◊ 18
Mentoring

CONCEPT

Mentor was a friend and counselor of Odysseus and later of his son Telemachus. Mentor's qualities of counselor and tutor are mirrored in his name and in the practice of mentoring. Business, with its laws of succession and the mingling of rookies and veterans, is a natural field for the ancient Greek's art.

Mentoring is productive because, among other things, it offers rewards to both teacher and student. The mentor gains the satisfaction of developing a mental heir and effective subordinate. The student gets the benefit of personal interest, instruction from the horse's mouth, knowledge, and a role model.

ACTION OPPORTUNITIES

Every organization concerned with its future human resources will consider mentoring as a way to prepare promising individuals for a fast track. An essential is the presence of qualified executives who are capable not only of passing along their knowledge and abilities, but who also will select their apprentices wisely. Top management may encourage mentorship and make managers aware of the opportunities for helping high-potential subordinates, even without a formal program.

EXAMPLE

Cal Fraley hires Lisa Redgrave not only because of her performance record both at college and in her previous job, but because he feels she has the potential to make a good marketer. The first weeks on the job confirm his belief: She is bright, quick and eager to learn. He decides on a close working relationship to expedite her training. Problems arise: Henry, a young man already on the staff, is a competitor. Lisa's good looks cause additional complications, suggesting a sexual factor in his interest, and causing male resentment toward a woman getting favored treatment.

Cal Fraley's boss stops by one day and casually mentions the rumors going around. The executive assures him that they are groundless, that Lisa Redgrave is a superior employee, deserving of extra training.

Fraley, sure of his motives and judgments, continues his mentoring. He is careful about two things: first, socializing. He goes to lunch with others, including Henry, but never with Lisa Redgrave, who understands. Second, he downplays the mentor relationship, neither trying to disguise it nor emphasize it in any way. As Lisa forges ahead, the arrangement is eventually accepted as a matter of course by the group.

HOW TO USE

Mentoring can be a method of passing along not only skills and experience but underlying attitudes and values as well. The following guidelines can help the process along:

1. Managers should recognize the difference between true mentorship and the less desirable practice of playing favorites. Part of the selection process has an unconscious base. For example, family background, ethnicity, and personality may be unconscious selection factors. A bias resulting from a kinship, pronounced or slight, is not unusual. As far as possible, the selection should be made fairly, on the basis of relevant objective factors such as potential, professional interests, aspiration, and so on.

2. Executives should assess their own mentoring proclivities. Some people have a natural desire to guide and teach, but there also may exist a negative impulse to overcontrol or to recreate one's own image. Here the mentor wants an extension of self rather than to develop the learner's talents. This tendency is basically destructive, and managers who find it in themselves should repress it or would do well to eschew mentoring altogether.

3. There comes a balance point at which the apprentice is ready to "graduate." This is an essential part of the development process, and should be expected and preferably welcomed by both parties, despite some wrenching of the relationship.

4. Mentoring can be different for women than for men, both as mentors or learners, as a result of business history. Women may not have had female role models, and so may have some problem accepting the responsibility and dominance of mentoring. And as apprentices to a male mentor, the oedipus factor may enter in as a complication. Awareness and open communication between the two parties can minimize the difficulties in either case.

Usually, mentorship is less structured than ordinary training, but it need not be. If the mentors prefer to map out, either on paper or otherwise, the areas and methods of imparting their knowledge, the arrangement is more likely to touch essential bases.

▷ 19
Minimizing Obsolescence

CONCEPT

The Industrial Revolution made us aware of obsolescence. Today, craftspeople are joined by brain workers as victims. Scientists, engineers, medical practitioners, and business executives are vulnerable. Training that once lasted a lifetime becomes outdated in ten or fifteen years. In high-tech professions, frequent refresher courses are required. In some cases updating must be continuous.

Margaret Zientara in *Computer World,* further clarifies the problem. She writes, "How can computer scientists and electrical engineers possibly keep up with the rapid technological change? The Institute of Electrical and Electronic Engineers alone published 200,000 pages in a recent year." But factors other than technological change may threaten executive jobs.

ACTION OPPORTUNITIES

Executives can use the obsolescence threat as a guide to remaining current. More than just new machines and methods are involved. For example, two things can happen: (1) Cultural shifts may damage an entire industry—the fate of the cinema as television burgeoned; and (2) Young people newly trained, tend to replace older people because of their updated skills and willingness to work for lower wages.

Particularly vulnerable may be those in middle management. One instance: computer-industry employment data shows that while the lower and top echelons retain their employability, middle-range executives whose experience is heavy in yesterday's equipment and thinking did not fare as well.

EXAMPLE

Computer and other high-tech fields are not uniquely prone to obsolescence. Consider how job security disappeared for one professional in the film and videotape field:

After winning a degree in film-making from New York University in 1955, Rita Cardine started as an assistant film editor and steadily progressed. In 1972 she became a producer of commercials for J.D. Emery Productions. But in 1975 Emery sold out to a competitor. Emery asked Rita whether she wanted him to make a pitch on her behalf to the new owners, but she said no. She had decided to quit and free lance.

Jobs came along. She produced shorts, including an award-winning film on teenage alcoholism, and films for industry. After a while, producing jobs dried up and she resumed film editing, renting cutting-room space and contacting former clients for contracts. Then Hank Keller, an old associate and now partner in a postproduction house that prepared film and videotape materials for broadcast, offered her a job selling company services, as well as doing some editing.

"Rita," he said, "you'll be great. You know everybody and they know you." Her professional friends were good leads and she did well, bringing in several major clients. But she began to feel out of place. In her early fifties, she was the oldest person around. One day, in a tape-editing room, she realized that the editor and his assistant, who were expertly doing operations she had tried in vain to master, were in their late twenties.

"O.K.," she told herself, *"you don't have to love your job."* But she did feel she deserved greater financial recognition and said as much to Hank Keller. He told her he would speak to his partner. Nothing happened. A few weeks went by and she told Hank's secretary she would like to see him. He didn't get back to her. Eventually she got the picture. Why give her a raise when they could give her job to a younger person, one who would project a younger company image and take a lower salary?

A friend had been urging her to go into the travel business with her. She hated to write off her training and years of experience, but it was time to change horses.

HOW TO USE

Career obsolescence appears in many ways and places. The manager's considerations should be made in the context of his or her own situation. Some guidelines:

1. Changes in your business. In some cases developments are rapid, in others, less so. The rate of progress—and obsolescence—should be judged on an industry-by-industry basis.

2. Age rollback. When the pace of change is rapid, a generation gap may be created. The experience of older people becomes irrelevant and younger competitors may be better qualified to perform.

3. Alienation. This factor can be a major handicap. It is a result rather than an aspect of obsolescence, and intensifies the older person's discomfort at being among "strangers."

4. Skill and salary competition. The older person can be at a disadvantage vis-a-vis a younger competitor. First, the latter benefits from updated training. Second, a younger person may take a job for less pay. Third, some companies favor younger employees to project a contemporary image.

For the dollar-shrewd employer, there may be other benefits. As one businessman points out, "Terminating an older, not-yet-vested employee may make it unnecessary to pay a pension. And if vested, it cuts down on the pension amount that will have to be paid for their length of service. And younger people are usually a smaller drain on medical coverage."

For executives who feel they are at some risk, an obsolescence-minimizing program is advisable:

- Ask yourself, "What do I want for the rest of my career? It's a basic question for any contemplation of future plans, not easy to answer, but worth probing.
- Check your organization's obsolescence-creating pattern. Consider both the company situation and your own profession or area of responsibility to determine whether the threat for you is real and imminent, mild and distant, or nonexistent.
- Keep ahead of the game. There are a number of options, such as:

Reeducation
Retraining
Courses, books, seminars, and so on
Shifting to a related, but for you more advantageous, field
Being a consultant in your area of expertise
Starting your own business

- Decide on your policy. Think through your situation and come up with a plan of action that can start a period of new growth and help improve your position for the present and future.

⊅ 20
Morale

CONCEPT

Contemporary management deals with the morale concept the way families of yore treated a relative hanged as a horse thief. Major management encyclopedias don't mention the term. The word may appear in management tracts, but only as a misspelling of the word moral.

This freeze reflects management's blighted hopes. Morale was once a glitter word in business vocabulary. Its two syllables promised to hold the secret of productivity, low costs, and job satisfaction—the ultimate trio of top targets. According to an expert of the 1950s, "Morale is the backbone of a working team, and sparks in a member the will to give the best of his talents for the organization." Unfortunately, untrue.

Authorities of later date, George Strauss and Leonard R. Sayles, see more clearly in *Behavioral Strategies for Managers*: "There is little evidence that high morale leads to high productivity. Just the reverse may be true. Morale may be low in a concentration camp, yet production very high. Similarly, workers may well be satisfied to 'goof off' in a department where the work pace is extremely slow. Numerous psychological studies show that the relationship between productivity and satisfaction is close to zero."

Paradoxically, the mistaken reading of morale benefits sprang from the Hawthorne Experiments, one of the most rewarding studies ever undertaken in industry. The astonishing jump in productivity that resulted from the test procedures was accompanied by high morale among the subjects. But morale didn't cause the improvement, it was only a coincidental result. Realistic managers as well as scientists knew the evidence didn't support the belief. As one executive pointed out, "The guys come back from a bowling victory and feel great. But the last thing in their minds is to buckle down and work, to say nothing of working better."

ACTION OPPORTUNITIES

But morale does have an important place in executive thought. The word means mood, or esprit de corps, and while high morale doesn't increase productivity, it can increase job satisfaction, in itself a worthy objective. In assessing your workgroup, morale is a vital sign you can use to gauge the success or failure of your leadership.

EXAMPLE

Professor Alex Bavelas and a group at MIT conducted an experiment in communication. Bavelas arranged a group of five people so that they communicated with each other in a circular pattern. This represented a democratic organizational structure. He set up another group of five in a hierarchal pattern representing an authoritarian chain of command. Both groups were given the same problem and were told to solve it by exchanging messages.

Bavelas found that the group in the circular pattern had high morale but was not efficient. The other group got better results but was dissatisfied with the procedure. In short, while morale doesn't improve output, the experiment suggests that good performance doesn't raise morale, either.

HOW TO USE

Assessing group morale may be in order when well-being, cooperative-ness, or creativity are unsatisfactory. Just thinking about the group in ob-jective terms may provide insights that could lead to worthwhile action.

To start, give the group an off-the-cuff rating. Ask, "Where does group morale rate on a scale of 0 to 10?" Note the figure and compare it later to the score for the factors listed as follows. The items are adapted from a study by David G. Moore and Robert K. Burns reported in *Factory Man-agement.*

Be objective in your ratings. For example, in the item, "Boss-subordinate relations," respond from a neutral standpoint if you are the boss. This is not easy, but do your best.

Factor	0	1	2	3	4	5	6	7	8	9	10
Job demands and pressures	—	—	—	—	—	—	—	—	—	—	—
Working conditions	—	—	—	—	—	—	—	—	—	—	—
Pay	—	—	—	—	—	—	—	—	—	—	—
Employee benefits	—	—	—	—	—	—	—	—	—	—	—
Friendliness of employees	—	—	—	—	—	—	—	—	—	—	—
Boss-subordinate relations	—	—	—	—	—	—	—	—	—	—	—
Confidence in management	—	—	—	—	—	—	—	—	—	—	—
Ability of boss	—	—	—	—	—	—	—	—	—	—	—
Effectiveness of department administration	—	—	—	—	—	—	—	—	—	—	—
Effectiveness of company administration	—	—	—	—	—	—	—	—	—	—	—
Status and recognition	—	—	—	—	—	—	—	—	—	—	—
Job security	—	—	—	—	—	—	—	—	—	—	—
Identification with company	—	—	—	—	—	—	—	—	—	—	—
Chances for growth and advancement	—	—	—	—	—	—	—	—	—	—	—

Instructions: Total all items and get an average. Determine how that average compares to the off-the-cuff rating you have given group morale before taking the quiz. If there is a big discrepancy, try to figure out why. Is your "impression" overly optimistic or unnecessarily low? Are you unclear about what shapes morale?

Now another question: Should you take action on your findings? Suggested answer: Not if you feel the assessment result is satisfactory.

This is one case where, "If it ain't broke don't fix it" probably applies. The answer could be "yes," if you feel you are depriving your people of the benefits of well-being, and yourself of the pleasure of leading a group with high morale.

What to do? Begin by talking to your people individually, in sub-groups, or in plenary session discussion. Pinpointing dissatisfactions and dealing with them can deliver worthwhile results.

▷ 21
Murphy's Law

CONCEPT

"When anything can go wrong, it will." The Murphy to whom managers owe undying gratitude may or may not have existed. The mists of time have hidden the moment when a creative individual milked the experience of countless disasters and enunciated it in this wise adage. But whether we're indebted to a real or a hypothetical Murphy, the wisdom bearing the name has won popularity because it has prevented countless accidents, errors, and failures.

Murphy's Law tells us that hoping for the best is less realistic than expecting trouble and preparing for it. It has three corollaries:

Nothing is as easy as it looks.

Everything takes longer than you expect.

Things will go wrong at the worst possible moment.

ACTION OPPORTUNITIES

Apply Murphy's law when:

- An untested undertaking or procedure is to be started
- A new element is added—say an inexperienced employee or an untried piece of equipment
- An operation is crucial—because of safety of individuals, cost, or other stakes whose loss would be highly damaging

EXAMPLES

1.   The head of Personnel suggests to the president, "This year, instead of holding our picnic on company premises, why not use the state park? We've outgrown the back lot. . . ."

There is no case on record of a company failing because someone forgot to bring the frankfurters or beer. But a successful company outing pays off su 'stantially in many ways, from boosting esprit de corps to increasing employee respect because "our outfit sure knows how to do things."

You'd think arranging a company outing would pose no problems. Murphy disagrees. A successful outcome, he states, requires that details must be carefully planned. A committee may be needed to assign responsibilities, make executives available to supply information and guidance, provide personpower (volunteers or otherwise), assign specific tasks, and so on.

2.   Murphy's Law applies to almost all planned activities. A vice-president, Research and Development may be staging a runthrough of a new process, your person in charge of systems may want to inaugurate a new method of organizing records, or you yourself may be planning a demonstration of a pet plan for improving maintenance services.

Whether it is a company picnic or a trip to the moon, countless elements are involved, each creating chances for failure. To play it safe, be guided by that genius, Mr. or Ms. Murphy.

HOW TO USE

Here is a procedure that helps invoke the benefits of Murphy's wisdom:

1. Become a pessimist, if only temporarily. Murphy's Law favors a mind set of expecting things to go wrong. Even if your positive thinking usually invites Lady Luck to play it your way, why take unnecessary risks? On operations where failure or serious trouble means hurtful loss, weight the outcome in your favor by reviewing your plans with awareness of possible points of failure, big and small. Take precautions. Try to anticipate difficulties.

In the case of the company picnic, for example, your planners should not depend on crossed fingers to prevent rain. It is said that hospitals and bankruptcy courts are filled with patients and litigants whose fingers are frozen in the crossed position. The question, "What if it rains?" needs a practical answer, whether it be setting a rain date or transferring the festivities indoors. Better to be in close quarters in a dry space than to have a washout of people, equipment, food, and the picnic spirit.

2. Plan thoroughly. Don't depend on last-minute improvisation, unless an unexpected development makes adlibbing necessary. Advance attention to detail is a better bet than spit-and-bandaid repairs to hold things together.

3. Spot crucial areas of operation. Major elements of an operation— a key machine, a capable operator, experienced supervision—should be checked out and in place. Minor details count too. Many a mission has failed because of the proverbial nail, an insignificant item which is essential for the operation to go forward.

4. Have backups available. This is not necessary for everything, but should be arranged for major subsystems, parts, and so on. Vera Mayer, vice-president of Information at NBC, exemplifies the executive with a realistic, one might even say Murphian, view of the need for duplication to make a system failsafe. When she switched her information-storage system from a manual, written one to microfilm with a computer retrieval capability, she fought off suggestions to get rid of the manual setup. "We're not going to eliminate the old system," she said. "Computers break down. We're not only going to keep the manual system, but we're going to keep it updated." There have been a sufficient number of instances when the manual system saved the day for her to be proved right. "A lot of us sleep more soundly. That's another benefit of the backup," she says.

▷ **22**
Natural Leader

CONCEPT

The "natural leader" is looked to by group members for guidance, command, and the spearheading of group action. Every echelon has its natural leaders, from front-line to executive staff. While the authority of appointed leaders usually goes unquestioned, natural leaders are regarded by their peers as *their* champions. Peers look upon natural leaders as their counter to the appointed leader, not necessarily as an antagonist, but more often as a mediator, negotiator, and interpreter of management policies.

The natural leader can be a resource, both for employees and management. To employees (this includes groups from bottom to top of the company), they can be a court of second resort when difficulties with company authority arise. An employee who is dissatisfied with management's treatment or judgments, may turn to the natural leader for counsel or use him or her as a go-between with management. For management, the natural leader may simplify negotiations and communications with employee groups. The potential for conflict between natural and appointed leaders is there, but is seldom ignited.

Union-management relations form a unique pattern of relationships and procedures in corporate life. In the early days of unionization, organizers sought natural leaders to head their drives, and natural leaders often become union officials. Managements also understood the potential of natural leaders and sought to recruit them into management ranks.

ACTION OPPORTUNITIES

Executives would do well to recognize natural leaders and seek their cooperation in implementing management policies and decisions. The acceptance of natural leaders can advance causes that are mutually beneficial.

EXAMPLE

Bea Farland is going to be fired because the work she was hired to do a year ago is being discontinued. But Bea has become a popular group member, and her friends want to argue her case with management.

"Let's get up a petition," says one. "Let's threaten to quit," says another. They turn to Hal Fort, asking "What do you think?"

Fort, a natural leader of the group, suggests that he tell the boss of the group's concern and try to arrange a transfer for Bea within the company. He presents the case in a direct and nonargumentative way, and the manager agrees to look into the matter. The next day he tells Fort, "There is an opening in Accounts Payable and it's hers if she wants it. And thanks. We may be able to hold on to a good employee."

A major area of participation for the natural leader is that of innovating change (see Resistance to Change, page 72). Also, when a company wants to have its values, attitudes, or actions understood by its employees, the natural leader can be an effective bridge.

HOW TO USE

Winning the natural leader's cooperation is clearly desirable. However, there can be a complication. If the individual seems too ready to cooperate, or seems to be self-seeking in going along with the company, the trust and regard of the group can be destroyed and the leader's power annihilated. To preserve the potential benefits of the natural leaders in your organization:

1. Know who they are. In some cases it's easy: He or she may be a standout, the first to speak up on employee-management matters, has the respect of peers, and can be seen to be the person the group consults on work matters. You undoubtedly can spot the natural leaders of your own group, perhaps you are one. Some additional qualities follow:

- *Know-how and savvy.* Whether based on experience, superior intelligence, or a shrewd understanding of people, the leader often can analyze and predict events.
- *Willingness to lead.* Natural leaders are self-confident and egotistical enough to feel comfortable in the leadership role. They accept authority and responsibility easily.
- *Ability to communicate.* They tend to be articulate and effective speakers. They can present a case, and argue and persuade for it, both to the boss and their peers.
- *Either ambitious or not.* It's a paradox, and a fact. Some natural leaders are aware of their effectiveness and use it as a means of advancement. But some who are equally effective seem satisfied with their status in the group and are content to remain in it.

2. Seek cooperation in appropriate situations. But do respect the fragility of their position. Some organizations have undermined their natural leaders by:

- Pressuring for the acceptance of ideas or moves which are not in the best interests of the group
- Offering rewards, even though disguised (for instance, good assignments or promotions) for cooperation. It is generally unwise to destroy the group's faith in their leader.

3. Remember what makes the natural leader tick. The qualities of the leader earns the respect, trust, and followership of the group. Weigh carefully the situations in which cooperation is sought. Touchy communications problems may yield to his or her intervention.

▷ 23
Parkinson's Law

CONCEPT

Some three decades ago, C. Northcote Parkinson, steeped in the tradition of English government and business, wrote *Parkinson's Law,* * a volume detailing some of his astute and humorous observations of people at work. The sage's ideas haunted and tickled the funnybones of English and American managers, and we haven't stopped laughing yet. He spoke before American business groups, was visiting professor to universities, and won many honorary degrees, including a Doctor of Laws from the University of Maryland.

The pearl of his wit and wisdom is known as Parkinson's Law: "Work expands to fill the time available for its completion." Having communicated this truth that both enlightened and embarrassed management, he went on to illustrate it:

An elderly lady can spend the entire day dispatching a postcard to her niece. An hour will be spent finding the card, another hunting for spectacles, half an hour in finding the address, an hour and a quarter in composition, and twenty minutes deciding whether to take an umbrella to go to the mailbox. And he adds:

"The total effort that would occupy a busy man for three minutes may leave another person prostrate after a day of doubt, anxiety, and toil."

Parkinson was not content to point an accusing finger. He also analyzed the factors underlying his law. He said there were two such factors:

- Managers seek to multiply subordinates, not rivals.
- Managers make work for one another.

He pictures an administrator who feels overworked. Whether he really is or only imagines himself to be doesn't matter. The reason for his decreasing energy, Parkinson suggests, may be a normal symptom of middle age. Regardless of the cause, there are three possible remedies:

- He may resign.
- He may ask that a colleague take some of the load.
- He may ask for two subordinates to assist him.

* Parkinson, C. Northcote (1957). *Parkinson's Law.* Boston, MA: Houghton Mifflin.

Never in history, says Parkinson, has a manager in this situation chosen any but the third course.

Having illustrated the first factor, he then goes on to the second: As a result of the addition of assistants, ". . . seven people are now doing what one did before." The seven make so much work for each other that all are fully occupied and the original overworked individual is working harder than ever.

ACTION OPPORTUNITIES

Parkinson's Law can be useful when staffing, organizing, reorganizing, or hiring for your department, branch, or company; or in work scheduling, work assignment, and deadline setting.

EXAMPLES

1. Executive Phyllis Layton becomes aware of a puzzling phenomenon. On her desk is a report she has asked a new subordinate to complete in time for a meeting with a key customer. Despite a deadline allowing only half a day for a task usually requiring twice as much time, the report is completely satisfactory. Why, she wonders, has the report been considered a full day's job?

2. Another task versus time mystery: Department head Harry Lord assigns six people to take quarterly inventory. That is two more than the usual crew, but Lord wants to get the procedure out of the way. The job still takes eight hours, however, and that's so even though inventory is down 10 percent from the previous quarter.

HOW TO USE

Some executives suggest, "Parkinson's Law is a purely scientific discovery, applicable only in theory to the business of today."

But some experts, appreciating the validity of the law, insist that there are applications. Here are some steps that can put it to work on your behalf:

1. Accept the law as a fact of life. Staffs tend to fatten up rather than to slim down. Managers have to develop a cool eye and a firm hand on their rosters and assigned deadlines.

2. Take the broad view. One cynical executive says, "If I don't get reasonably frequent complaints about overwork, I suspect the Parkinson syndrome has struck."

Here is one executive's prescription: "Every six months I match up the total work performed in my department to our objectives; the amount of goods and services delivered." (He's in Purchasing.) "I then compare these two elements to those of previous periods, and if I seem to be slipping, I start looking for ways to tighten up."

3. Take the narrow view. Another executive tries to assess work done compared to work objectives on a person-by-person basis. "The trick here," he says, "is to be hard-headed. Few employees have major amounts of idle time on their hands, but that's not the point. The real question is how much of their time is spent on productive assignments. This isn't to favor keeping employees' noses to the grindstone every hour of the workweek. But there is a difference between boondoggling and normal efficiency."

4. Test. For managers who suspect that either because of laxity or changes in the work situation, such as new methods or equipment, present task-time balances are off, probing may reveal inequities. In some companies, work contracts may limit a manager's freedom to act. Even in nonunion companies, however, employees may resist efforts to change time allowances. But tightening up procedures, like innovating new ones, is part of the continuing drive for effectiveness on which survival depends.

C. Northcote, your combination of wit and wisdom has helped many managements keep work more productive and workers more meaningfully employed. Idleness is the most boring and unsatisfying activity there is.

◊ **24**
The Peter Principle

CONCEPT

In 1969, Dr. Laurence J. Peter propounded the "Peter Principle," and it became an instant catch phrase, active in our vocabulary today. We knowingly diagnose the Peter Principle when a skilled operator flops as a foreman because he can't manage people, or when an accountant can't cut it as comptroller because she is unable to relate to top management.

The following is Dr. Peter's statement of his idea: "In a hierarchy every employee tends to rise to his level of incompetence." It suggests that in a system based on rewards, those who do their jobs well are pushed up the ladder, and eventually into jobs beyond their abilities.

Dr. Peter drew on his years as teacher, counselor, school psychologist, prison instructor, and university professor to develop his concept. The book, *The Peter Principle,** written with Raymond Hull, a playwright and satirist, became a bestseller. Most people suspected that Peter and Hull's respective tongues were neatly tucked in their cheeks as they wrote, but there is considerable insight behind the humor.

Like all generalities, the Peter Principle doesn't mean to imply that all people are victims of overpromotion. What Dr. Peter has uncovered is a tendency in organizational life, not a fate that awaits all employees. The Principle is sufficiently valid to help managers in the important areas of promotion policy and individual careers, however, including their own.

ACTION OPPORTUNITIES

The Peter Principle comes into play when:

- Considering an employee for promotion
- A previously good employee is not making it in a new job
- Comparing two candidates for advancement
- Planning a career path in your company for a promising employee
- Planning your own career

* Peter, Laurence J. & Hull, Raymond (1969). *The Peter Principle*. New York: Morrow.

EXAMPLES

1.   Judy Singer was an excellent reporter. Her copy required little editing, her stories came in on time, she covered all the key questions, and included the best quotes. When the chief editor left suddenly, Singer's boss gave her the job and she was pleased to be a manager. But troubles began to mount. Despite her efforts to the contrary, writers missed deadlines, were often superficial in their coverage, were careless, and depended on rewrite to fix up poor copy.

Judy Singer longed for the good old reporting days. Managing people? She didn't care for it.

2.   Norman Beane was a brilliant research scientist who had made important discoveries for his company. A grateful management decided to make him director of research. Used to solitary effort, he now had to work closely with others, both subordinates and higher-echelon people. He chafed at being tied to a desk. The big crisis came when he was asked to prepare a budget, got hopelessly bogged down, and his boss had to step in and do it for him. He had the qualities to be a brilliant researcher. He was at best a poor administrator.

HOW TO USE

Peter and Hull did not spell out serious solutions to the crucial and widespread problem they spotlighted. They did suggest humorous remedies, however, such as avoiding promotion by creative incompetence, dressing shabbily or using too much make-up, refusing to drink coffee at the coffee break, or parking one's car in space reserved for the company president.

But the Principle applies to an important business reality. Ability and performance must be distinguished from potential.

The Peter-Hull idea can be used to prevent major waste of your organization's human resources, and destruction of individual careers. Use it for:

1. Yourself. Don't let the American Dream, the mythical pattern of rising to the top, push you past your optimum rung on the ladder. You will do better for yourself and your organization by growing in your job and enriching it than by moving up into a no-can-do, no-win position. These specifics can help:

   ■ Know when to hesitate over a proffered promotion. No matter how tempting the benefits—higher pay, status, and so on—examine the job requirements and decide whether you have what it takes to fill it.

- Remember that more than ability is involved. Are you willing to shoulder the additional responsibility, possibly longer hours, and separation from old friends and work patterns?
- Get your boss's ideas as to your capabilities and qualifications for the new job.
- Realize that the final judgment is yours. No one can tell you how much you like your present job, or how much the new one will offer you in overall satisfaction.
- When in doubt, consider a test run. It may not always be possible, but if it is, make the change on a temporary basis and check the key points: your ability, suitability, the "feel" of the job in terms of the workstyle it demands; new associates and working relationships. Finally, after weighing the pros and cons, estimate your net satisfaction and then decide.

2. Subordinates. Consider both company policy and your own views on promotion:

- Does company tradition favor promotion for merit?
- Is there an overeagerness for promotion from within, so that homegrown mediocrities win out over hiring new blood from the outside?
- Is loyalty to the home team interfering with an objective long-range view that may require major shifts of human resources needs, and the people to fill them?
- Is the executive staff alert to the kind of forward thinking that will remedy and cure the Peter syndrome? (In other words, avoid promoting people who will just get by in the new job.)
- Do you let your subordinates know that outstanding performance in the present job is appreciated, and may be earn pay increases and other rewards, but that it's only half a recommendation for advancement? The other half consists of developing and refining the qualifications the next-level job demands?

To Dr. Peter and Raymond Hull, the management community owes thanks for adding humor to the presentation of a serious and constructive idea.

▷ 25
Pretesting

CONCEPT

Business undertakes a vast number of projects, programs, new products, and plans. Some are routine, but many are untried with millions of dollars at stake. A winning innovation can mean rejuvenation, while a losing one can run the organization into the red and possibly into bankruptcy court. Pretesting—of people as well as other factors—reduces the risk.

The pretest is a trial that simulates actual use as far as possible and provides a basis for a decision whether or not to go ahead, or just as crucial, pinpoints needs for correction and adjustment.

ACTION OPPORTUNITIES

Any innovation with consequences in terms of money, reputation, or ability to operate lends itself to some form of testing. The planners' need to penetrate the screen that separates us from the future can be partially satisfied by testing. Two requirements are willingness to invest time and effort, and availability of someone who can devise appropriate methods.

EXAMPLES

Industries tend to develop their own approaches to testing. For instance:

*1. **Housing.** A developer buys ten acres of suburban land intending to build twenty homes. What style will sell, and what features will get the customers excited? A furnished model is opened to the public, sells on the second day, and buyers are ready to put cash down on the basis of lot selection and blueprints. The builders have not only tested the house style, but have learned two additional things: An extra half bathroom would increase appeal, and could bring in $5,000 more per house.*

*2. **Detergents.** The manufacturers of a line of kitchen and laundry detergents decide that a lemon-scented laundry liquid would hit home with homemakers. They test market the product, complete with scent and new container, in a typical area. "Lemon's a lemon," they conclude. The package moves, but not fast enough. "Back to the drawing board," Marketing and Research and Development are told.*

HOW TO USE

A large range of devices and methods are available to test undertakings, large or small, inside or outside the firm. Consider these tools:

1. The real thing. The model home tested the actual product in its natural setting. The same principle applies elsewhere:

The president of a chemical company decides the organization needs a house organ. His staff splits: One faction favors a publication that emphasizes company news and plays down social and personal items, while the other wants the emphasis reversed.

The executive has samples of each version printed and distributes copies to a key group of employees, whose opinions are surveyed. The group strongly favors the business-orientated publication, and the decision is made accordingly.

2. Blueprints, drawings, sketches. Fashion designers are experienced hands at quick sketches of their ideas, ditto architects, toy makers, and so forth. Layouts can also help managers in improving storage or the movement of materials in the department.

Another application concerns a move to new offices: Who shall occupy how much space? Where should that space be? Who shall be next to whom? These are some of the questions. Floor plans can enable people to see how needs will be met, but there is a caveat. Some people can't visualize from two-dimensional drawings, even with elevations. For them the next device may be the answer.

3. Models. A model home is usually the actual structure. But models can be the item reduced in size. They can be rough, or an exact replica of the original, made to scale, working or nonworking. Manufacturers of everything from ships to furniture make table-top replicas to assess eye appeal and check for design and function. Exact models of autos and boats may check such qualities as wind resistance and structural strength.

4. Performance tests. New products stand or fall on the single question of how well they perform in use. Food, perfume, tires, and paint are tested for durability, nose appeal, taste, and so on.

Trials are performance tests of an entire complicated product. There are two versions:

- **"Dry run."** This is a check for the general feasibility and basic aspects of an item.
- **"Wet run."** The headline read, "Experts Study Explosion In Crash Test of Airplane." Behind the headline: A fuel additive developed by

government engineers to prevent fire and explosions after plane crashes had been tested exhaustively in the laboratory with good results. The final check was a crash landing of a four-engine Boeing 727 operated by remote control. It blew up. Moral: Where possible, pretest under actual conditions. Disappointing though it was, the fireball saved lives and money.

◊ 26
Quality of Work Life

CONCEPT

Quality of Work Life (QWL) developed from the seminal Hawthorne Experiments (see heading, page 200). As the human relations movement strengthened, the conviction grew that the twin goals of employee satisfaction and improved productivity could be achieved by enriching the job and tailoring it to the practical and emotional needs of workers. QWL is the logical next phase of the job enrichment approach, made larger and more inclusive.

QWL seeks to improve the working experience for employees by replacing some traditional methods, everything from authoritarian management to management-dominated decision making, by new procedures, values, and attitudes aimed at enhancing employee status and dignity. For instance, workers share in discussions of company objectives, planning, decision making, and work methods. The overall purpose is to create a climate of freedom, participation, and autonomy in which the worker is regarded not only as worth his or her hire, but as a capable partner sharing in common objectives.

The concept got a big push when an official of the United Automobile Workers introduced QWL in negotiations with General Motors and it was eventually included in the 1973 contract. After a start in one plant, GM reported these results:

For employees it noted greater commitment to the company and its goals, increased self-esteem, stronger work involvement, and enhanced personal dignity. Corporate benefits included better labor-management relations and improved productivity and quality of product.

ACTION OPPORTUNITIES

QWL is a way of thinking as well as an approach to managing. It is a company style rather than a style for individual managers. Managers could apply the concept in dealing with subordinates, but the ultimate benefits depend on a response to the total work environment. Familiarity with QWL can afford executives: (1) understanding of an important management idea; (2) knowledge of the elements that constitute the approach; and (3) deeper insight into the human realities of life on the workscene.

EXAMPLE

General Motors' 1973 contract with the UAW included Quality of Work Life provisions which the company implemented in its Tarrytown, New York assembly plant. The move may have been taken out of desperation. Product quality there was the worst in the entire organization. The company explained the objectives and procedures of the new approach to all personnel. Major elements were participation in problem analysis, problem solving, and decision making.

As a result of the new approach, the company reported improved labor-management relations, improved productivity, and most important, a transformation of quality output from the worst in the company to the best. Workers went on to join management in the design of production facilities for new plants. GM's favorable experience created QWL action not only in other automobile companies, but in other industries as well.

HOW TO USE

Richard E. Walton of Harvard Business School was an early formulator of the QWL approach. In an article in the *Harvard Business Review,* he spelled out the factors relevant to the improvement of working life as follows:

1. *Fair compensation.* Pay and benefits sufficient for the employee to lead an acceptable life, and comparing favorably with that paid for similar work in similar circumstances
2. *Safety and health.* Absence of health-threatening facilities, substances, odors, noise, and so on
3. *Self-development.* Enabling employees to develop themselves

4. *Growth and security.* Career path designed to stave off obsoles-cence, encourage use of advanced skills, and utilize promotion potential
5. *Social integration.* Freedom in the workplace from prejudice, en-couragement of upward mobility, and an atmosphere of community and openness
6. *Constitutionalism.* Rights for the worker and the means to protect them, absence of favoritism in recognition and rewards
7. *Life space.* An employee's worklife should be a balanced part of his or her total life. The impact of work on the family and its needs should be minimized
8. *Social relevance.* The company should be responsible in such mat-ters as its product, marketing, respect for the environment, employ-ment practices, and its ethics in general, for its own sake, as well as that of its employees and society at large

While the objectives of the Quality of Work Life concept are salutary, people and society itself pose difficulties:

1. Implementation procedures such as participation and assignment of tasks and roles are not foolproof and may misfire.
2. Some people, for reasons clear or unconscious, may not go along, or may pretend they do but drag their feet. This resistance may exist at all organization levels, including top management itself.
3. Initial enthusiasm may cool.
4. Rearrangement of roles and status may well upset those who feel they have benefited less than others.

Dr. Harry Levinson, in his book *Executive,** describes a difficulty that might apply to the power transfer in QWL;

> *There is a hazard with bosses who pretend they do not have power over others. . . . People do not know where they stand with a boss who has power but doesn't want to be dictatorial.*
> *Bosses who pose as peers are like wolves in sheep's clothing. Even when they mean well—and when the last thing they want is to be wolves—the disguise frightens people and throws them off balance. . . . Even when the boss seems to want group decision-making, subordinates fear that he or she will snatch off the lambskin and reclaim the boss's power and pre-rogative.*

* Levinson, Harry (1981). *Executive.* Cambridge, MA: Harvard University Press.

Despite the difficulties, many companies have adopted QWL as company policy, and scored gains for themselves and employees.

▷ 27
Resistance to Change

CONCEPT

Early observers noted the resistance of workers to change in their jobs or conditions of work, small or large. People resisted the change of the color of the office walls just as strongly as they resisted a reorganization that threatened their jobs. Even top management wasn't immune. Executives resisted office relocations and shifts in job responsibility with vigor equal to that of their subordinates to comparable changes.

Awareness of the depth of the problem makes management of change an area of general concern. Most management training courses treat the subject fully, and it appears regularly in seminars and business books. The attention is not misplaced. Surprised managers repeatedly face unexpected rebellion by individuals and groups over alterations that seem minor. But to those affected, the threat of change is real, even though the reactions seem disproportionately strong to those in charge.

The phenomenon was of special interest to psychologists. Kurt Lewin, an outstanding innovative investigator, simplified the change problem by graphically depicting the opposition of forces:

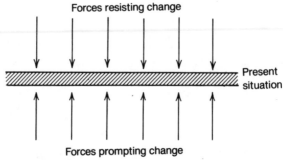

Forces resisting change

Present situation

Forces prompting change

Figure 3. *Lewin's force field analysis*

Lewin's chart represents the factors that make a change desirable, pitted against those that resist it. The How to Use section, which follows shortly, adapts the chart as a tool to help v/in acceptance of the new.

ACTION OPPORTUNITIES

Any time conditions of work, procedures, physical surroundings, or traditions are to be altered, suspicion of the people involved should be expected. Even if the reaction seems irrational, and this may be the case, playing it safe requires anticipating complaints and knowing how to prevent or minimize them.

EXAMPLE

A publishing company was to change location, moving from a deteriorating neighborhood to an area with new office buildings, one of which was to be its new home. After months of study and planning the experts had worked out office and space arrangements so that all the editors, secretaries, and administrators had adequate space and working facilities in the new setup.

On the first day in the new premises complaints were rife. Incredible as it seemed to management, people whose offices were bigger, brighter, and certainly cleaner than the ones they had left behind were grumbling. One senior editor told the publisher, "I hate air conditioning. The windows don't open and I feel as though I'm choking." Another pointed out that the copy equipment, previously near her office, was about 50 feet away, requiring a lot of extra walking. That seemed like a rational complaint compared to one editor's demand that his old desk be retrieved because the shiny finish of the new one gave him a headache.

"I'd have gotten less griping," the publisher told his wife that evening, "if I'd cut their pay ten percent." Probably true, particularly if he had taken the proper steps to explain the need for the reduction.

HOW TO USE

Here are guidelines that can help ameliorate the difficulties:

1. Understand the psychology. These three major factors make change threatening:

- **Surprise.** Sudden announcements and unexpected developments throw people off balance. When people feel unprepared and out of control, resistance seems the only means of coping.

- *Usurpation.* The self-styled victims see change as an invasion of their turf.
- *Loss.* Lowered status, sacrifice of privileges, uncertainty about the future, and decreased personal convenience, as well as material losses are typical deprivations, real or fancied.

2. Be aware of the terms in which people see the threat of change. The kinds of doubts that assail employees are:

- Will I lose my job? A change in departmental setup or a new boss or assistant may cause worry.
- Will the new method, a change in equipment or facilities, be difficult or impossible for me to handle?
- Will I have to change my way of doing things? People get fond of their habits. Interference with traditional practices may cause discomfort.
- Will new people in the department lessen the possibility of promotion or advancement?
- Will the new situation mean more work for me? Harder work? Less desirable work?
- Do the rumors of organizational moves mean my job will be affected or even lost? Job security is often the economic and psychological foundation of employee well-being. Any shake-up becomes a major concern.

3. Use a step plan to inaugurate change:

- *Cooperation.* In the earliest planning stage, keep in mind the need to get the cooperation of those who will be affected. Part of the planning should include ways and means of minimizing the trauma.
- *Announcement.* This need not be a formal statement, but can mean informing employees individually or in small groups of the general plan: "We've been thinking of swinging the division over into a two-shift operation . . ." An important part of what is said is the explanation of the need, and reasons for the change.
- *Participation.* In cases where it is feasible, those who will implement the innovation should become involved in:

> Giving opinions about the idea
> Pointing out problems
> Offering suggestions
> Taking on some of the planning

- *Acceptance.* Use the "minimax" approach to get acceptance. This means minimizing the negatives and maximizing the favorable factors that make the change desirable. Kurt Lewin's force field analysis chart below can be adapted for a visual rendering of the minimax technique:

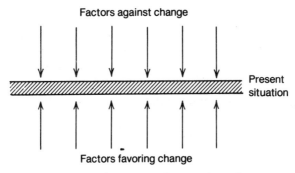

Figure 4. Confrontation of pro and con factors

Here is an example of the chart in action: Executive Peter Lund wants to bring in a new boss for the Order Department from outside to replace the incumbent who is retiring. He feels no present employee is qualified. He anticipates that after going through the steps of an announcement, and explaining why the new manager has been recruited from outside the company, the factors will shape up like this:

Unfavorable factors: The staff feels resentment toward an outsider. Two individuals feel they should have gotten the job. There is general uneasiness about how the new boss is going to run things.

Favorable factors: The new boss is good at working with people, morale and trust is high, and the business outlook for the company in general is strong.

Using the minimax technique, Lund works to *minimize* the negatives. He explains that the new boss, because of his experience, will build up the department, thus creating advancement opportunities. He talks to the two people who aspired to be boss, suggesting directions in which they might develop their qualifications. He has a special talk with Paul X, the natural leader of the group, and after a frank exchange about the future of the department, he swings him around to an optimistic view of the change.

Lund *maximizes* the positive factors. He makes capital of the fact that the company is doing well, and that there are promising things ahead for Order Processing. He also suggests that under new leadership he hopes that the staff will be able to raise its level of pay: "No promises, but . . ."

- **Trials.** It's not always possible, but in some instances of change you can overcome doubts and suspicions by tests and trials that answer employees' questions.
- **Monitoring.** The executive instituting the change, and as many assistants as are necessary, should be on hand to see that plans go ahead as anticipated and that unexpected developments are dealt with.
- **Cooperation.** Remnants of resistance sometimes show up in the form of foot dragging or discreet sabotage. This can be a sufficiently important factor to get the monitors' full attention.
- **Follow-up.** Some changes get started and just keep rolling along to everyone's satisfaction. But it's wise to schedule a review to make sure the new method is being used as planned, and that backsliding is not undercutting the effort.

An important part of follow-up is a comparison of actual performance with expectations. If the results aren't there, the whole purpose of the change may be lost. The original planning may have to be second-guessed, and readjustments made. And, of course, if results are on target, or better, compliments are due to the planners of the change.

◊ 28
Retirement Readiness

CONCEPT

Retirement is both a goal and a way of life. A key question that wage earners at every level ask themselves in their fifties is: "When do I start thinking about retirement?" Some related questions are: "Should I retire?" "What preparations should I make?"

The self-appraisal questionnaire that follows in the How to Use section will help answer questions like those.

ACTION OPPORTUNITIES

For anyone pondering the retirement option, a review can be a check on readiness. For those over 50 who haven't given the subject any thought, it is a reminder that planning is the key to making retirement a promotion instead of a disaster.

EXAMPLE

Rick Baird and Clarence Lynch were long-time friends. Baird worked for a pharmaceutical firm and Lynch was owner and manager of a large service station and car-repair shop. Both were relatively well off, and they hit their middle fifties before they discussed their retirement. Baird said his company had a full-fledged retirement benefits program and he began to attend information meetings and take advantage of a financial counseling program conducted by the company's extreasurer. Lynch kidded Baird: "They going to sign you up to an old age home next week?"

Baird took early retirement at 62 and thrived. Lynch expected to continue right on running his shop, but painful arthritis forced him to sell out. Facing an unexpected future, with his finances in disarray and not a glimmer of what to do with himself, he and his wife began having some bad times.

HOW TO USE

The Retirement Readiness quiz that follows is designed to bring the retirement situation into sharp focus for those who will be facing it. When does that happen? The experts suggest that 50 is a good time to start thinking and planning. Isn't that premature? No, because some things, like finances and health, benefit from early planning.

A word about the questionnaire. It covers seven key factors on which retirement depends. Check the statement that comes closest to describing your situation for each. Each statement has a number or score assigned to it. These are weighted to give them their realistic relative value. For example, finances is a vital factor. If you can't afford to retire early, you have to forget it, no matter how favorable other factors may be. That's why the finance items are scored so heavily.

The more accurate your responses, the more useful the result. You will find scoring directions and interpretation at the end.

Your Retirement Readiness Rating

Finances

− 50	( )	I don't have enough reserves on hand to make it now.
5	( )	I have just enough to scrape by.
10	( )	I can make it if I live "cheaply" and cut back on extras.
15	( )	I'm O.K. for the foreseeable future at my present level of living.
25	( )	I will do fine in almost any event.
50	( )	Money is no consideration.

Health

− 5	( )	My work keeps me zipping along, gives me exercise, and forces me to watch my diet and personal habits.
5	( )	I feel that my work favors my health in that it keeps me busy and on a regular schedule.
15	( )	My work generally leaves me dragged out at the end of the day. If it weren't for weekends, I'd be in a bad way.
50	( )	My work is a terrible strain. It drains my energies, keeps me on edge, and doesn't let me sleep nights.

Relationships

− 5	( )	If I retire now, I suspect my personal relationships will suffer badly—for example, I expect my wife and I will get on each other's nerves, I will lose some of my job friends, and so on.
0	( )	I'm not sure if I have enough, and good enough, friends to make for a satisfactory social life if I stop working now.
10	( )	I've never depended very much on people I met on the job for socializing, and I have a well-rounded group of friends and relatives who always have and will continue to make for a full social life.
25	( )	The minute I stop working I'll be able to improve and devote more time to practically all of my relationships.

Emotional Outlook

− 10	( )	I'm emotionally unprepared to stop working. If I retire now, I won't be able to make the many adjustments that are necessary.
5	( )	I don't believe retirement is going to be much of a threat for me. I'm pretty flexible.
15	( )	I find the prospect of retirement kind of exciting, an attractive adventure.
30	( )	I can hardly wait for retirement. There are so many things I want to do.

Housing

− 5	( )	If I stop working now, I'll have to give up my present living arrangements for something much less desirable.
5	( )	My retirement won't affect my housing arrangements much one way or the other.
15	( )	I expect benefits from my retirement: I'll be able to do a lot of work around the house that I've been putting off for years, which will mean not only enjoyable activity but also an increase in the value of the place.

Your Retirement Readiness Rating   *(Continued)*

20	( )	If I retire now, I'll be able to move to another site in another part of the country (or whatever) that will give my whole life a lift.

Work
− 15	( )	I would miss it terribly. There is so much more I want to achieve before I quit.
0	( )	Work? I can take it or leave it.
15	( )	I'm proud of my work record. However, I feel my job achievement is behind me.
25	( )	The day I leave the job will be one of the happiest of my life.

Activities
− 10	( )	I know I'll never find anything else to do that I will enjoy as much as I do my job.
5	( )	I enjoy my life on the job as much as anything I might do on the outside.
10	( )	I like the idea of getting into new things.
20	( )	There are any number of things I've been eager to do, and when I leave my job, I'll finally have enough time to get to them.*

* Adapted from *Over 50—The Definitive Guide to Retirement* by Auren Uris. Chilton Book Company, 1979.

Evaluating your score. Go back over all your checkmarks (it's assumed you've made a choice for each factor), and total the numbers alongside them. Fill in the blank:

Total Score: _____

Interpretation. If you scored over 100, chances are you are both practically and mentally ready to consider retirement. But don't act on this appraisal alone. To get a different perspective, discuss the results, both the total and factor by factor with interested parties like your spouse, family, and friends.

A score between 75 and 95 means that there are advantages and disadvantages, and you have to see exactly how they balance out. Start by reconsidering the answers you checked off. Make sure they represent what you *really* think and feel. Give special attention to the most important factors: health and finances.

A score below 75 indicates that you are not ready for retirement. In this case you may want to take steps that will improve your prospects. For example, if housing is particularly important consider actions that can change the picture favorably.

Your situation with respect to these factors may change. In that case, go through the quiz and recheck the factors. You may come up with a new score that changes your retirement prospects.

◊ 29
Rumor Handling

CONCEPT

Reputations have been shattered, careers smashed, and companies forced out of business by the crushing force of rumors. It is essential to understand the rumor pattern in order to deal with it effectively.

Wherever the winds of rumor blow, upset and turmoil may follow. Executives should be prepared to deal with this force if it should rear its insidious head in their areas of responsibility. Rumors may be favorable too, but the majority are destructive and may demand intervention. But even favorable rumors can cause unjustified expectations that may require attention.

The dictionary defines rumor as: "An unverified or unfounded report or story circulating from person to person . . . often based on gossip or hearsay." Two facts that studies have revealed is that rumors are unexpectedly troublesome to deal with, and that the obvious remedy, finding and eliminating the source, is often impossible.

ACTION OPPORTUNITIES

Rumors may flourish at any echelon. The target may be an employee, executive, department, or the entire organization. It is up to the executives in charge to spot the danger, evaluate it, and decide on a suitable action.

EXAMPLE:

Ron Lambert is hired to run the Purchasing Department. Behind the move are the need to clean up a mess, inefficiency, favoritism shown some employees, and suspected graft. Shortly after Lambert takes over, these stories circulate:

He has laid violent hands on his secretary.

He had been divorced one more time than a famous, often-married Hollywood star.

He is about to replace all of Purchasing's employees.

Lambert emphatically denies the rumors, but the facts fool no one. For instance:

The "assault" on the secretary: He had spoken sharply to the woman after she continued a procedure he had ordered stopped. Later it became known that the secretary had an "understanding" with a supplier and hoped to place an important order "right under the boss's nose."

"Divorced often:" Lambert had only one divorce. The fact that it was recent may have exaggerated it in the mind of the rumor starter.

"Wholesale firing:" Lambert had found many inefficient procedures, which he was eliminating. Redundant employees were being transferred.

Eventually the rumors died down. Six months later Lambert and the president, his boss, reviewed the situation and the purchasing executive said, "I should have taken some action to counter the stories. We could have cut down the time it's taken to get back to normal." His boss agreed.

HOW TO USE

The basic problem is to act or not to act:

1. Should you attempt a remedy? Some rumors are silly, more a gag than a threat. These usually can be ignored. But act when:

- The rumor is costly in terms of dollars—the "news" that your company is in desperate financial straits may kill the possibility of a needed bank loan, the company's image, or its reputation.
- A crisis looms. Customers start to cancel orders. Morale and performance problems intensify.
- Individuals' reputations are being damaged, relationships are suffering, and so on.
- Are people taking them seriously? Some rumors are such patent distortions that they fall flat of their own weight.
- How widespread are they? Some rumors spread like oil on water, others are restricted. Those that cause trouble and threaten to get out of hand demand corrective action.

2. Recognize types of rumors. There are three categories:

- ***The bogey.*** It is founded on fear; fear of layoff, unacceptable job changes, bankruptcy, reorganization.
- ***Pipedream.*** This results from wishful thinking. For instance, at Christmas one employee tells another he is expecting a bonus amounting to ten percent of his annual salary. It is a hope based on a friend's news that her company is giving out large bonuses. When a

bonus comes through and it is one percent, some employees are bitterly disappointed.

■ *Hate.* Al X, a new employee, tells his boss that he is quitting and he does. It has been whispered that he is the petty thief who has stolen the small items that have been disappearing from the office. A month later the real thief is caught. Who had started the original rumor? Someone who had it in for Al. The character-assassination rumor is the easiest to spread and the hardest to curb. Reputations can be ruined overnight. Behind the whispers is someone with a peeve, or worse, a "professional hater."

3. Dig out the facts. This is the first step in assessing the seriousness of the situation. The rumor itself will usually tell you where to start. A rumor about John Jones, for example, pinpoints him as the first one to query. What can he tell you relating to the "information" going around? Be circumspect. If Jones incriminates Sam Smith, you can't assume the suspicions are correct. And in questioning people, try to avoid spreading the rumor. As far as possible limit your conversations to those who already know, but if you do question those who turn out to have nothing to contribute, explain that you are trying to squash a falsehood.

4. Seek the source. The type of rumor may provide a clue as to the originator. But don't jump to conclusions. Go from link to link, but don't be surprised if you come to a dead end: "I heard it in the lunchroom but my back was turned and I didn't recognize the voice." Your investigation may find you in a standard dilemma: You are pretty sure who the culprit is, but he or she denies it. And if you don't have proof, the most punishment you can mete out, if there is to be any, is that the rumor originator will feel uneasy knowing your suspicions.

5. Truth. This is your strongest weapon. Usually facts are the best counter. But stating the facts may not be enough. Instead:

■ *Convene the group.* Getting people together formalizes and adds weight to what you have to say. Include the natural leaders and those who may be involved. Emphasize that your primary purpose is to prevent damage and unfairness.

■ *Repeat the rumor.* Get others to agree with your wording, then refute the story by stating the contradicting facts. And be prepared to back the statements with proof.

6. Deal with the identified culprit. Punishment for a certified rumor monger depends on the circumstances. People have been fired for a lot less than starting damaging stories in the organization. But if you plan to stop short of firing, put it squarely: "We can't permit that kind of behavior. It creates ill feeling, hurts people, and interferes with getting the work done. There had better not be a next time."

7. Take advantage of a major cause you can control. Studies show that rumors flourish in the *absence* of news and information. Your strongest antirumor weapon is a well-informed group able to separate the lie from the truth on their own. Here are the elements of a positive policy:

- Establish open, two-way communications channels. Encourage and reasonably answer employee questions. This yields a double dividend: The doubts and fears that cause rumors are lessened, and rumors are more likely to reach you quickly, while they can be more easily squelched.
- Give advance notice of contemplated changes.
- Keep people informed of progress and prospects on such key matters as sales, finances, future plans, new products, and so forth.

▷ 30
Selective Leadership

CONCEPT

In earlier days, especially during the 1950s, enlightened management favored the democratic approach to leadership, by which employees were encouraged to discuss problems and participate in decision making. But an experiment by one of the outstanding contributors to management theory, Kurt Lewin, changed that. Lewin, then at the University of Iowa, decided to test leadership methods by an experiment involving two groups:

- Members of one group were divided into several subunits run by "autocratic" leaders who decreed policy, decided on the work and how and by whom it was to be done. These leaders were personal in their praise and criticism and general supervision.
- The subunits of the second group were run by "democratic" leaders who brought up matters for discussion, encouraged individuals to join in making decisions, and allowed group members to work with

whomever they chose. Comments about work performance were objective and directive rather than critical.

Lewin noticed, however, that one of the democratic leaders used a different style from the others. He exercised practically no control over the group and allowed members to work by themselves and develop their own solutions to difficulties. The psychologist tagged this group under a third heading, "laissez-faire."

Differences in atmosphere, feelings, behavior, and accomplishment among the three groups were significant:

- The autocratic groups were quarrelsome and aggressive. Some individuals became completely dependent upon the leader. When he was absent, work ceased. Work progressed at only a fair rate.
- Democratic group members got along in friendly fashion. Relationships with the leaders were freer, more spontaneous. Work progressed smoothly even in the leader's absence.
- The free-rein (Lewin's "laissez-faire" term anglicized) group worked haphazardly and at a slow rate. There was considerable activity, much of it unproductive. Time was lost in argument.

Using Lewin's study as a basis, this writer, in *Techniques of Leadership,** developed Selective Leadership, which proposes that each of Lewin's three methods has utility. Managers may use each as appropriate, just as a golfer uses different clubs, like the driver, niblick, or spoon.

ACTION OPPORTUNITIES

Selective Leadership is a practical, day-to-day approach by which managers can guide subordinates. Being both comprehensive and utilitarian, it has been adopted by companies and managers. An imaginative instructor at Boston College used *Techniques of Leadership* in a course on family relations, and the National Training Laboratories prescribed the book for graduates of their sensitivity-training programs.

EXAMPLE
Manager X selects one of the three techniques according to the requirements of the particular circumstance:

* Uris, Auren (1964). *Techniques of Leadership*. New York: McGraw-Hill.

- *He directs (autocratic method) a secretary to make a report.*
- *He consults (democratic method) with his employees on the best way to deal with a jamup of work at the copiers.*
- *He suggests (free-rein method) to his assistant to look into ways to improve order processing in the department.*

Note that Manager X uses all three techniques and that each is appropriate in the situation involved.

HOW TO USE

Mastery of the Selective Leadership technique lies in knowing when to use which method. Four considerations should guide you:

1. The situation. Your technique varies with needs:

- A fire breaks out in your department. You can't waste time, you need fast action: "Tom, get the fire extinguisher. Helen, notify security. Paul, see to it that everyone gets out into the corridor . . ." You have used the autocratic method effectively.
- Costs in the department are getting out of hand. Everything from paper towels to telephone use is over budget. You describe the problem to your entire staff and ask for suggestions on stopping waste and minimizing expenditures. This is the democratic procedure.
- You need an idea for new products to fill out the middle of your price line. Ordering people to be creative won't work. Your best move: Put two or three of your best people on the assignment, and give them their heads. This is the free-rein method.

2. Response desired. Situations may include an element that provides a clear cue as to method, the kind of response you want from the subordinate. For example:

- *Compliance.* If a subordinate's task is routine with well-established goals, the autocratic method is appropriate.
- *Cooperation.* When you want teamwork, people working along with one another, the democratic approach is usually best.
- *Creativity.* When new ideas and the imagination to produce them are needed, free-rein is your likeliest tool.

3. The individual. The kind of person you are dealing with is a consideration. For example:

■ **The hostile subordinate.** The employee is characterized by unco-operativeness and resistance to you and to your ideas. The autocratic method is called for. This isn't meant to bar attempts to overcome the negative attitude by discussion, but the firmness of autocracy has the effect of channeling aggression and steering energies to constructive ends.

■ **The team player.** The individual who likes to work with others will probably function best with democratic leadership.

■ **The individualist.** The solo player who likes to develop his or her own work procedures and come up with fresh approaches is likely to perform best if you use the free-rein technique.

4. Your own personality. Managers tend to have a natural affinity for one of the three basic techniques. Psychologists have studied human personality and established three prototypes that roughly correspond to the three types of leadership:

■ **The "authoritarian" personality.** People in this category are strong-minded, even rigid in outlook. They like things as they are, want conformity, and tend to "go by the book." Managers in this group usually prefer the autocratic method.

■ **The "egalitarian" personality.** These people feel that subordi-nates should be respected and treated on a par with each other. Democratic leadership practices would suit managers in this category.

■ **The "libertarian" personality.** "Live and let live" is this type's conscious or unconscious slogan. Managers in this category prefer loose supervision and encourage subordinates to operate on their own. The free-rein approach is compatible with their outlook.

In using the selective leadership method, the question may arise, "If I'm an authoritarian type, can I readily use the democratic or free-rein methods?" Answer: Regardless of the personality group in which you place yourself, there should be little trouble.

Remember, you are expected to change your *actions,* not your *feel-ings.* Everything else being equal, follow the style, autocratic, demo-cratic, or free rein, that you prefer. True, in practice you may have to behave out of character, and, for instance, be firm, unyielding, and autocratic when you are an egalitarian. You may also let a subordinate follow his own hunches when you'd rather make him toe the line if you need that subordinate's creativity.

The key to resolving the occasional conflict that may arise in selecting among the three basic methods is to adopt the one most likely to give you the essential results you're after.

You may have to modify some impulses or accept behavior from subordinates that rubs you the wrong way, but Selective Leadership offers a time-tested approach that can resolve many of the contradictions and weaknesses of working with people.

▷ 31
Skinner's Behavior Modification

CONCEPT

Motivation theorists McGregor, Maslow, Herzberg, and most others stress the "why" of performance: McGregor's Theory X Theory Y assumes that workers' feelings and attitudes determine effort. Psychologist B. F. Skinner stresses *what* is done, behavior, as the key. Improved performance, says Skinner, can result from modifying behavior rather than manipulating the psyche.

Skinner's major tool of behavioral change is reinforcement, positive and negative. Positive reinforcement acts as reward, negative as punishment. His ideas are based on extensive experiments. He changed the behavior of rats and pigeons by operant conditioning, that is, evoking a desired action by training the subject to expect a reward for doing it. A pigeon is trained to peck at a dot by giving it a grain pellet after each peck. A worker, then, could be motivated to perform a task by knowing it would be positively reinforced, that is, rewarded. "Reinforce the behavior you want repeated," became a catch phrase.

ACTION OPPORTUNITIES

Skinner's innovations further extend the field of motivation and provide you with additional ideas for consideration and workscene application.

EXAMPLES

A number of companies developed performance-improvement efforts based on Skinner's concepts:

Emery Air Freight launched a program in its shipping department. Workers were encouraged to set a production goal, which usually turned out to be higher than the goal the manager would have set, of the number of pallets they would stack with packages preparatory to shipping. Fulfilling or surpassing the goal won commendation and eventually, material rewards. Sub-par performance was not mentioned. Productivity improved significantly.

A supermarket chain used Skinner reinforcement in training checkout clerks. The trainees were applauded for what they did right, poor or incorrect performance was ignored. Result: shortened learning time and higher skill levels.

HOW TO USE

Even Skinner's detractors admit the scientific discipline and success of his experiments. He was able to train pigeons past the dot-pecking to elaborate dance movements. A key disagreement concerned Skinner's claim that people could be trained as his laboratory animals had been. But the attempts to apply behavior modification suffered from the same problems as other theories:

- The procedures represented the addition of elements that were seen as artificial. Praise, for example, an effective traditional stimulant, eventually wore out its effectiveness when used repeatedly as positive reinforcement.
- It was necessary to continue positive reinforcement to prevent extinction, the gradual diminution of the conditioned response.
- It was difficult for some supervisors and trainers to witness unsatisfactory work, such as errors and sloppy performance, without making a negative comment.
- Attempts to use both positive and negative reinforcement overlooked the dictum that negative reinforcement cannot elicit desired behavior, it can only discourage unacceptable behavior.

The basic question as to whether success in conditioning animals could be duplicated with human beings is still unanswered. The human race, its behavior still reminiscent of its origins, may be viewed merely as an intelligent animal. But the human brain and psyche's sensitivities, imagination, potential for spirituality, ability to create, aspire, and even its laxities and self-indulgence, represent forces weaning it away from purely mechanistic behaviorism.

For managers, Skinner's ideas contribute some practical elements, for example, his view of punishment and reward (the old carrot-and-stick idea in modern dress). The examples of Emery Air Freight and the supermarket chain suggest the possibility of successful application. But attempts to duplicate these have not been satisfactory. This suggests that unidentified variables are at work.

At any rate, Skinner's ideas have a broad and provocative appeal. If motivation interests you, Skinner's ideas might make worthy fare. Among his books is a novel, *Walden II,* that dramatizes his theories and is an ongoing backlist title. His major works, in order of fame, are *Beyond Freedom and Dignity,* 1971; *Schedules of Reinforcement,* 1957; *Analysis of Behavior,* 1961; and *About Behaviorism,* 1974. The novel, *Walden II,* was first printed in 1948, with many editions to follow. Also of interest is a book about Skinnerian psychology, *Behavior Management: The New Science of Managing People at Work,* by Lawrence M. Miller, 1978. (Also, check Motivation in the Index.)

▷ 32
Stress

CONCEPT

Stress is a physical and mental state. It is both subjective: "One more foul-up and I'm ready to snap," and objective: It can show up in our respiration and heartbeat. According to Dr. Hans Selye, the Canadian world authority, long-term stress can contribute to coronary heart disease, peptic ulcers, suicide, nervous disorders, insomnia, pill popping, marital discord, and a host of emotion-centered misbehaviors.

Dr. Selye identifies two types of stress:

- Distress, which is painful and destructive
- Eustress, or good stress, which invigorates and makes superior effort possible. Athletes are familiar with eustress: "I feel psyched up," they say, referring to their tension before a race.

Dr. Selye's pioneering work and that of other investigators in the past 30 years has greatly increased our understanding of the stress phenomenon and its alleviants.

ACTION OPPORTUNITIES

None of us is free of stress, and minimizing its destructive consequences can raise our health and performance levels. The work setting is rife with sources of stress—insecurity, deadlines, competitiveness, and the urge to excel. This is one area where we can be our own patients, and with patient-doctor cooperation, get helpful results.

EXAMPLE

Ed Linton comes home after work and his wife Ann hands him his martini. He drops into his armchair. "I'm bushed."

Perhaps because it's spring Ann suddenly says, "I've seen you come through that door a thousand times, played out after work. And it's not physical, because the things that throw you are your nagging boss and obstreperous subordinates. Can't you cut down on the tension?"

Linton, urged on by Ann and their doctor, begins finding answers that eventually reduce the wear and tear on a man whose main problems are being overly conscientious and too hardworking.

HOW TO USE

Understanding the causes and alleviants of stress can increase enjoyment of eustress and lessen distress. Some key points:

1. A revealing study. Dr. Daniel H. Funkenstein, author of *Mastery of Stress,* performed experiments at Harvard in which he analyzed people's emotions after being scolded and chided.* He found:

- *Anger.* This included annoyance, irritation, and "being sore." Some subjects directed the anger outward, others inward, against themselves.
- *Anxiety.* This also appeared in two different forms. The first was severe anxiety reflecting fright, panic, and apprehensiveness, and the second, performance anxiety, in which the subject reported feeling excited and geared up, "as before an athletic contest."
- *No emotion.* Some individuals reported no awareness of feeling.

According to Dr. Funkenstein, "The most efficient way of handling stress is either with 'No-emotion' or with 'Performance anxiety.' The

* Funkenstein, Daniel H. (1957). *Mastery of Stress.* Boston: Harvard University Press.

least efficient way is with 'Severe anxiety' which disorganized the personality. Between these extremes is 'Anger,' with 'Anger out' being more efficient than 'Anger in.'"

In working terms the findings translate as follows:

- The executive who doesn't get emotionally worked up about pressure in the first place makes the best showing.
- Next best off are executives whose response is like that of a contestant before a race. They feel keyed up, but energies and thoughts are focused on reaching their goal.
- Third come those who get annoyed, irritated, or angry, and express their feelings in griping or complaining.
- Executives who feel the anger but "swallow their feelings" don't do as well as those who vent their feelings.
- The executives who make out worst are those who become upset, lose their heads, and lose control of the situation.

2. Remedial steps. A group of executives attended a meeting on the subject of stress. At the end of the session they were asked to suggest steps that in their opinion could depressurize the executive job. Their list:

Analyze and minimize immediate problems

Put some order into the chaos

Delegate

Systematize procedures

Be good-natured about things

Consider the crisis as a temporary situation

Backstop the people who get rattled easily

Improve team spirit and teamwork

Develop relief devices for rest and relaxation

Set priorities

Lend a hand to struggling subordinates

Explain causes of pressure to subordinates

Have someone you can gripe to; a boss, colleague, or the like

Deal with irritants in the early stages

Don't transmit your feelings of pressure to others

Break bottlenecks

3. Three basic alleviants. Analyze the list above and you will see that the items fall into three approaches to neutralizing stress:

■ *Change the situation.* The work setting itself may be a major cause of pressure. Bad layout, inadequate equipment, toleration of interruptions, and inefficient systems may increase both the burden and pressure of work. Causes like these are controllable.

■ *Change the people.* Reshuffling assignments, refresher training, and getting increased cooperation can smooth operations. Monitor your subordinates' stress responses. An executive says, "I put my stronger people at key pressure points."

■ *Defuse yourself.* Here are some methods executives use to calm down:

"When things get too tough I go outside for a breather. When I return, I'm relaxed and have a better perspective on things."

"I take the time to analyze the causes. Even when I can't cut the pressure, I can accept it more easily."

"I just accept stress as the emotional cost of doing business. In some cases I'd even say it helps get the work done."

David W. Ewing of the *Harvard Business Review* comments:

Tension . . . does not signal breakdown or failure. The opposite of tension—harmony, serenity, equilibrium—does not represent an ideal. Tranquility in an organization may be viewed with alarm, associating it with sick enterprises and vulnerable departments. Tension may not only be acceptable but desirable.

Effective executives echo this turnabout view of stress. Two typical opinions: "It's part of the job, and I'm satisfied to put up with what I can't eliminate." One more point: This executive doesn't pass the pressure down the line or drop it into his boss's lap.

An executive is discussing her job with the vice-president, Personnel, who asks, "Would you be interested in an assignment with less pressure?"

There is a moment's hesitation, then a sudden burst of realization. "No. I guess I really enjoy the pressure of my job."

4. Self-monitoring. Dr. Karl Albrecht, author of *Stress and the Manager,** strongly advocates paying close attention to your physical sensations: "Become intimately familiar with the signals that tell you the status of your arousal level. From these signals you can infer a great deal about your overall reaction . . . which may not be obvious by simple intellectual analysis." He states that most people assume they are calmer than their body signals imply. And people who suppress symptoms by trying to "keep a stiff upper lip," may suffer emotionally.

* Albrecht, Karl (1979). *Stress and the Manager.* Englewood Cliffs, NJ: Prentice-Hall.

The signals he refers to are "nervous stomach," clammy hands, perspiration not caused by physical exertion, and headaches. He warns against pills used to dull awareness of body signals. A cover-up may actually worsen a condition better treated by facing up to it. He favors "DR," deep relaxation techniques, as bringing about a restful condition that, in some cases, results in feelings of optimism, cheerfulness, and general good humor.

▷ **33**
The "Why Not?" Rejoinder

CONCEPT

Your responses to proposals by your subordinates can signal more than a simple "yes" or "no." In addition to the tone of voice, there are other words or phrases, like "maybe," or "let me think about it," that delay the decision. For some executives the phrase, "Why not?" in addition to acquiescence, has connotations that give it special force.

ACTION OPPORTUNITIES

In your responses to subordinates who suggest ideas or recommend courses of action, consider the special effectiveness of "Why not?" And the same holds true when you consider a daring course of action for yourself.

EXAMPLES

1. A subordinate says to Pete Brand, "Instead of relocating all the storage shelves, how about cutting a new entrance through the wall into the stockroom?" Brand, instead of saying, "That's a good idea," as was his first intention, gives recognition to the breakthrough quality of the idea, and says with enthusiasm, "Why not?"

2. Manager Gert Sample says to herself, "I wonder how Bill" (her boss) "would react if I suggested that while he's on his vacation, I take over the planning of the customer-relations campaign we've been working on

*together?" She knows its a chancey question but concludes, "Why not?"
She makes the request and gets a green light from Bill.*

HOW TO USE

Understanding the meanings of the "Why not?" rejoinder will help you
decide whether and when to use it. Some of its connotations are:

"I think it's worth the risk."

"What have we got to lose?"

"Nothing ventured, nothing gained."

It can suggest a joint venture: "Let's us undertake it."

It implies that there are opposed forces to be dealt with, but these
become a challenge. A motivational element grows out of that challenge. A let's-go-for-it attitude creates encouragement and enthusiasm.

Consider its use not only for others, but for your own proposals for
yourself. The previously mentioned Gert Sample case illustrates how it
works. The "Why not?" response can clinch your decision and raise the
level of your resolve.

▷ 34
Work Climate

CONCEPT

Work climate can be a key factor in employee well-being. It consists of
two elements:

- **Physical surroundings.** This includes everything from good lighting
  to ventilation, from a comfortable chair to pictures on the wall. (See
  Office as a Tool, page 271.)
- **Emotion-influencing factors.** These include the boss's smile, or the
  absence of it, group feeling, and friendliness or the cold shoulder.

ACTION OPPORTUNITIES

In assessing the atmosphere in your department, don't assume that moves to improve it will influence productivity. That idea is based on the paternalistic fallacy that somehow survives in management thinking: "I'll treat you like a generous parent, and you'll become more devoted to my interests." Frederick Herzberg explains that, as a hygiene factor, climate does not motivate. (See Herzberg's Motivator/Hygiene Concept, page 26.) It is a factor in job satisfaction, however.

EXAMPLE

1.   While Pete Tell doesn't believe that neatness is next to godliness, he does feel it is important. And so he is disturbed when Avery Pruitt, a promising new employee, keeps his office in a mess. Pruitt's feet on the desk ruin a high-gloss finish, a book tossed at a book-shelf smashes a picture on the wall.

Just as Tell winds up for a serious confrontation, Avery completes his first project and it's a winner; innovative, ingenious, and highly practical. Tell thinks perhaps he should go around messing up the offices of some of his other engineers.

2.   "I've given them the best working conditions anyone could ask for," complains a Research and Development chief, *"and a more surly, unproductive lot I've never seen."*

The report is accurate but incomplete. Not mentioned is authoritarianism, constant pressure for results, and labeling of any relaxed or spontaneous behavior as boisterous and unprofessional. The staff feels mentally imprisoned and creatively stultified.

HOW TO USE

The executive in the second example voices the apparently ineradicable idea that if you "give them the best working conditions" you will get improved performance. In a limited sense this may be true. Better lighting and equipment, more convenient layout and workplaces might improve efficiency, but not motivation. Be realistic in your expectations. These points will help:

1. Understand how climate influences attitudes and performance. One manager says, "I finally realized that a good climate doesn't make people work better, it makes them feel better." But results are highly individualized. Consider these reactions:

Employee A: "I give 100 percent for my boss. . ." For him it's rapport with his superior that triggers his willingness to do his best. Under unattractive surroundings he might still outperform an unmotivated worker in the best-furnished office in town.

Employee B: (an exhomemaker) "The peace and quiet in my office is like heaven. I feel I could do anything, and I try to show it in my work." To her, physical surroundings are important because she has been sensitized by her housekeeping experience.

Employee C: "My boss is a slave-driver, but I'm no slave. I'll do just enough to get by." Boss pressure is a turn-off for her.

2. Don't underestimate the emotional component. Review your management style. Your supervision of subordinates is often the key to the department's atmosphere. For example:

■ *Individual recognition.* "Eye on the sparrow," is the way one manager puts it. Each of your subordinates from the stars to the minimum performers should feel that you are interested in what they do and how they do it.

■ *Reward.* B. F. Skinner's idea (See Skinner's Behavior Modification, page 87.) that you should reward behavior that you want repeated is both logically and psychologically correct. Everything from praise to promotion is both a real and symbolic demonstration of appreciation.

■ *Encouragement.* A pat on the back or approving nod combines recognition with "I know you can do it," a vote of confidence. Encouragement is as necessary for some workers as gasoline is for a car.

3. Procedures. How you work with subordinates influences their attitude. One executive says, "To me, climate is the externalization of the superior-subordinate relationship." This means he can create a beneficial rapport by the way he gives assignments, sets objectives, checks progress, helps resolve obstacles, and comments on completion of a task. How you perform these influence your group's performance.

◇ 35
Zeigarnik Effect

CONCEPT

Industrial psychologists have studied the need for closure, an individual's wish to finish a task once started. This urge to complete is called the "Zeigarnik Effect" after its major investigator, whose finding explains why people tend to resist interruption.

ACTION OPPORTUNITIES

The Zeigarnik phenomenon clarifies unexpected workscene behavior, such as:

- Why people don't like to "change horses in midstream"
- Why some employees will work after hours—overtime pay aside—to wrap up a project in which they are involved
- Why employees sometimes balk at stopping one task and starting another, and even the higher priority of the superceding job doesn't seem to be a satisfactory reason

These problems are in area of scheduling and assignment, in which the Zeigarnik finding can be helpful.

EXAMPLES

1. Manager Tom Gray gets word from Sales to put a rush on an order for television chassis for a key customer. He goes out on the factory floor to stop the workers on their present jobs and have them set up for the rush order. Some shrug and set about making the changeover, but Bill Mercer comes over and says, "I've only got another hour to go. Can't I finish up on what I'm doing?" Another employee comes over with the same request.

Gray says they must make the change. Never having heard about Zeigarnik, he goes off muttering, "I never can understand why they make such a fuss. It's not costing them a cent."

2. Executive Elsie Moore tells the office manager: "We've got to get that special mailing out before the end of the day."

The office manager says, "Let's see, the job will take three and a half hours, it's two now and we've got until five. We'll manage."

Moore says, "If my arithmetic is correct, you'll need extra help to make the deadline."

The office manager, an old hand, says, "My group will do the job." She doesn't know the word for it, but she is familiar with the concept. She has put the Zeigarnik Effect to work on her behalf. The group, reinforced by the need for closure, will put out a bit extra to make the deadline.

HOW TO USE

Here is how to avoid the negatives of the Zeigarnik Effect, and how to benefit from the positive:

1. Build a tradition of flexibility. One manager says, "From the first minute a new employee comes aboard, I make it clear that our schedules are subject to change without notice. Once they understand that it's not our convenience but the customers' that's important, they seldom question a reshuffle of priorities."

2. Be creative about deadlines. "I try to have time goals coincide with regular breaks in the day, lunchtime, quitting time, for end of the week, and so on," says a drafting supervisor. "Somehow, the deadline becomes a more tangible—and reachable—target." This same manager tries to set subgoals at convenient points rather than at times that mean leaving the work in disarray overnight or over a weekend. Halting a job at a regular workbreak makes for a smooth halt and an easier startup.

3. Explain the change. A phrase, a sentence of explanation as to why tasks are to be reshuffled will water down the Zeigarnik reaction. There are few employees who don't understand the practical necessity described by the phrase, "A top customer wants us to . . ."

Priority is one of the basic factors in Zeigarnik-involving action. Having employees participate in working out their own schedules—which also means re-scheduling—should keep cooperation high, and performance likewise. (See also, Prioritizing, page 163.)

PART TWO

PROCEDURES

Countless activities help do the world's and your department's work. The Ideas in this section include the best way to work with an Assistant To to the concept of Zero Defects. Here also you will find Participative Management, a method invented in the United States, exported to and refined in Japan, which rocketed that country to industrial preeminence and gave Americans considerable food for thought.

You will find of particular interest those Ideas that relate to present problems, while others should refresh your outlook and stimulate thinking about work in general. This part contains the following Ideas:

*   *   *

▷ **36**
Assistant To

CONCEPT

In the 1950s and 1960s, management's growing sophistication created the "Assistant To," to fill the gap between executive responsibilities and the ability to encompass them. (See Delegation, page 120.) The assistant position differs from the executive secretary in emphasis. While the latter is often given considerable responsibility, duties consist largely of secretarial and detail work. The assistant to's job is broader and more varied in content.

Peter Drucker's dictum that executives are only as good as secretaries help them to be, is even more true of the assistant. In an article on assistants, the term "multipliers" was used, suggesting that assistants don't merely add to, but multiply their bosses' effectiveness. The pivot on which the benefits hinge is the executive's ability to coordinate the working relationship.

ACTION OPPORTUNITIES

The following assumes that you do not now have an assistant. If you do, your reading can serve to check your present practices. Assistantless executives with a large workload and a fair personnel budget should consider the advantages of adding one to staff. And every aspiring pre-executive who might benefit from the apprenticeship should, if the opportunity arises, consider the benefits of serving as an assistant.

EXAMPLE
Showing what can go wrong in the relationship between executive and assistant emphasizes its flexibility.

Executive Phil Starr is interrupted by his assistant, Bill Robbins: "Would you like me to go down to the treasurer's office and check last week's figures?" Starr suppresses his annoyance, says "Yes," and wonders why he ever thought Robbins would make a good assistant. At exactly what points the relationship failed aren't clear, but the consequences are. Robbins hasn't fitted into his role. Two months after starting he still asks questions about procedures he should have picked up weeks ago, has trouble working with other departments, isn't accepted by the rest of the staff, and adds to Starr's workload instead of diminishing it.

HOW TO USE

Boss-assistant teamwork is the key to the benefits. Here are the steps that can help you hire and train an assistant to your mutual satisfaction:

1. Think through the assistant's job. Study your own job, its content and ramifications. Then, on paper or mentally, list the assistant's possible areas of responsibility, eventually boiled down to specific tasks.

2. Visualize the team at work. Consider all the details, from where you will put the assistant physically in terms of office space and equipment, to what you want done.

3. Construct a profile. There is no such thing as an "ideal" assistant. You must sketch out the individual qualities that will satisfy your needs. For instance, if your assistant will be required to take on surrogate duties and help you at some meetings and occasions, the individual you choose must be tactful, have social poise, and be able to communicate effectively with others. On the other hand, if you want a problem solver, investigator, and report writer, intelligence, creativity, and writing ability will be important qualifications.

4. Recruit and test. After you list qualifications and have gone through the prehiring procedures, you should find a candidate who satisfies you. In a sense you are hiring for two jobs; performing assigned tasks, and getting along with you. The latter is largely unpredictable because it depends on "chemistry," that irritating word that intimates the indefinable something that creates rapport. If you can, consider a trial period. A test of about three to six months will help you evaluate the assistant and allow him or her to assess prospects of permanence.

If there is a probationary period, undertake it wholeheartedly. Unless you reflect optimism on the outcome and build the assistant's self-confidence, ability to perform will be undermined.

5. How much responsibility? It's a key question. One top executive says, "Some executives want assistants who 'know how to follow orders.' This helps, but the operation of the 'system' then requires that the boss be constantly at the wheel. My preference is for someone with ability and initiative, who can sub for me within reasonable limits and liberate me for more important matters."

6. Open communication. A free-wheeling give and take helps build a good relationship. Remember, training for the assistant never stops, since both executive and assistant grow and change. This requires a two-way flow of questions and answers.

7. Workstyle. Another executive, wise in the ways of the "assistant to" team says, "There must be an adjustment between the two people's methods of operating. This doesn't mean that the assistant develops the same values and behavior as the boss. This may happen. But an assistant may complement the boss, and in effect fill the gaps in the other's capabilities."

8. Personal relationship. Walter Mondale, as vice president to Jimmy Carter, held the biggest "assistant to" job in the country during the Carter years. In a speech at the University of Minnesota, Mondale discussed the essentials for being vice president, and especially the unique affinity between boss and assistant:

> The relationship is intensely personal. It is founded on professional need but it thrives on personal respect. For any vice president to play an active useful role, he must have the confidence and trust of the president.

9. Loyalty. Talk to executives about their assistants and sooner or later the word "loyalty" emerges. The prevailing view is that loyalty to the principal is essential. One executive says, "Unequivocally, if you have somebody who doesn't feel committed to you and the job, the arrangement just doesn't work. And it goes the other way, as well."

10. The fate of assistants. In a community college in upstate New York, a system is used whereby the president takes on an assistant for one year. This is as much a training period for the assistant as a help to the educator. At year's end the assistant, whose abilities and horizons are now raised, qualifies to advance in the organizational setup. He or she usually does.

⟶ 37
Authority

CONCEPT

The dictionary defines "authority" as the right to command and enforce obedience, the right to decide and act. Work must be performed in a controlled setting, and authority must exist to maintain the order necessary for productive action by eliciting cooperation and acceptance of orders, directions, and guidance.

The authority to which employees turn for information and help is vested in supervisors, managers, and executives who represent the company. Usually, they are given the power necessary to carry out the tasks for which they are responsible. Although authority is the power base on which the organization rests, like the steel hand in the velvet glove it only appears during crises.

Some authorities, notably Chester I. Barnard, in his classic *Functions of the Executive,** suggest that it is acceptance by subordinates that gives management its power. But this authority-from-below theory is more a "manner of speaking" than a fact. The proof of the proposition would lie in instances where a group has rejected management's representative in favor of it's own candidate, which is so rare that it becomes the exception that proves the rule. But it is useful for managers to consider the employee-acceptance factor in their leadership approach.

Managers may possess three different degrees of authority:

- *Complete.* The manager can act and decide without first consulting others
- *Limited.* The manager may act, but is obligated to notify the boss afterwards
- *None.* The manager must go to the boss for an O.K. before taking action

ACTION OPPORTUNITIES

Every manager must have concise knowledge of the limits of his or her authority. Not to do so may complicate and damage the manager's

* Barnard, Chester I. (1938). *Functions of the Executive.* Cambridge, MA: Harvard University Press.

standing and relationships up and down the ladder. Knowing how, when, and when not to exert authority is a job essential.

EXAMPLE

"Be here the first Monday of the month," Executive Ruth Wesley tells Greg Byrnes, whom she has just hired.

"One point I'm not clear on," Byrnes says. *"I've been interviewed by several people. Who will I be reporting to?"*

"To me," the executive replies. Obviously, it's a surprise to the other. *"Does it make a difference?"*

"I've never taken orders from a woman before."

"Think it over and let me know by noon tomorrow whether you're in or out."

Even in the "soulless organization," authority can be a highly personal thing. The person who wields it, how it's used, and the nature of the individual who responds to it, are all factors in whether it is a force for good or a source of trouble.

HOW TO USE

Here are the things you must know in order to handle authority wisely:

1. Know the basis for your authority. Power derives from four factors, that vary from manager to manager:

■ *You represent management.* And management directs the entire organization, making decisions central to organizational life.

■ *Your group's respect for your expertness.* Managers are often looked up to because of skills that subordinates can see and appreciate. A bumbling boss may be accepted in a patronizing way, but his or her power is diminished by visible ineptitude. Message: be as competent as you can be.

■ *Being personally liked.* In a way, it's unfortunate, and certainly not businesslike, but a group may be more responsive to a popular boss than to an unpopular one. But woe betide the manager who tries to substitute goodwill for respect, since favor is likely to melt under the heat of controversy. Managers must build their position on stronger ground.

■ *Threat of punishment.* The power to punish is also the power to reward, and in some situations, it is punishment that represents the teeth of authority. "Tough but fair" is not a bad reputation for a manager. It implies respect and acceptance of authority.

2. Know the five crises. These are the situations you must be aware of to operate constructively:

■ *When authority should be used but isn't.* "Why aren't you wearing your safety gloves?" the foreman asks an employee.

Employee: I don't think they're necessary.

Foreman: They protect your skin from harmful chemicals.

Employee: I'd rather not wear them.

Foreman: Well, O.K., Just be careful.

The foreman risks two kinds of trouble by not putting his foot down, the possibility of a health hazard, and the loss of the respect and obedience of his subordinates.

■ *When the manager acts without authority.* "Yes, you can take the afternoon off for Christmas shopping," Buck Trent tells his secretary. Next day his boss is at his door. "I understand you gave Lena permission to take yesterday afternoon off. Don't you realize we've kept the work going through the holidays only by insisting on everybody keeping regular hours? I've already gotten a dozen complaints and everyone wants the same privilege. You didn't have the authority . . ."

■ *When managers don't know if they have the power to act.* An employee asks his boss, "Can I come in to finish up some work on Sunday?" The manager realizes there may be problems of security, overtime pay, setting an undesirable precedent, but it would be helpful if the assignment got finished. However, he had better check with his boss before saying yes.

■ *When a manager's action is not backed by his boss.* A misstep here can rock the rafters. For example: "Frank, I'm going to ask you to rescind that promotion you gave Tess. I don't think you picked the right person for the spot."

"But C. B., I evaluated the three candidates very carefully. It's my considered opinion that I made the best choice."

"Some of the people upstairs don't agree. You'll have to break the news the best way to Tess you can. Gayle is the one."

"I disagree. Don't I have the authority to promote?"

"Usually. But in this case, I can't back you up."

Eat crow or quit? Frank has a tough choice.

■ **When authority is challenged.** Once or twice in a manager's career, an employee is insubordinate. What you do or don't do can be crucial to your image, even your standing in the firm.

"No one," oldtimer Al White asserts, "is telling me how to handle this customer."

"I'm telling you," his boss says calmly. "I'm the last one to say the customer is always right, but in this case you have to give him the benefit of the doubt and tell him the complaint is justified."

"I refuse to do it."

Al's boss has four choices: He can (1) fire Al, (2) give in and let him proceed as he wants to (and risk losing the customer), (3) walk away and hope a second conversation later on will yield some kind of agreement, or (4) go to *his* boss and dump the problem in his lap. The first action is preferred and is best done by saying, "I'm responsible for our relations with that customer. I've told you what should be done. Refusing may cost you your job." Now the decision is up to Al, and the boss is being boss.

(See also, Responsibility/Accountability, page 227, and Delegation, page 120.)

◊ 38
Bossing

CONCEPT

The bossing concept explains a major mystery: Why do business school graduates—even those from the best schools—flounder and grope in their first jobs, trying to master the practicalities of the workscene? The answer is, their education prepares them to *manage,* not to *be boss.* Bossing is more subtle than managing, a matter of touch rather than technique, of mastery of people rather than of things or systems.

Bossing is the art, as opposed to the science, of management. It covers such things as establishing rapport with individuals and the group, getting cooperation, trust, and respect for your authority, and knowing how to inspire people, which is considerably different from understanding theories of motivation.

ACTION OPPORTUNITIES

Anyone who looks forward to heading a workgroup, as supervisor, department head, head of a division or of an entire organization, will benefit from, and indeed, must have, the ability to boss. Understanding the bossing concept—and even those who have been doing it for years might gain from a review—is central to working effectively with others, maximizing your leadership potential, and getting increased cooperation, participation, and contribution to overall goals.

EXAMPLE
Dennis Short goes fresh from business school to the job of assistant to the head of an electronic firm's director of systems design. His superior spends most of the first day showing him around, introducing him to the department's personnel, and explaining the department's objective and work procedures.

At the start of the second week Short's boss gives him an assignment, to work along with a group on a design project. The respect and friendliness he expects for someone in his position fail to materialize. His reception ranges from matter-of-factness to faint hostility. When he reports this dismal fact to his boss and voices his disappointment, the response is, "When I started, I got the cold shoulder for months. It's a problem of learning, Dennis. You're in a new world and have to understand its people, ways and values, not in the abstract but in your bones and guts. If you're lucky, time will be on your side and you will be able to use all the things you learned at Harvard."

HOW TO USE

Fortunately, bossing can be learned in the head as well as in the muscles, with a consequent shortening of on-the-job learning. Some practical tips:

1. Becoming a boss is a democratic process. You are made a manager by the authority vested in management to make you one, but being a boss depends on establishing good relations with subordinates.

2. Leadership doesn't come with the job, no matter what your job description says. Rookie managers too often see their starting role as leader when it may be follower. Your subordinates usually have to teach you what you need to know, then decide whether they will accept your authority. Once they do, you are free to use whatever type of leadership you like. (See Selective Leadership, page 83.)

3. Ten subordinates mean ten different bonds. The boss's relationship with subordinates is individual and personal. Although each has the same ingredients, and you're probably friendly with all to varying degrees, you develop openness and trust, confidence and closeness, respect and two-way communication based on factors subtle and practical. For instance:

- Form a reasonable number of contacts to discuss the work.
- Develop a teaching relationship that shows interest in their growth.
- Recognize their off-job interests, hobbies, family, and so on.
- Talk about your off-job interests as you might with any friend. Don't hide the fact that you're as human as they are.
- Show that you consider the group a team, talk of group objectives, performance and achievement, to build team spirit.
- Above all, show your interest in their work and recognize special effort and achievement such as a tough job accomplished, or contributions above and beyond job requirements. More on this point:

Don't take your people for granted. A good working bond depends on a continuing appreciation of the subordinate's activities. Some bosses make the mistake of recognizing faults and failures while efforts and successes are taken for granted. B. F. Skinner, a great contributor to motivation theory, asserts that the reverse is desirable, that you should recognize and reward the behavior you want repeated. Criticism or punishment may get people to avoid repeating faulty behavior, but will not necessarily cause them to perform successfully. (See Skinner's Behavior Modification, page 87.)

◊ 39
Brainpicking

CONCEPT

Here is a good idea with a bad name. The term "brainpicking" is pejorative, and in the popular mind suggests exploitation of colleagues and friends. The feeling is that they are being deprived of their time and the fruits of their thinking. However, when brainpicking is done constructively, everyone, including the organization, benefits.

The practice of brainpicking is widespread and simple. It involves:

- *An information gap.* There is a felt need for knowledge, a problem in search of a solution.
- *The Picker.* He or she is an individual seeking advice, opinions, ideas, or experience relevant to the matter at hand. He or she is willing to appeal to others for help.
- *The Pickee(s).* Previously innocent bystanders, those at an adjoining desk or office or codiners at lunch may qualify.

ACTION OPPORTUNITIES

Use brainpicking any time your mental problem-solving equipment proves inadequate, your thinking lags, a deadline approaches, and someone who may help is at hand.

EXAMPLES

1. Linda Bell gets a hurry-call from her boss: "We're having a special meeting at 3 P.M. to assess our flooded warehouse situation. I'd like you to come up with suggestions for making up the product loss from your department in the shortest possible time." It's a tough and unprecedented problem, and Linda needs all the help she can get. She taps three of her brightest colleagues to get their ideas for a crash program to turn out the greatest amount of product in the shortest time. She enters the meeting much better prepared than she otherwise would be.

2. Reggie Greene has been trying to solve a scheduling problem, going from two to three shifts in a computer operation. There are a lot of angles and Reggie suspects he may not be aware of all of them, despite briefing by his boss and Personnel. Security, increased threat of drug use, and maintaining support services after midnight suggest details with which he has had no experience. He knows managers who have worked on the third shift, however, and makes a point of consulting them to get their ideas about handling these problems.

HOW TO USE

Keep in mind that brainpicking is different from brainstorming and calling a meeting. Both of those are group procedures. Effective brain-picking is best done when you are closeted with a single person, and so avoid group procedures and pressures. A systematic approach can give you the full benefits:

1. Be clear on the need. You have many problems and occasions for seeking information, not all of which suggest the brainpicking route. Since brainpicking is easy to do, it may be overused. Use these points to validate the choice:

■ The information you want is not available from other sources. For instance, if you want to know the distance from Cannes to Nice you're more likely to get it from an atlas or a travel service than by knocking at the doors of colleagues.

■ People are available who will be glad to help if they can. "Never brainpick an enemy," is the way one executive puts it.

■ Don't give the other person an "assignment" that is really yours. "I got pretty angry with Bill," reports one manager, "when he asked me to get some information from Marketing because he hesi-tated to do it himself." Chestnut snatching should not be foisted on others.

2. Be sure you're welcome. Even a friendly colleague will resent being interrupted at an important task. While brainpicking is often impromptu, check for the other's convenience.

3. Announce your purpose. Although some people simply say, "I'd like to pick your brain," the pejorative sense of the term may create an unnecessary hesitation. An opener such as, "I'm stuck with a problem and I though you might help," or, "I'm stumped by a personnel situation I think you've had experience with," is clear, direct, and gets the conver-sation off to a fast start.

4. Don't be led into an argument. Remember, you are seeking the other person's opinions, ideas, and judgments. Some people fall into the trap of asking for an opinion and then criticizing it if it seems wrong. The savvy brainpicker knows better. Obviously the other is justified in resenting finding himself or herself in a battle when he has been generous enough to try to satisfy a request for help.

5. Show your gratitude. The other person is helping you. The way you receive the information as well as your thanks at parting make the point.

6. Take notes. It may be desirable to record the conversation. One reason: the details may be technical, and you want to be sure you get them straight. Another has to do with giving credit. There are instances where an idea or information from a colleague was a stimulant to your further thinking rather than useful in itself. If a question arises as to the origin of the material, your record of the conversation could clarify matters.

7. Give credit. The person giving useful information should get recognition, particularly if the contribution leads to an outstanding achievement. Even if there is no great payoff, an expression of thanks, possibly in the presence of others, in addition to anything said in the interview shows your appreciation. It also helps you remain a brainpicker in good standing, and assures future cooperation from colleagues.

▷ **40**
Brainstorming

CONCEPT

Brainstorming was conceived in the 1950s by Alex F. Osborn, cofounder of the advertising giant, Batten, Barton, Durstine & Osborn. Osborn's *Applied Imagination,** the bible of brainstorming, put the procedure on the map and in countless corporate meeting rooms. Brainstorming is essentially a form of group thought, a procedure to mobilize a group's creative resources to solve problems and develop ideas.

Organizations went for the Osborn approach because, with American enterprise becoming increasingly technical, ideas were needed to hasten the development of new products, processes, and services. To many,

* Osborn, Alex F. (1979). *Applied Imagination.* New York: Scribners.

Osborn's approach seemed a godsend. No longer was it necessary to depend on inspiration for answers. Groups could meet, go through the brainstorming agenda, and quickly produce ideas and possible solutions to problems. These could be evaluated, the useless discarded, and the gems polished and put to work.

Eventually the concept, like many others in management, ran through its lifecycle (see Lifecycle of an Idea, page 209) and its popularity faded, but its inherent vitality continues to recommend it to managers.

ACTION OPPORTUNITIES

Every business problem, practical or hypothetical, and every situation in which ideas are required, lends itself to the brainstorming approach. It works better for short-term, highly focused problems than for those with deep roots or complications. It has proved a worthwhile expedient when executives have had "rush" problems and want to mobilize their group's mental powers to solve them.

EXAMPLES

1. *Company A, a cosmetics firm, decides to enter the competitive perfume field. Al Lane, marketing director, tells the president, "The labs have come up with an essence that seems to be just what we're looking for. Now we need a name for the product." The president agrees to assemble ten or twelve of the most creative staff members. The meeting is held, the brainstorming procedure inaugurated, and after an hour, 150 possible names have been suggested. Now the marketing director has something to work with.*

2. *"Number three press is down, Boss." Manager Joe Smith decides it's the last straw. He has all the equipment turned off and calls a meeting in the open area in front of his desk. He has used brainstorming a couple of times before, and briefly reminds the machine operators of the "rules." Then he says, "Here's the problem. In the last month we've had more breakdowns than ever before. I'd like you to give me as many ideas as you can for remedies. How can we prevent our machines from going down?"*

Once the group gets into the swing of the brainstorming pattern, the suggestions come in a flood. In half an hour Smith has gotten dozens of suggestions and feels that among them he can pull out five or six that can improve the equipment record.

HOW TO USE

Here are the steps for the brainstorm procedure:

1. Focus on a problem or situation that needs a remedy. Osborn suggests, "A problem like 'How to introduce a new synthetic fabric' is too broad. This should be broken down into three sub-problems such as: a. 'Ideas for introducing the new fibre to weavers and mills,' b. 'Ideas for introducing the new fibre to dress houses and cutters,' and c. 'Ideas for introducing the new fibre to retailers.'"

2. Get yourself a conference room, a conference leader familiar with the brainstorming technique, and a qualified group of conferees. It's all right to include peripheral or offbeat people, but exclude those who have no competence that relates to the problem. Their silence will make them uncomfortable and may dampen momentum. Still worse, they may try to participate and throw the meeting off track.

3. Appoint someone to record the suggestions. You have several options, but don't use a tape recorder alone. You may want to refer back to something that's been said, and that would cause an undesirable delay. Have someone write the basic idea either on an easel chart—this makes possible collecting the sheets at the end of the first phase of the meeting—or on paper. A tape recorder may be used in conjunction with the written notes, as a backup to clarify unclear notations.

4. Instruct or remind the group of the meeting rules:

- People should be as spontaneous as possible, and pop out ideas as fast as they come.
- There are no restrictions. "Feel free to say whatever comes to mind, no self-censoring. Don't worry about an idea being too far-fetched or wild."
- No criticism! This is especially important. The leader should condemn negative comments, ridicule, wise-cracking, put-down phrases like, "That's old hat," "Won't work," and so on.
- Quantity is desirable. This is one case where there's value in numbers, and quantity may be the road to quality. If a tendency to coattail develops, a conferee adding a modification of a previous idea, that's O.K.; this often produces a winner.
- See to it that the person doing the recording notes every suggestion, using just enough words to catch the basic idea.
- End the session when you feel the group has run dry.

5. Evaluate. This is best done by a small group, even one person, capable of separating the useful ideas from the total gathered. A 5 to 10 percent yield of good ideas is average.

6. Refine, combine, improve. The "evaluation committee" should regard the retained ideas as raw material for further improvement by means of editing, rewording, adding, subtracting, or possibly putting together two ideas into a single effective one.

7. Report back. The group should get feedback on the results of their efforts. This is desirable in any event, but essential if you plan to ask the members to participate in the future.

⋫ 41
Bypassing

CONCEPT

Bypassing is a communication in which someone—sometimes you—has been dropped out of the communications chain. You can be involved in three ways:

- Your boss or another employee may contact your subordinate without your knowledge or permission on a matter that ordinarily would claim your attention.
- Your subordinate may contact your boss or another higher-echelon executive without your knowledge or permission.
- You may want to bypass your own boss.

ACTION OPPORTUNITIES

Bypassing is a communications anomaly. Damage may be minor or may represent a serious challenge to status and authority. You should be prepared to deal with its various forms.

EXAMPLES

1.   Harriet Drew's subordinate, Jim Perry, has been after her for permission to take a course in art history at the company's expense. Drew has checked and confirmed that although the company funds work-related studies, Perry's course doesn't qualify.

Drew gets an angry call from Personnel: "Perry was in here this morning. I thought you gave him a negative answer . . ." Drew lets Perry know she resents his going behind her back. She is more upset than the incident seems to warrant, and tries to figure out why. For a starter she realizes it makes her look bad to the Personnel people. She suspects her sense of damage involves her leadership status.

2. George Lister has been trying to sell his boss, Tom Borden, on an idea that he believes would open a new market for the company. Borden is not encouraging, and eventually Lister stops trying. But one day he meets Ed Thorn, Borden's boss, in the elevator. Thorn learns Lister is free and suggests a joint lunch. During the lunch conversation, Lister describes his idea of a new marketing approach. Thorn is interested and asks the manager to send him a memo.

Back at work, Lister realizes he has bypassed Borden and goes to him and explains what has happened. The boss is clearly resentful. Lister feels he's got a boss problem that goes deeper than the bypass situation itself. Apparently Borden feels his standing with his boss has been hurt.

HOW TO USE

In a narrow sense, bypassing is a flouting of accepted channels. It can also be viewed as a means of opening blocked communications. But its impact is due to the threat to the established order. To deal with it:

1. Understand the causes. There are two sets:

■ Good reasons:
The manager was bypassed because he or she was unavailable.
The matter had considerable urgency.
The bypasser felt there was a good deal at stake and was willing to take the risk to get the message across.

■ Bad reasons:
The authority of the person bypassed is questioned or flouted.
The bypasser is dissatisfied and hopes for a more favorable hearing by circumventing the manager.

2. When you are bypassed. Don't act in haste or anger.

■ Find out the reason for the bypassing. It may be acceptable to you, or it may be a hostile act.

- If you feel it is unjustified, assess the motive of the bypasser. If it was thoughtless, explain the breach and the desirability of sticking to channels. If malice is involved, you are faced by insubordination and probably hostility. These, as much as the bypassing, should be dealt with. Talk to the other person. Negative feelings should be assessed. You may decide to ignore the bypass, issue a warning, or take disciplinary action.

3. When you bypass. You are sufficiently sophisticated in matters of status and company politics to consider the negatives before going over your boss's head. If you decide to bypass:

- At a minimum, be prepared to justify your act.
- Be ready to cope with possible resentment and reprimand.

4. Questions. Ask yourself the following if you are bypassed:

- Are you too slow in dealing with subordinates' requests?
- Is the higher echelon too slow in giving you answers? If you don't get reasonably quick answers for your staff, you may be considered the bottleneck.
- When responses to subordinates are delayed, do you explain and set a deadline for the answer?
- Failure to listen. Employees may be unassertive. Increase your level of receptivity so as to catch even the fainter voices.
- Are you tough enough with your boss? When managers don't swing their weight with their superiors, employees may feel compelled to bypass to get action.

When your boss or other executives go directly to one of your subordinates without letting you know, ask yourself:

- Was it an emergency? If so, it's generally acceptable.
- Was the bypassing a reaction to delay? Do you handle queries expeditiously? If time is a problem, perhaps you can have an assistant or delegate get the answers.

Is your relationship with your boss at issue? A practical discussion of the possibility should touch on:

- Your willingness to cooperate
- Explanation that your authority is being undermined

If the discussion doesn't end amicably, the underlying situation must be hauled into view and faced up to by both parties.

▷ 42
Crisis Management

CONCEPT

Organizations face two kinds of crises. The first is in the business area, and involves things like major product failures, marketing shifts, cash drain, unfriendly takeover attempts, and so on. The second is managerial and involves dangers like fire, flood, serious equipment malfunction, accidents with and without physical injury, earth slides, earthquakes, terrorism. To have them happen is bad enough, but to be unprepared is—unmanagerial.

Professor Gerald Meyers, a teacher of crisis management at Carnegie-Mellon University says, "Crises are becoming more visible more severe and of greater general concern. The media, our volatile economy and rapidly changing world have evolved to a point where managers can no longer ignore business disasters nor down play business vulnerabilities."

ACTION OPPORTUNITIES

Crisis management takes on dangers by preparing the countermeasures against them. Crisis planning and crisis teams can protect your organization from costly and even life-threatening events. No organization and/or department is free from fire hazard, equipment malfunction, physical injury, or health crisis. Flood or terrorist attacks have varying degrees of possibility for individual firms. Management should review preparedness in relation to its situation. Crisis plans and crisis-control elements—trained people and adequate equipment—must be ready as needed.

EXAMPLE
Workers in a small furniture plant in a suburban area are suddenly assailed by noxious fumes. A huge tank truck has crashed off the road and into the yard. The tank splits open and a toxic mist starts to penetrate the factory.

The company is lucky. An alert executive has seen the accident and activates the fire alarm system. He rushes through the corridors shouting, "Everybody out!" A foreman runs up. "Shall I shut down the machines?" An employee says, "There's a sick woman in the ladies' room." The fumes are getting thicker and people are gagging as they flee. "Did anyone call the fire department?" someone shouts. "Should I phone the hospital for an ambulance?" yells another.

The company's luck holds up. The fumes aren't toxic. The worst casualties suffer from tearing eyes and irritated throats. Fire trucks and two ambulances arrive and the few people who feel sick are treated on the spot. The truck driver is badly shaken up but not badly hurt. He says the chemical isn't poisonous and management decides to let skeleton crews return and close down for the day. The big hero is the sweeper who went into the ladies room and carried a fainting clerk out to the parking lot.

"We'd better get organized," says the vice-president who sounded the alarm. "We might not be so lucky next time."

HOW TO USE

Experienced managers know that catastrophes come in two sizes; department-wide and company-wide. Typically, a single department must have the capability to respond to a fire or accident. If the crisis involves two or more departments, the organization must be prepared to add its capabilities.

The department head can't prepare for all contingencies, but he or she should prepare for appropriate ones, for example, a toy factory in Bluebell, North Dakota needn't worry about a terrorist attack. The manufacturer of light machine guns in the next town might be a target, however.

An overall approach by industrial psychologist Harry Levinson supplies helpful perspective. He says, "Everyone in the organization should recognize the four steps in managing crises: Impact; Recoil-turmoil; Adjustment; Reconstruction." Some suggested steps follow:

1. Call in a security consultant. Top management should consider employing the services of an expert, preferably one with experience in its industry.

2. Top management must take over the responsibility for overall crisis planning and implementation. And the effectiveness of measures adopted will depend on how skillfully the information and motivation is passed through management levels. Since the taskforce members will include a large percentage of rank-and-file employees, it is advisable to have them participate in the development of plans at their own level.

3. Companies should see to it that every department head has a hazards list. Here is one made by an insurance office manager:

- **Fire.** Wires to equipment may short out, hot plate in coffee area, careless smokers
  - **Water.** Break in ceiling pipes, or from sprinklers
  - **Injury.** Sprains or broken bones from slipping or falls
  - **Health crisis.** Heart attack, stroke, fainting, and so forth
  - **Emotional crisis.** Rage, depression, fear

This is a good start for most departments. Add your own: _____

---

4. Organizing for trouble. A crisis group consisting of the most capable and cool-headed employees should be appointed. The taskforce approach of cutting through regular organization lines to get the people you need is suitable. (See Taskforce Management, page 168.)

5. Special equipment and the skills to use it. Taskforce members should get whatever training they need. In one company, the president, who had recovered from a heart problem, saw to it that at least two people in each department were trained to deal with heart attack victims. Organizations shouldn't require that motivation to take this useful step, however. Whether it is handling a fire extinguisher, or pushing the alarm bell, make sure that even simple knowledge is not assumed. Under the pressure of events people lose abilities that haven't been fully mastered.

6. Maintenance. After your plans and preparations are in place, they shouldn't be permitted to deteriorate. Check equipment and have occasional drills to test the taskforce operation.

7. Take the time element into account. Conditions may change, and so may personnel. Yesterday's suitable taskforce may be depleted by people leaving or being promoted to other departments. Update regularly, retrain, and improve methods.

▷ 43
Delegation

CONCEPT

No matter how talented or hard working they are, executives can't do everything themselves. The diagram below explains why. Executives' job responsibilities exceed their grasp, and so they must work through others. This process is called delegation.

The dictionary definition is helpful. To delegate means, "To entrust to another; to appoint as one's delegate," or substitute.

ACTION OPPORTUNITIES

Delegation is a multipurpose tool. A principal use is the one already described, that of handing over some of your tasks to prevent your workload from getting out of hand. But there are additional benefits:

- To use special skills of your subordinates. An executive works on a report that will eventually reach the president and the board of directors. His assistant is an excellent writer, and he asks her to do the final editing of the draft.
- The tasks delegated can provide training for subordinates.
- They can also prepare assistants for expanded job responsibilities.
- Delegated assignments can prepare subordinates to take over your routines to give you more latitude in the field to visit suppliers,

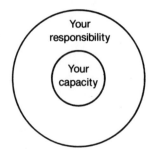

Figure 5. Reach-versus-grasp chart

customers, and so forth. This is also advisable for vacation and absence for health reasons.

- Delegation can test subordinates' capabilities, such as problem-solving, ability to take initiatives, and so on.
- Finally, it can free you for long-range tasks, planning, developing new procedures, and so on.

Few executives use delegation for all these purposes, but the more applications, the better perspective you can get of your own area of responsibility and the abilities of your staff.

EXAMPLE

After three months of experience, management trainee Cal Bates is put in charge of a small statistical unit. He does well and is made manager of a larger accounts receivable department.

One of his favorite sayings is, "If you want something done right, do it yourself." And so, as in his previous job, he handles all the mail, does the follow-up on inquiries, takes on special problems with some customers, etc. A bulging briefcase is his constant home companion. Of course, Bates knows about delegation, but he wants to impress his boss with his huge appetite for work.

He awakes one morning unable to get out of bed. His wife drives him to the doctor's office. After listening to Bates' description of his work habits the doctor advises slowing down: "And start by taking two weeks off to rest."

Reluctantly, with his boss's help, he hands key responsibilities over to subordinates. "Call me if any problems arise," he says. He is surprised to receive few calls. He heads back to the office refreshed, half hoping things are in a mess. But everyone seems calm, and going quietly about their work.

His boss shows up, telling him how great he looks. And knowing the other's problem with delegation, says gently, "You did a good job of assigning the work. To my mind, delegation has always been a key to executive sanity."

Cal Bates learns the lesson.

HOW TO USE

The best executives invariably delegate. Behind cases of burnout often lies the inability to do so. (See Burnout, page 249.) The following steps can help sharpen delegation practices:

1. Be aware of the psychological factors. Cal Bates and others who neglect delegation seldom do it out of ignorance. They know about it, but they are deterred by:

- *Loss of control.* Some people are threatened by the feeling that they no longer control activities for which they are responsible.
- *Egotism.* It takes two forms, first, the belief that no one will perform as well as they can, and second, the possibility that a subordinate will do the job better.
- *Knowledge is power.* Some delegators are reluctant to share their know-how.
- *Advancement.* Executives generally understand that having an able successor favors their own advancement. But there are some for whom the capable subordinate is a spectre of competition.
- *Bad experience with delegation.* This is an understandable cause, but effective delegation seldom backfires. Master the procedure, and built-in controls will prevent misfires.

2. Pinpoint the task. Delegating the right tasks brings benefits, while a poor selection creates difficulties. Use these guides in making your choice:

- *Know why you are delegating.* For example, is it to ease your workload, give an assistant useful experience, or challenge a bright employee? These are all good reasons. A few questionable ones are the chance to goof off for a while, or to avoid an onerous task. There are some tasks that should never be delegated:
- *The hot potato.* It is unwise to pass one along just to take yourself off the spot.
- *The power to discipline.* This is the backbone of executive authority, and is not transferable.
- *Responsibility for morale.* You may assign tasks aimed at improving morale, but it is the executive's responsibility to maintain it.
- *Know-how.* Don't delegate tasks you alone have the technical knowledge or the judgment to execute properly.
- *When a trust or confidence is involved.* Cost data, or the personal affairs of a subordinate, may be for no one else's eyes or ears.

3. Select the right person. There are two considerations: the nature of the task and the abilities of the individual. You will make different matches depending on your purpose. For example, if you want a job done well and fast, you give it to A, your most capable subordinate. But B will get it if you want an ambitious employee to stretch his or her capabilities. Other factors include:

- *Present activity.* You may choose someone with time on is hands over one who is rushed.
- *What the subordinate can contribute.* An ingenious employee who is familiar with the task may come up with new ideas. An experienced one can avoid known hazards.

4. Smooth the path. The way you make the assignment can help the delegatee. You give assignments all the time, but with a delegated task:

- *Add how-to.* Since the job may be unfamiliar, give instructions for critical elements, add cautions, and indicate sources for additional information: "If you want help with the calculations, see Pat Harley in Statistics."
- *Clear interdepartmental activity.* "I'll tell Miss Temple in Engineering that you may call on her for help . . ."
- *Make clear your availability.* This is as much for reassurance as for possible need.

5. Retain control. Since you must retain responsibility, you must keep control without needlessly limiting the delegatee's freedom to think and act.

You have to depend on the other's judgment on when to come to you for advice, information, and discussion. And you should be told of unexpected developments, delays, and problems.

Progress reports will help you and the delegatee. You keep your finger on the pulse, the other has a chance to assess the quantity and quality of performance, and note how deadlines are being met. Where complete independence is possible, give it. Then all you need do is ask for results.

What do you do when a delegatee falters? When do you step in, and how? Lack of skill, or an unanticipated development may require your intervention. Some key questions are:

- Is the situation remediable?
- Can you support the delegatee, so that the failure is not permanently destructive?
- Can you help the individual limp across the finish line, rather than step in and take over?

Finally, there is one benefit to delegation whose importance should not be underestimated: It can make you a better delegator and bring you the attendant benefits.

(See also, Responsibility/Authority/Accountability, page 227.)

▷ **44**

Executive Communications Network

CONCEPT

Management experts or executives themselves, in considering the communications function, feel they do it justice when they speak of it as two-way, meaning incoming and outgoing. This is factually correct, but is an over simplification that disguises a more useful view. In this author's recent publication *Executive Excellence,** I suggest that a more comprehensive analysis reveals that the executive communication network consists of five channels, each of which are incoming and outgoing. The chart below illustrates the communications network available to managers.

These are the people and groups represented:

1. Upward. To your boss, other higher-echelon executives, the CEO, Board of Directors

2. Lateral. To your peers, others in the organization who are approximately at your own level

3. Downward. To your subordinates.

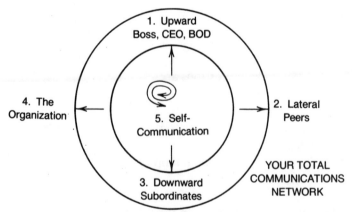

Figure 6. *Communications network available to managers*

---

* Uris, Auren. (1985). *Executive Excellence.* New York: Alexander Hamilton Institute.

4. The organization channel. This involves contacts with people and departments at various levels and functions in the organization. For example, a memo to Joe Smith, who is in charge of the benefits program, can help you resolve a policy matter. Contacts like these deserve separate consideration because they depend on and help you learn your way around the organization. Especially in larger companies, knowing the right person to ask about specific company matters helps get things done. One executive says, "The right person is not always the one in charge. When I want a fast inventory check I call Charlie. That's O.K., because I've cleared it with Charlie's boss."

5. Self-communication. This personal and self-contained area of executive functioning is often utilized but with little objective awareness. It involves the procedures you use in thinking, creating, gathering, recording, and being able to access information, all essential for executive action. (For more on this key channel, see Self-Communication, page 280.)

ACTION OPPORTUNITIES

Developing an effective pattern of communications for sending and receiving the myriad messages your work requires is a key to professional capability. Considered in visual terms your network becomes a guide, and like a roadmap for a traveler, helps you get around in a communications sense. The five-way network concept can assist in refining the communications aspect of your job.

EXAMPLES

1.   Lila Keynes has a good image in her company. She has developed impressive visibility by taking on tough assignments and completing them well. Given the opportunity to address the management group at an annual meeting, she gets a rousing reception for her witty and trenchant presentation, "Reaping as We Sow," her critique and suggestions for improving the company's reward policies.

But her boss doesn't give her an expected promotion. He knows there is a dark side to her performance: She gets hopelessly tangled in routines. "She is a poor administrator," he explains to the CEO to justify his action. "She has bad work habits, and I must confess that I haven't been able to train her."

Analysis of Lila Keynes' work difficulty would reveal that her self-communication system is at fault. She is forgetful, has no simple system for keeping information available, and is poor at solving work problems due to an inability to come up with relevant ideas, a self-communications function.

2.   Seth Pearson comes into a large computer software company and after a year, as one colleague puts it, "All he knows about this place is where the men's room and cafeteria are." His orientation in the company is hampered by his ignorance of the many elements of the organization channel, for example, who to see about a special computer program or who is in charge of Payroll. Maybe ostriches don't really bury their heads in the sand, but Pearson's ignorance of the organization world about him achieves the same result.

HOW TO USE

Get the five-way concept to work on your behalf:

1. Recognize its utility as a visual tool to help familiarize yourself with the opportunities and obligations relating to your work.

2. Conduct an informal review of your use of the five channels. Few jobs require extensive use of every channel. Each executive's job is different, and so no one can prescribe an ideal formula of usage. The practical question to explore is, "Am I making satisfactory use of each one, suitable to my special requirements?"

3. Don't overlook the possibilities of the self-communication channel. While some aspects deal with habitual practices such as note-taking, the idea can help improve your results. An executive for whom decision making was a special problem developed a method of putting the pros and cons of a given course of action on tape, and then playing back his own words. Listening to himself created an objectivity and perspective that cast a new light on the matter.

4. Consider a check of those channels you suspect are not well utilized. Let's say it is the first, communications to your boss and the higher echelons. Make a chart using the following elements:

- People and/or offices comprising my communications targets; boss, company president, and so on, (list them).
- Estimate (or keep a record for a period of time) the number of memos or letters sent, memos or letters received, phone calls made and received, frequency of face-to-face conversations.
- Estimate frequency of problems, such as unanswered queries or excessive delays in your exchanges.

Decide on the adequacy of the *quantities* you have indicated. You can use a rating scale from one to ten, for example, or satisfactory, unsatisfactory, or don't know.

■ Next, assess the adequacy of the *quality* of the communications, using a rating scale as you did for the quantity factor.

■ Finally, develop a program of changes you feel will improve your communications results.

One more thought: A simple assessment of a channel's health of communication index may be made among three choices; overcommunication, undercommunication, and satisfactory level of communication. You might apply this test to all five areas for a quick overall review.

▷ 45
The Exception Principle

CONCEPT

Also called "management by exception," this approach is a time and effort saver, helping you control an activity by bypassing acceptable performance and concentrating on the exceptional and unacceptable. In a manufacturing operation, for instance, once the dimension of a mechanical part has been specified, along with limits, (1.5 inches, plus or minus .001), managers need only investigate the exceptions, those outside given limits.

This physical example can be extended to general situations involving employee behavior, performance, and so on. Items within the given range require little attention, while you concentrate on the exceptions that demand remedy.

ACTION OPPORTUNITIES

Almost any ongoing activity, from job performance to behavior in the lunchroom, from output of a punchpress to quality of letters produced by a correspondence department, can be controlled by the exception idea. Once the errors, misoperations, and/or unsatisfactory performance is isolated, remedial action can be taken.

EXAMPLES

1. Manager Tess Ames is in charge of Traffic for a construction company. In checking costs for messenger and carrier services, she notices a gradual increase. Overall figures show a 15 percent rise from six months ago. And the number of items shipped is about the same.

Further digging shows that while rates for many items are stable, there are exceptions. Costs are higher for small, lighter items, and for large ones over 25 pounds. By digging into expenditures for these two groups, she learns that rates have been changing and that failure to route packages to carriers whose rate structures favor smaller and larger items has led to unnecessary expense.

2. The exception principle often requires the setting of standards by which "exceptions," or nonacceptable work or events, stand revealed.

Manager Bill Trent, head of an inspection operation in a computer parts division, finds that third-shift operations are unsatisfactory in both quantity and quality. A meeting with the supervisor gets a one-word explanation: "Discipline. I have trouble making the inspectors follow regular procedures."

Trent comes in early next morning, and as agreed, the supervisor has had his group stop work half an hour early. Trent explains his concern over the quality and quantity of work done. "I'll put it simply," he says. "We can't afford to operate the way we've been going. Does anyone feel that the bad work is the result of poor equipment, facilities, or procedures, or poor management? Tom, you're an old-timer. Any comments?"

Tom says, "The way I see it, Mr. Trent, some people just aren't suited for third-shift work. They eat wrong and sleep wrong, and when they come in, they can't cut it."

Trent thanks Tom and says he and the supervisor will see what can be done. No one else speaks up and the meeting is adjourned. Trent and the supervisor talk it over. The latter is apologetic: "I should have realized that some of the newcomers were having trouble adjusting." Trent asks him to check individual performance among newcomers as compared to old-timers. The former show notably poorer records. Trent says he'll get Personnel to print up eating and sleeping schedules recommended for the night workers. "We have that information, but didn't pass it along to new third-shift people."

One employee among the new group quit. As a result of the attention to the problem and the help in establishing better living and working *patterns, the poor performers improved to the point where their work eventually rose to normal range.*

Changing from group to individual performance measurement made it possible to spot the exceptions, and determine and alleviate the cause of failure.

HOW TO USE

Lester R. Bittel, in *Management by Exception** describes six steps to implementation:

1. Assign values, often numerical, to performance. Without standards of some sort, it is impossible to identify exceptions.

2. Projection. Analyze those measurements that are keys to your objectives and extend them to future expectations. For instance, what is the percentage of "exceptional" items, and how much must it be reduced to make performance acceptable?

3. Selection. Pinpoint the criteria you want used to monitor progress toward objectives. In other words, focus on the qualities or aspects that tell you how your remedies are working.

4. Observation. This is the measurement phase that tells you of the current state of performance. The closer to actual performance time your figures are, the more useful the feedback.

5. Comparison. A comparison of actual performance with expected performance identifies the exceptions that require attention.

6. Decision. What action must be taken to:

- Bring performance back into control, or
- Adjust expectations to reflect changing conditions, or
- Exploit opportunity by creative change

* Bittel, Lester R. (1964). *Management by Exception.* New York: McGraw-Hill.

▷ **46**
Feedback

CONCEPT

The dictionary defines feedback as, "the return to the input of a part of the output of a machine, system, or process." Lester Bittel, professor of management at James Madison University, explains more specifically: "Relaying the measurement of performance back to the individual or unit causing the performance so that action can be taken to correct the variance."

Both statements suggest a systems approach. Of equal importance is the psychological aspect. In general, people want to know how they are doing. The mayor of New York City, Ed Koch, starts many of his personal appearances before his constituents with the trademark question, "How am I doing?" Everyone who does a job wants to know how he or she is doing, not only for reasons of redirecting effort, but for the satisfaction that comes with the sense of accomplishment.

Also, feedback is said to "close the loop," to make a system self-assessing and self-correcting. For example, the sales department tells Production the reactions a new line is getting in the market, so that design, quality, color, and so on can be evaluated and modified if necessary. When the output involves a person, "closing the loop" takes on a second meaning. When individuals get feedback on how they are doing the loop is closed psychologically; their desire for closure is satisfied. (See Zeigarnik Effect, page 97.)

ACTION OPPORTUNITIES

Any performance of work can benefit from feedback to the point of origin. An automatic machine that gets no feedback that compares results with what is desired could turn out parts that are 100 percent bad. Feedback, with adjustments it may suggest, helps keep the machine producing within acceptable limits.

In addition to the mechanistic aspect, people themselves need feedback to stay on track. Presidents and CEOs are as dependent on feedback as anyone else.

EXAMPLE

Bittel describes an instance of self-administered feedback in an AT&T operation. Keypunch operators began to verify their own output and keep track of their own errors, with a significant improvement in error percentages. Also, turnover was cut and productivity improved.

HOW TO USE

As experienced managers know, there is feedback and feedback. These qualities insure effectiveness:

1. **Proximity between point of origin and feedback source.** For instance, if an inspection procedure is performed close to the production unit, the inspectors will have more direct contact, and will understand both the sources of error and the remedies better than if they were removed and had little contact.
   2. **Immediacy.** Donald J. Fletcher, a director in the Holyoke area of the Massachusetts Department of Mental Health, says, "The shorter the timespan between operation and feedback, the more helpful it will be. First, the person remembers the task better, and if the job is repetitive, the sooner necessary adjustments can be made. Second, fast feedback suggests that the work is important enough to warrant the supervisor's close attention."
   3. **Specificity.** "It's O.K., I guess," may be feedback, but it is less useful than spelling out the details, for example, "The report is fine, but the introduction is long, and the points made would come through better if they were numbered and given tagline titles. The conclusion is an excellent summary, and I would only suggest that you add a paragraph asking the people who receive copies if they would like to have a meeting to critique it."
   4. **Authoritativeness.** In formal situations, the feedback should come from a person or persons in authority. While comments and criticism may help a project in its formative stages, formal evaluation is less meaningful coming from the boss's secretary than from the boss.

Feedback can be technical, expressed in numbers or degrees of quality, or may represent subjective reactions in the form of opinion and comment. As long as it satisfies the basic requirement of monitoring output to keep the work within given limits, or to improve it,

feedback is an essential part of the process. The psychological effects—recognition and potential for helpful criticism and praise—
should not be underestimated. The feedback-conscious manager, who
can also supply information up the ladder by letting his boss know
reactions to new company policies and procedures, is one of the more
effective kinds.

▷ 47
Flextime

CONCEPT

Flextime (also called "flexitime") was developed in Europe to ease jam-
ups on public transportation during rush hours. Staggering employee
working hours permitted people to leave their homes and offices at
nonpeak periods. Another advantage of flexible work schedules is that
employees could improve home arrangements for child care, nursing of
ill family members, and so on. And there were operational advantages
for employers as well.

ACTION OPPORTUNITIES

Transportation overload, overcrowded restaurants, and other service
facilities can be mitigated using flextime. Employees with conflicts between personal concerns and work hours, for example, their own medical treatments, family members requiring attention, child care, and so
on, may also benefit. And employers are able to diminish absenteeism
and lateness caused by employees' personal situations. Flextime can be
applied company-wide or departmentally, with employees who have
special time needs.

EXAMPLE
*Sally Hayes and her husband Ron both work. Their two children, aged two
and four, require day care. A neighbor agrees to take over for five hours,
saying, "More would kill me." Sally and Ron plan schedules with their
employers. Sally leaves home at 10 A.M. and finishes at 6 P.M., while Ron*

works from 7 A.M. to 3 P.M.. The arrangement works well, except for emergencies. If the neighbor can't fill in, Sally has a nonworking friend who agrees to be on call as needed.

HOW TO USE

Flextime has strong advantages if its drawbacks can be avoided. It doesn't satisfy all employees and companies. Employers who have no need to undertake flextime schedules would be wise to weigh the negatives. Some employers got on the bandwagon just to be fashionable, and regretted the administrative burdens that ensued.

The following checklist identifies advantages and disadvantages:

Difficulties for the employee

( ) Mandatory change can bring resistance to altered hours for personal reasons, including interference with established routines.

( ) Schedules desired by the employer may not suit employees' requirements.

( ) A workgroup may lose its unity of time and place, and continuity is fragmented as early and late personnel lose touch with the main group and possibly with the supervisor.

Benefits for the employee

( ) Flextime can improve the quality of an individual's worklife, eliminating the crunch of rush-hour commuting, making eating and other local facilities more readily available, and tying in better with personal activities.

( ) Home and family scheduling can be done more easily.

Difficulties for the employer

( ) Record-keeping of hours worked, work done, and so on, becomes more complicated.

( ) Squabbles may arise among employees over preferred hours.

( ) Irregular workhour patterns may complicate work scheduling, and problems may arise from the need to supervise employee activity over a longer period of time, either overburdening managers or forcing makeshift fill-ins, an inexperienced senior employee, for example.

Benefits for the employer

( ) Longer operating periods may solve some scheduling and operating problems, and lead to greater productivity.
( ) Absenteeism and lateness can be reduced.
( ) In some cases morale and employee-management relations are improved as a result of joint planning of flextime schedules.
( ) Some companies note an improvement in morale because employees were given the chance to choose their work hours.

Despite generally favorable results, flextime may place unaccustomed burdens on management that should be balanced by benefits, for employees and for the organization as a whole, to be justified.

▷ 48
Management by Objectives

CONCEPT

So-called "management by objectives," (MBO) was greeted enthusiastically by executives who saw it as a solution to some of the following intractable problems:

- *Vagueness of performance targets.* MBO would help the employee and his boss discuss and agree on specific goals together.
- *Uncertainty in work planning.* With goals clearly set the subordinate and boss could lay out appropriate work procedures.
- *Resistance to performance appraisal programs.* It was thought that MBO, by permitting employees to set their own goals, would then provide an acceptable basis for performance measurement. Also, judgments were often by self-appraisal.
- *Unacceptability of critiques.* In the traditional appraisal interview, the approach usually stressed errors and weaknesses. In the MBO context, the boss was seen as a helper or coworker rather than as a judge.

- *Subjectivity of measurement.* Assessments of performance traditionally were subjective, consisting of the boss's opinion, with which a low-rated subordinate often disagreed. MBO emphasizes performance rather than personality or other peripheral factors, and also emphasizes future action rather than past behavior.

The MBO system that promised to accomplish this basic transformation of employee attitude and performance consisted of a series of simple steps:

1. Explanation of the MBO concept to the subordinate
2. A work session in which subordinate and boss develop realistic objectives
3. Agreement on the means by which the goals will be achieved, set forth in relatively specific plans
4. At the end of a subgoal period (monthly, quarterly, etc.), actual results are compared to expected results
5. Achievement is noted, and plans are reviewed and adjusted if necessary to assure satisfactory performance for the next period

MBO, when faithfully followed, is thorough, specific, focused, realistic, and flexible. If conditions change, objectives and methods must change accordingly.

ACTION OPPORTUNITIES

MBO may serve in four areas:

- *The organization.* The company as a whole sets objectives, for example, increase of profits from Product X of 10 percent by midyear. Top-echelon managers and operating heads participate.
- *Unit.* The procedure is used by a group, department, division, etc. For this application and the next two, managers may proceed on their own and develop their own version of the standard procedure, if the organization is not the sponsor.
- *Individual.* Employees deal with their own job goals.
- *Personal.* Goals may be set for promotion, salaries, or other personal career objectives.

In addition to job performance, the system may be applied to the following:

Profits	Cost reduction	Human resources buildup
Productivity	Sales volume	Share of market
Safety	Quality	New Products
New markets	Community relations	Quality of working life

EXAMPLE

Divisional president John Franklin and general manager Harry Black meet to discuss Black's job objectives. They have a wide-ranging conversation about past performance, problems, and opportunities, and then decide mutually to aim for an increase in production and sales of Product X of 5 percent by year's end. They discuss implementation, including the promotion campaign, amount of sales effort to be devoted to X, methods of getting cooperation from the service departments (all departments from Credit to Shipping), and end up with a written plan on which the push for Product X will depend.

Every two weeks Franklin and Black hold progress reviews to see if subgoals are being met. Profits go up 5 percent by the end of August, but fall to 2 percent in September. The managers reevaluate the situation and devise extra steps; putting a little more pressure on Sales, making sure Credit is being reasonable, and checking with Advertising to see if the best media mix is being used. Sales improve, and by January the figures show a 6.5 percent overall increase. "Let's see what we did right," Franklin says, "and try to spread it across the board."

HOW TO USE

Application of MBO these days is not so much a matter of procedure, for the steps are clear, but of knowing what is needed to make MBO the problem-solver it can be, and of knowing how to avoid the destructive factors. The following points can guide your thinking:

1. The procedure must be understood, including weak points and critical points, by all echelons and individuals.

2. It is crucial that there be commitment at all levels, especially at the top-management level, for a company-wide program.

3. Where MBO is being used by individual managers on their own, the system will necessarily reflect their personal biases. It requires intelligent and concentrated effort to make the procedure productive.

4. Remember the needs of employees. Don't make reviews too frequent, or let them be seen as punitive or overly judgmental. Maintain a supportive, constructive atmosphere. Stress successes and suggest remedies for failures. Point to the future and its opportunities for achievement.

5. Be clear about responsibilities. Don't be vague with yourself or with subordinates. Lack of clarity or failure to deliver expected help can leave responsibilities falling between the stools.

6. Keep communications lines open. Check on key points in an operating plan, and subordinates should be free to call on you when a complication arises.

7. Who really sets the objectives? You have to be clear in your own mind that, although you may exert influence, the performer must accept the goal wholeheartedly, or the effort will be halfhearted. Goal setting, a crucial element, can be as simple as a quick agreement on a numerical target, for instance, "The department will process 100 customer requests a day," or as abstract as a subordinate's assurance that he or she will come up with a replacement for a whole product line that has gone sour. The more positive the employee feels about the target (it should neither be too low or high, but it should be challenging), the better the auguries.

▷ 49
Management Consulting

CONCEPT

Need for outside expert help grew from the early 1900s to the point where, after World War I, client demand created a body of practitioners. In 1929 the need for ethical and service standards became evident to those in practice, and ACME, the association of Consulting Management Engineers, was formed. In 1981 a more representative designation, the Association of Management Consulting Firms, was adopted but the acronym ACME was retained.

ACME's major objectives:

- To develop and maintain standards and ethics of the profession
- To serve as a public relations and research center for the management consulting profession

Management consulting has become a much used tool in American business. From individual practitioners to full service companies, experts offer help in every management function and operational specialty, plugging gaps in a company's expertise.

ACTION OPPORTUNITIES

Consulting is indicated when: (1) an organization has a policy or operating problem that exceeds its grasp; (2) a new venture demands planning for which present staff is inadequate; (3) profitability or other basic objectives are not being achieved; and (4) an organization has difficulty in pinpointing reasons for key failures.

EXAMPLES

1.   "Computerize," the board of directors advises the CEO of Company X. The move would be radical, requiring changes in human resources, systems, equipment, and so on. The CEO decides that a consulting firm with experience in planning and implementing this kind of transition is the way to go.

2.   Company Y decides to start up an overseas branch. The problems, which include everything from legal complications to practical problems such as that of language, fall outside the experience of Y's staff, and thus suggest the need for consultants. At the very least a preliminary survey of physical requirements, personnel, organizational changes, and an estimate of the investment needed and potential profitability is advisable.

HOW TO USE

Consulting services come in all sizes, ranging from day-long conferences to intricate relationships and multipronged activities that go on for years. In addition, it must be said that engaging consultants doesn't necessarily assure a satisfactory outcome. It can help to be up on the kinds of failures that may occur and to keep expectations to realistic levels. Executives have voiced negative opinions:

"They picked the brains of our own people and rehashed these opinions to us. They didn't tell us anything we didn't already know."

"All we got was a nice report. The suggested improvements were too theoretical. We couldn't implement their recommendations."

"They want to come in and install prepackaged solutions to our problems. They are not aware of our particular needs."

"Their work dragged on far too long for what we got."

"The consultant picks up all the experience. When the consultant leaves, the experience goes with him. We should have the capability for doing these things ourselves. I would rather have our own people learn whatever there is to be learned."

"Some consultants don't know how to work with clients."

"Consulting firms should be more careful about their staff. Some individuals give the impression they know it all and we are naive not to see things their way. However, decisions had to be ours and they assumed no responsibility for them."

Forewarned is forearmed. Alertness to the pitfalls and care in the key steps of the undertaking can help make the effort successful. Consider the following steps:

1. Full discussion in your own organization. In the preliminary stages not everyone need be involved, but, if it is to be a first experience for you, or one of large scope, all those in the policy-making group and those executives who will be in contact with the consultants should participate. The basic pros and cons should be discussed so that the final go-ahead reflects the fullest possible understanding. Particularly important is the probing and elimination of negatives. It's impossible to anticipate all difficulties that may arise in working with the consultants, but the effort should be made.

2. Defining the project. Why do you think you need a consultant? What do you want him to do? What don't you want him to do? It's quite possible you can't state the problem clearly—sometimes that *is* the problem—but you should expect to state as well as you can what you think the problem is. This statement should include information about the conditions for its solution—costs, time, for example—the end results sought, and company rules or limitations within which it must be solved. Usually, the definition of a problem is achieved only after the consultant has studied the situation and determined underlying causes.

3. Selecting the consultant. "Hiring a consultant," says one executive, "is not too different from hiring an executive for your staff. You want someone with relevant experience who you feel you can work with and who seems to promise results."

Objectivity, integrity, and qualifications that suggest he or she is able to work effectively on your problem are obviously desirable. The matter of fees can be touchy since neither you nor the expert can be sure of the payoff. A low figure may mean a total loss, a high one an excellent investment. Listen carefully to how the service is presented. Are you getting a realistic pitch or an exaggerated one?

4. Agreement on mutual obligations. You're in a joint venture with a consultant you hire. In most cases, the client company must be an active participant. If the requisite time and effort is not forthcoming, the results probably won't be either. Usually management shares responsibility with the consultant for definition of the purpose and scope, general time, and cost of the study. But follow-through is important. Conclusions are practical only to the extent that management reviews them, understands and challenges them, and accepts those suited to its requirements.

A final report on findings should be followed by a discussion as to whether your personnel can implement the recommendations or whether you need the consultant's help. Finally, it is often desirable to request a post-installation review of the recommendations after they have been in operation for three to six months.

5. Supporting the consultant's work. It helps to maintain an active interest in progress, to evaluate the findings of the consultant, and to make sure efforts remain on track. Ask for interim reports, first, to keep management in the picture, and second, to help clarify the consultant's own thinking.

The consultant, an outsider, may seem to presume to tell people of experience how to do their work more effectively. To prevent resentment and get cooperation, you must smooth the way. This means: (1) support from the top; (2) strong liaison with one or more key people through whom the consultant can get help when needed; and (3) advance notice and indoctrination of personnel as to the purpose of the project, its relationship to their job assignments, and the importance of cooperation. (See Resistance to Change, page 72.)

6. Follow-up. "File and forget" is sometimes the fate of consultants' reports. One way to get a payoff is to request periodic feedback from your people as to how implementation of accepted recommendations is progressing. Ask for both positive and negative factors to ensure a balanced assessment.

7. Measure results. Some will be obvious, others less so. Here are some checkpoints of the consulting experience:

- How much disruption or productive stimulation is evident afterwards?
- How do cost and time estimates look in retrospect?
- How do you assess the completeness of the final report?
- Has management come out of the experience better, smarter?
- Would you employ the same consultant again?

▷ 50
Management Meetings

CONCEPT

Management meetings are the backbone of organizational communication and management effectiveness. The face-to-face situation, in which three to fifteen conferees gather for any one of several important purposes, permeates managerial activity. Nevertheless, there are two opposing views on meetings:

- They are a vital method of group communication
- They are a waste of time

Informed opinion suggests that poorly conceived and run meetings explain the latter view. The well-run meeting justifies the more favorable statement.

Contemporary meeting procedures benefit from the pioneering work of social psychologist Kurt Lewin, whose investigations of group dynamics made clear the psychological interaction that affects behavior. (See Group Dynamics, page 23.) The insights of group dynamics pushed meeting techniques to higher levels of sophistication.

ACTION OPPORTUNITIES

Meetings may be held for a range of reasons, each a key area of management action:

- *Introduction.* Of new personnel, new products, etc.
- *Announcements.* New policies, organizational changes, etc.
- *Reports.* Of progress, performance, special projects
- *Problem solving.* How to raise morale, improve quality, deal with a destructive rumor, improve line-staff cooperation
- *Decision making.* What to do about a serious customer complaint, where a new plant should be built, when to launch a new program
- *Idea development.* Brainstorming (See Brainstorming, page 111) to produce anything from the idea for a new product to a name for it
- *Planning.* Long-range and short, at all levels

- **Motivation.** To improve attitudes in the group, create enthusiasm for a goal, build team spirit
- **Cost cutting.** Methods improvement, programs, indoctrinating employees
- **Security and safety improvement.** Attitudes, procedures, equipment
- **Training.** Either for review, or to improve abilities
- **Testing ground.** On which people can display thinking ability, sharpen verbal and interpersonal skills in a group setting

EXAMPLE

This negative example shows how meetings can go wrong, and illustrates the demands the medium makes on its users:

Conference leader Harry Landon enters the conference room late, prepared to apologize, but finds he's the first to arrive. Then the others trickle in. "Let's start," Landon finally says.

A latecomer stands in the doorway. "I'm not sure I should be in on this," he says. "What's the subject?"

"You got an agenda sheet this morning."

"I didn't. Mail was held up on our floor."

"How to improve materials storage in the annex."

"Not my thing. See you next week."

Landon steps up to the easel chart and says, "Let's list the problems we're having with our present storage system." A number of hands go up. The door opens and in comes Mr. Grace, Landon's boss, with a stranger in tow. "Harry, hope it's O.K. Mr. Hansen is from Norway, and he's interested in how we run our meetings."

"Glad to have you," Landon says, although he isn't. The next fifteen minutes are a good demonstration of how a meeting dies. Landon asks questions, no one responds, he tries to get members of the group to speak up. No one volunteers.

Pete Sherman sees an opportunity to get attention for a pet idea and says, "Why don't we do what I suggested last month, and use that old shed near the parking lot for storage? I bet in the long run we'd save a lot of money . . ." He hopes the cost angle will go over with the "big boss."

Sally Lane points out that the shed is in poor condition and couldn't be used without considerable repairs.

At this point Mr. Grace rises and thanks Landon, the visitor from Norway adds his thanks and they depart. Seth Black suggests they reschedule the meeting for next week, the group applauds, and Landon agrees. Meeting adjourned.

Granted, the advent of the visitors was beyond Harry Landon's control, but their presence only ended a meeting that started badly. The section that follows can help foolproof meetings.

HOW TO USE

On the average, managers spend fifty percent of their time in meetings. On the basis of pay-per-hour alone, meeting time is a huge investment of human resources. More positively, the purposes served offer a potential for highly constructive activity. Here's how to make meetings effective:

1. The leader. Meeting-wise managers agree that the person who officiates is a major determinant of results. A capable leader mobilizes the group toward achieving desired objectives. It is up to the management level above that of the leader (who is often one level above the group members) to select qualified ones.

2. Preparation. Key matters should be attended to in advance:

- The leader should be clear on objectives.
- The roster should be checked to eliminate unnecessary attendees, and conversely, to insure the presence of key people.
- The size of the meeting should reflect its purpose. Experts suggest that for problem solving or decision making, small odd-numbered groups of five, seven, or nine are best. Brainstorming aside, creativity is helped by maximum freedom and cooperation with five members. As the group gets larger, individual participation shrinks. For announcements and introductions, your entire group may be invited.
- The meeting place should be reserved if necessary, readied, extraneous materials removed, essential supplies provided, seating arranged, public address system and projection equipment checked, refreshments ordered, and so on.
- Those who are to give reports or make presentations should be checked for readiness, queried to ascertain that their contribution will be on track, told how much time they'll have, whether they are to field relevant questions, and so on.
- Guest speakers can inject new vitality and pace into a meeting schedule. Select the right people and help them choose and slant their subject to your needs. Don't overlook the talent within your own organization, from board members down.

3. Meetings not to hold. Experienced leaders recommend avoiding matters like these:

- **Mystery agendas** unless they are an intentional come-on. The antimeeting conferees will have cause to gripe, "If I'd known the subject, I wouldn't have come." Others may justifiably protest inability to prepare as they would have liked.
- **The misidentified problem.** "Our subject will be how to increase interdepartmental cooperation." Cooperation may be the problem, but the underlying difficulty may be poor discipline, or inability of some departments to meet deadlines. Statements of purpose that are meant to be euphemistic—possibly the leader wants to avoid hostility by some—are O.K. if intentional. But then the leader should start with the announced subject.
- **Public punishment.** A gathering ostensibly called to determine "How to set up a liaison with Department A," is intended to demonstrate what stinkers Department A people are. It is unlikely that this will prove a step toward peace and improved operation.
- **Wrong medium.** Subjects dealing with delicate or confidential matters might fare better when handled in individual conversation. Information that involves considerable detail, requires considerable thought, or that may arouse undesirable reactions might better be conveyed in writing.

Elements within the meeting may also threaten its purpose. Some standard reefs are the hidden agenda, in which a member injects a subject of personal interest into the discussion (see Hidden Agenda, page 72); mixed echelons, that almost invariably witness the intimidation of the lower-status individuals (note the chill of conferees in the Example at the entrance of Mr. Grace); and signs of disinterest, such as lack of participation or sagging attendance.

4. Structure. Meetings should have a crisp, direction-setting start, a logical on-track development, and a constructive wrap-up. On the way to accomplishing these there may be various kinds of features, such as visual presentations, oral reports, and guest speakers.

The leader must avoid two undesirable extremes: (1) Laxity: Discussion that wanders or lags incites disinterest and boredom. (2) Rigidity: Insistence on a single narrow focus. Stay on track, but permit some digression to enrich the subject and add to its interest.

A three-part structure expedites problem-solving conferences:

- **Identification.** The problem is clarified and pinpointed
- **Analysis.** The problem is examined, and causes are sought
- **Solution.** Out of the probing, one or more solutions emerge

5. Wrapup. The conclusion of a meeting is often the key to its benefits. The following points should be covered:

■ *Summarize.* A rundown of points that have been accepted, rejected, or postponed prevents misunderstanding. Important items should be noted in a written record.

■ *Follow-up.* Clarify actions to be taken: "Karen, we'll depend on you to check the figures and send copies to each member."

■ *Progress reports.* "Greg, keep track of how the new method works and bring in the data at the next monthly meeting."

■ *Bridge.* In a meeting series, build interest in the next session: "Next week we'll end discussion of security problems and start on an action program to submit to the front office."

▷ 51
Media Selection

CONCEPT

Seldom is an executive action undertaken that doesn't require telling, asking, checking, proposing, disagreeing, or responding. For these and other messages eight communication media are available, each with advantages and disadvantages. Practical problem: Which medium is best suited for which communication?

ACTION OPPORTUNITIES

Usually the choice is made effortlessly. If you want an urgent meeting with your boss, a phone call can arrange it in seconds. If you have been investigating a product-breakage problem in truck shipments, a written report best conveys the detailed findings. But in many cases there is a question as to how to best communicate. These require a scanning of the choices to decide on the best medium for the message.

EXAMPLES

The two following cases illustrate the consequences of poor choice:

1. *Al Merrit wants to let Ben Lee know that he has made reservations for their flight to California. He scribbles a note and drops it into the interoffice mail. There is a jam-up in the mailroom and instead of being delivered that evening it arrives the next day. But before he gets the memo Lee also calls the airline for plane tickets and stops by to tell Merrit he has done so. After a few acerbic words the mixup is straightened out, but it wouldn't have happened if Merrit had phoned Lee about the ticket purchase.*

2. *Harriet Blue calls a meeting of her staff to describe a new public relations project for a client. Her concept is innovative, but, as it turns out, controversial. There are five people in the group and five opinions on every point. The project gets lost sight of in the argument. "I should have talked to the group individually," she realizes, and terminates the session. Meetings can be time-savers, but not if they get lost in irrelevancies. Meetings are a bit like a genie. Before summoning one up, be pretty sure you can keep it under control.*

HOW TO USE

The determining factor in selecting a medium is suitability: "Which is best for this particular message?"

The Media Selector helps you weigh the pros and cons of your choices. Five of the eight avenues are more or less standard, while the following three require some explanation:

1. Meal meetings. These are held at breakfast, lunch, or dinner. Even though much used, meal meetings have advantages and disadvantages that are rarely thought through, with benefits unavailable in other media. Increasingly, managers exploit the special tableside climate. In New York City, hotels that cater to business people report major adjustments in planning are necessary to accommodate the increasing breakfast influx.

2. Audio tape. Along with the office machine, technology has produced the good quality, pocket-size tape recorders that offer instant recording of thought. With word processing services widely available, transcription is seldom a problem.

3. Video tape. The advantages of sound, sight with color, and the proliferation of cameras and replay equipment continue to spread the number and variety of applications.

Advantages	Disadvantages

Phone

Speed. Permits questions and answers. Can be done with your personal touch. Several calls can be made in sequence.

Person at the other end might not be available, or subject to interruption. Also, in most cases, there is no record of the conversation.

Face to Face

Personal contact.

You can set a mood by a show of friendliness and relaxation. You can show and discuss visual material. Conversation is two-way.

One or the other individual may be subject to pressure by a powerful personality or outmaneuvered by a higher fluency. May not be easy to terminate.

Note or Memo

Brief. A tangible record can be filed. You can prethink your message.

One way. No control over its respondent at the other end. A rigid form, limited by permanent words on paper.

Formal Report

Can be comprehensive. Material may be organized at your leisure. Can be disseminated widely by means of copying. Provides you or a subordinate with an opportunity to show his or her stuff. Indexing and other summary devices help reader grasp scope of piece, locate specific subsections.

May require considerable time in reading. Problem of actual writing may be discouraging to a time-hungry executive.

Meetings

You can develop a two-way flow; also permits use of visuals—charts, films, and so on—you can show and explain.

Permits discussion and better meeting of the minds. And you reach several minds at once.

Time-consuming, possibly inconvenient, and sometimes difficult to keep a meeting on track.

Can be a field day for the long-winded individual.

Media Selector   *(Continued)*

Advantages	Disadvantages
Meal Meetings	
Informal, relaxed atmosphere. Moods and attitudes tend to mellow, and subjects of a confidential, "let's-drop-our-guard" nature may be broached. Being off company premises provides a new perspective. Some espouse lunch get-togethers as excellent for ending feuds, patching up misunderstandings.	You must find a restaurant that is convenient and suited to conversation, with cuisine good enough to add a pleasant note to the occasion. Noise, poor service, poor food, and fear of confidential matters being overheard, interfere.
Audio Tape	
Dictation can be done out of the office on mini-recorders, while traveling, and so on. Has immediacy of one-on-one conversation. May be listened to during off hours.	Inputter should be good at dictation. Irreplaceable material should be duplicated before mailing. Some voices are monotonous.
Video Tape	
Creates a feeling of human contact. Charts and other visuals may be shown. Excellent for illustrating procedures, training sequences, and so on.	More costly than paper and ink, and requires equipment for playback. Although complete run-throughs go smoothly, accessing a specific point takes a little time, not true of a typed report.

These media are not mutually exclusive. Executives may use more than one method for a reinforcement effect.

⯈ 52
Minimax Technique

CONCEPT

The "minimax" idea originates in the field of economics, where it refers to an action aimed to minimize the maximum loss in an undertaking. But the term also suits a strategy psychologist Kurt Lewin recommends in dealing with resistance to change. Lewin shows how the resistance is best overcome by minimizing the forces that oppose the change, and simultaneously maximizing the favorable forces, hence "minimax." (See Resistance to Change, page 72.) This double-action principle may be used in various situations in which there is a face-off between opposed views.

ACTION OPPORTUNITIES

The minimax gambit can be used in situations where a new status quo is sought, and matters may be improved by minimizing some factors and maximizing others. The resistance-to-change situation is a particularly apt application, but there are other situations which may be resolved by the combination of minimizing and maximizing the influential factors.

EXAMPLE

Bob Brell and his partner Tony Lewis own a suburban sanitation service. Brell tells Lewis, "We must raise our charges by 10 percent. The accountant says if we don't, we'll soon be operating at a loss."

Lewis says, "Our customers don't like us and if we boost the fees, we'll lose the borderliners, weekenders, and those who will go back to dumping their garbage in the woods."

Brell knows Tony Lewis is right about the community attitude. An irate customer once described their building and surroundings as a "smelly eyesore." The partners think the problem over and discuss it with the accountant advisor. Together they work out a program to improve community relations. Lewis, an old-timer, had tried to win goodwill by handouts to the fire house and the police force at Christmas time, and by paying for the tree in front of City Hall. The new approach consists of minimizing the company's unpopularity, maximizing favorable points:

- *Building a high, opaque fence around the parking lot where the garbage trucks are stored.*
- *Putting $500 into plantings and flower boxes around the front of the building and giving the whole structure a paint job.*
- *Buying spray equipment that provides a high-power stream of water plus deodorant for the trucks. Each one is now cleaned every third day of use, alongside the building, in full public view.*

The next step was maximizing not the cash contribution—that stayed at previous levels—but the partners' participation in community activities. Brell gave talks to the Parent-Teacher's Association on the problems of protecting the local environment and the need for planning for future waste disposal. Lewis and his wife organized a social activities program in the local senior citizens' center. The press gave them coverage.

Some time later, the firm announced a rate increase for the new year. Only four customers canceled, but new ones signed up at a steady rate.

HOW TO USE

The minimax approach is effective because its double action provides considerable leverage. These points help in applying it:

1. Determine whether a given problem lends itself to minimax by asking, "Are there negative factors that can be made more favorable by minimizing them, positive factors that can be maximized?"

2. List the factors under two headings. Here is how the sanitation service situation breaks down:

- **Minimize.** The "eyesore" and "nosesore" problems; the "ruining the neighborhood" problem resulting from its fleet of garbage trucks cluttering the landscape
- **Maximize.** The images of the partners, their interest in the community, an alternative to seeming to "buy" goodwill

3. Plan and apply a program of weakening the negative factors and strengthening the positive ones for the strongest possible total effect.

▷ 53
The Pareto Principle

CONCEPT

Vilfredo Pareto, a nineteenth century Italian economist, analyzed the distribution of wealth in his time. He discovered that most of it was in the hands of a small number of people, whom he called "the vital few," while the rest existed in poverty. These he called "the trivial many." Pareto's idea is sometimes called the "80-20 rule," meaning that 20 percent of the known variables will produce 80 percent of the results.

This simple but revealing fact is relevant to important executive concerns. It suggests that analyzing a cause-effect situation makes it possible to isolate key factors, either positive or negative, for remedial action. Either the vital few or the trivial many may hold the secret of improvement.

ACTION OPPORTUNITIES

Pareto's principle can be used where managers seek to improve an operation or performance area such as costs, sales, customer evaluation, quality control, accident reduction, employee productivity, and so on.

EXAMPLES

1. A computer parts manufacturer analyzed 2753 orders. The top 13 percent accounted for 66 percent of the sales volume in dollars, while the bottom 69 percent brought in only 7.1 percent. Here the vital few, while accounting for 66 percent of the results, incurred only 15 percent of the sales costs. The trivial many, bringing in only 7.1 percent of the sales, were responsible for 62 percent of the costs. In this case it is clear that in order to cut sales costs most effectively, management must deal with the trivial many.

2. Paul Greene, head of Production in a furniture factory, sees that absenteeism is rising. In the worst departments it ranges from 10 to 15 percent, with consequent loss in output, and scheduling and delivery problems. Greene asks heads of departments with unsatisfactory attendance to keep careful records and send them to his office weekly.

Analysis of these reports shows that in each case about 10 percent of the roster causes about 75 percent of the absenteeism. The findings were spelled out to the department heads and a program developed by which each manager would work closely with the vital few, the individuals who were a major cause of the problem. As a result, the reasons for their staying away from work were pinpointed—they ranged from travel difficulties to need for infant daycare—and minimized. Attendance improved significantly.

HOW TO USE

The Pareto Principle can be applied to any management problem that has a clear cause-effect core. Five simple steps lead to its application:

1. Develop a record or list of factors, units, or components involved in the matter being investigated.

2. Arrange the items in order of importance relative to the problem. In the computer parts example, the 2753 orders were sequenced by dollar volume—largest first, smallest last. In the attendance situation, the department heads recorded absentees weekly, and after a month or so it became possible to list the worst offenders in order of days absent.

3. Identify the vital few.

4. Identify the trivial many.

5. Act on the findings. In some cases your remedy will focus on the vital few, in others on the trivial many. For example, in one case the managers got results by dealing with the vital few causing the excessive absenteeism. In the example of cutting sales costs, it was the excessive expenditure by the trivial many that required action.

▷ 54
Participative Management

CONCEPT

It has become difficult to discuss participative management without describing the Japanese effort, which has refined the art. Accordingly, Japanese practice will be touched on but coverage will focus on the American context.

Here is an enthusiastic description of participative management:

"Few techniques have been as successful in developing harmony and the attainment of common goals as has the development of participation. . . . It is an amazingly simple way to inspire people. And its simplicity lies in the definition of the word: 'to share in common with others.' . . . You must share knowledge and information with others in order to get their cooperation. . . . You must share the decision-making process itself so that employees can do some things the way they'd like to."—Lester Bittel, professor of management at Madison University School of Business.

The benefits that Professor Bittel indicates may be won, but success doesn't just happen. It usually results from good procedures. Likewise, in failure the unfavorable factors often haven't been anticipated.

Japan has been a major educator for today's American managers. Some observers assert that Japan's participation practices account for that California-sized country, with few natural resources except people, becoming the third most powerful industrial nation, after the United States and the Soviet Union.

The Japanese experience has made us aware of two facts:

- Americans developed participative management decades before it appeared in Japan in the 1960s, but the Japanese deserve full credit for their imaginative transplant and further development.

- In Japan, participative management is not simply a procedure but a practice rooted in national culture and education. Some experts feel that talk of our replicating Japanese methods, such as quality circles, is unrealistic. One executive uses as a parallel, "buying four wheels and thinking you have an automobile."

ACTION OPPORTUNITIES

Activities involving a substantial human element may use participation to good effect. Where the procedure is already practiced, a review may reveal ways to make it work better. Department heads have used participative management as an aspect of personal leadership. For broader application higher management's backing is necessary.

EXAMPLES

1. *A negative case taken from an interview of an office worker quoted by Professors George Strauss and Leonard R. Sayles in their book* Behavioral Strategies for Managers* *makes its point.*

* Strauss, George & Sayles, Leonard R. (1980). *Behavioral Strategies for Managers.* Englewood Cliffs, NJ: Prentice-Hall.

"We have meetings once a month. The office manager asks if we have any questions or suggestions. Sure, we have lots of complaints, but no one has the courage to bring them up. Once in a while someone who is looking to make a good impression asks some silly question, although he already knows the answer."

2.   Here is the success story of a word processing department as told by its supervisor:

My boss called me in and said, "Bill Grey tells me he sent down a tape on Monday morning and didn't get the transcription back until Tuesday afternoon. You've got to cut turnover time" (the time between receipt of copy or tapes by Word Processing and their return) "to no more than three hours."

I got my group of seven people together, told them about the complaint, and that we were going to get the whole department to work at improving things. I announced we'd start regular meetings to develop new methods.

In our first meeting I explained that I was going to be an observer. They would elect a chairperson and work out their own agenda. Actually, I planned to be out of the room most of the time. Mary Santini was elected leader, and she knew her stuff. An entire session was spent discussing operating problems, and Mary listed them on an easel chart. Later they analyzed them and developed solutions. I encouraged them and mostly stayed out of the way. In two weeks they came up with a 12-point program of changes, some for our operation, some for the executives to follow. We then worked out just how to implement them, and did. We now average a two-hour turnaround.

This second example represents almost full autonomy for the participants. The supervisor had properly assessed the group and its abilities.

HOW TO USE

When company climate poses no complications and objectives are realistic, a good leader and responsive people such as in Example 2 make satisfactory results likely. Note the encouraging free-rein leadership of the department head.

In appraising the possible use of participative methods:

1. Understand the Japanese situation. Some authorities feel that Japanese managerial practices cannot be duplicated here. Pervasive paternalism, guaranteed lifetime employment, racial and cultural homogeneity, uniform education, a tradition of consensus decision making, and especially important, government and unions in nonadversarial relationships with business, create a unique climate.

2. Consider the elements that may travel. Some practices, especially those relating specifically to participation, may be copied, for instance:

- *The manager's role.* Generally, it is not to give orders, but to facilitate group action. This is not for all American managers, but to many it is a natural style. And with this approach comes the expectation that subordinates, as group members, should think and participate responsibly in the department's operations.

- *Training managers.* Starting at the lowest echelons, the techniques of participation may be taught so that it loses its threatening aspect and is accepted as a useful tool.

- *Training employees.* Employees are trained not only in their jobs, but in the things they must know to operate as responsible group members. In Japan's quality circles, for example, workers are taught statistical analysis methods so that they can understand the figures, trends, and checks used to monitor and control quality.

3. Degrees of participation. The list below, adapted from *Behavioral Strategies for Managers,* by Strauss and Sayles, spells out five kinds:

Types of Participation in Increasing Order of Employee Involvement

Boss solves departmental problems with minimum participation from subordinates.

Boss gets data from subordinates, then makes the decision.

Boss shares problem with subordinates, asks for ideas and suggestions, then he or she makes final decision.

Boss shares problem with subordinates and together they work out a decision.

Boss specifies problem and asks subordinates to develop solutions and to make the final decision.

You choose among the methods above, depending on: (1) the nature and attitude of the group; (2) the nature of the problem; (3) such aspects as time, cost, and priority of other matters on the department's agenda; and (4) your own leadership preference.

The subject matter to be dealt with may vary widely, from a behavior problem like absenteeism to an operating difficulty like "How can we handle customer complaints more efficiently?" or one involving creativity: "How can we improve our packaging so as to lessen breakage?"

4. Target the benefits. Well-managed participation should yield the following gains:

- Superior decisions
- Minimized resistance to change, especially change that the group has helped devise and will implement
- Improvement in worker satisfaction, since the participation is a form of job enrichment
- Increased productivity, from improved work attitudes and the better methods developed
- Increased trust between employees and managers

5. Remember the possible obstacles:

- Managers' fears of losing control
- Employees' wariness of change and management's motives
- Lack of sufficient savvy for new roles participation may require of both employees and managers
- Misunderstanding of objectives. "Plan a company tour for five customers' representatives, with lunch included," may seem a simple matter, but if no more information is supplied the lunch may be hot dogs and beer instead of a meal at the local gourmet restaurant. Moral: Autonomy may be a fine thing, but some guidance is usually required.

An organization may change when participation becomes a way of work. Not only do manager and employee attitudes get out of traditional ruts, but employee-management cooperation may create a perceptible difference in atmosphere. This only happens, however, when top management is committed to the participation philosophy, and both managers and subordinates master their roles in the participative procedures.

▷ 55
Personnel Testing

CONCEPT

Hiring is one of the most crucial executive acts. Choose the right candidate and you're in good shape, the wrong one adds to your troubles.

Consider David and Goliath. Even today's sophisticated manager couldn't have seen much potential in David the shepherd boy as a challenger for Goliath. King Saul was unimpressed: "Thou art but a youth, and he a man of war from his youth." Or in the language of today, "Sorry, we can't use you."

Luckily David was not subjected to testing, for example, how large a tree he could cut through with the swing of a sword. He had job-related experience and told the King how he had saved a lamb from a ferocious lion: "I went out after him and smote him and delivered it out of his mouth." Apparently King Saul knew people. David got the job.

In the absence of kingly perceptiveness, management often depends on personnel testing to improve the odds. However, in recent years (since the 1971 Supreme Court ruling against discriminatory hiring practices) some companies avoid legal difficulties by abandoning testing entirely, or use practical tests of job skills like typing, shorthand, manual dexterity, and mathematical abilities. Organizations seek to meet government criteria for nondiscriminatory hiring procedures by

- Content validity, relating the test content to job needs
- Construct validity, which avoids screening out applicants who fail because the test questions themselves aren't understood

Testing still offers legal and effective tools for evaluating applicants.

ACTION OPPORTUNITIES

Testing of some kind is desirable for every hire. Even taking the top three contenders out to lunch can strengthen the hirer's hand in making a final choice.

EXAMPLES

1. There is a famous case—perhaps apochryphal—of a candidate failing the "Dining Test." Henry Ford took a plant manager candidate out for a "size-'im-up" dinner. The man was subsequently rejected. Ford explained, "He wasn't careful in his judgments. He ordered soup and added salt without first tasting it."

2. Fred Watson is looking for a person to take charge of the London office. The potential job is bigger; president in five years. The board of directors is monitoring Watson's choice.

Elliot Widdoes is the prime prospect. Watson circulates Widdoes's resume to key staff members, arranges for them to meet him, and then flies him to London to meet the executives he'd be working with. In addition, he gets Widdoes's consent to take a battery of tests given by a psychological testing service. The report is favorable. Widdoes is hired and works out well. Watson is pleased, but tells the board chairman, "I knew he was the man from the first moment. Why did we bother with all those procedures?" Partial answer: they reassured the board.

HOW TO USE

Fred Watson suggests that all the evaluation efforts used on Widdoes were wasted. Not so. If Watson had hired on a hunch, he would have been regarded as irresponsible, and had Widdoes failed, Watson would have been judged replaceable. As experienced observers say, testing and evaluation procedures not only tell you about applicants but add a margin of safety by using professional techniques to reinforce judgments.

Testing isn't the whole answer—some people test well and can't perform, and vice versa—but the more you have to go on, the better your decision will be. Testing should be suited to individual situations. You will proceed differently in the cases of a receptionist, a programmer, and a chief financial officer, although the objective in all cases is the same; a profitable hire. Some helpful methods:

1. Record review. Evaluate the applicant's work history, education, job training, professional and related experience, jobs held, and so on. References or similar data adds another perspective.

2. The interview. The face-to-face meeting between a job candidate and organization representative—in most cases, the potential boss of the applicant—is the most used, flexible, and helpful procedure. But there are interviewers and there are interviewers. An experienced person can come out of a session with accurate evaluations of the candidate's appearance, manner, interpersonal abilities, emotional stance, life values, and ability to stand up under pressure. An inept interviewer may emerge with bland and useless observations like "I think she's O.K.," or with distortions that represent personal bias, like the comment "She's too aggressive." Meetings with two or more interviewers can provide a desirable range of reactions that can be blended for a consensus.

3. Performance tests. For measurable skills such as in word processing, drafting—for managers, an "in-box" exercise is sometimes used to gauge administrative and decision-making capability—performance trials offer a promising check.

4. Trial period. In some cases a test or probationary period permits a check on ability to do the actual job. But remember, it is then incumbent on management to make the trial a fair one by preparing the candidate adequately.

5. Critical-point testing. Some jobs demand a specific capability. For instance, an inspector may need unimpaired eyesight with or without glasses, and a person selling by phone won't do well with an unpleasant voice or manner. Inadequacies here would represent a knockout factor. The hirer should analyze the job for critical areas and test for the essential qualities needed to perform them.

6. Psychological or personality testing. This approach attempts to predict performance on the basis of personality. Widely resorted to in the 1960s and 1970s, it is still used when hiring for professional or top management jobs where the individual's emotional makeup is a key job asset or liability. Excerpts from a psychological testing service report suggest their approach:

■ *Appraisal of John X.* The search: A person is needed to head up a new unit which is to expand present product lines, requiring both product development and marketing ability.

Key excerpt from the report: This candidate has fine intellectual capacities, especially along creative and technical lines, but has little to offer in terms of the initiative, practical-mindedness, or enthusiasm, essential to selling ideas. His attitude towards superiors is characterized by a "chip on the shoulder." He seems to go on the assumption that one always fights losing battles with people in authority. Potential: limited. He lacks the practical judgment and understanding of people required by a top-level position, and seems to think his best years are over and the future is unpromising.

■ *Appraisal of Henry Y.* The search: Here the question is whether a present employee, now comptroller, should be moved up.

Key excerpt from the report: Mr. Y is brilliant, conscientious, a sober-minded introvert with a flair for mathematics. He is generously endowed with a talent for logical, straight-line thinking. He certainly has the intellectual power to deal effectively with the kind of problems he would encounter in his present job or on a higher echelon. Potential for upgrading: Excellent. He is eager for additional responsibility and should make a good corporation treasurer.

7. Executive recruiters. Headhunters are a standard factor in searches for key personnel at the professional and managerial level, but keep in mind that they require intelligent cooperation. Like computers they work on the garbage in, garbage out principle. Only when management is willing to provide not only the basic needs but also the nuances of the job, and the nature of the organization with its inbred requirements, can the professional recruiter deliver. Among other things, recruiters help management think through both the kind of individual needed and the job context.

◊ 56
PERT

CONCEPT

When the U.S. Navy wanted to expedite the Polaris missile program the spotlight was turned on its management methods. A key idea for improving efficiency was "PERT," an acronymn for "Program Evaluation and Review Technique." Basically this is a method for programming and controlling operation or production procedure. While the Navy used it for its missile program, many organizations apply the approach to office and factory procedures.

Essentially, PERT's approach is like that of the homemaker preparing a multicourse meal. Several burners of the stove are used simultaneously. The things that take longer are begun first, and all items end up ready to serve at dinner time.

ACTION OPPORTUNITIES

PERT can be of great value in coordinating a production schedule or a project of several lines of action conducted in time and space. It helps prevent costly overlaps or shortfalls.

EXAMPLE

PERT can handle operations involving large numbers of people and large amounts of equipment and materials. A simple example demonstrates the basic procedure:

Manager Len Doyer wants to reorganize his storage facility. A key change requires a transfer of cartons from one room to another. He makes a list of the things he must have in readiness and the procedures which must be gone through:

Provide hand truck
Two employees to do the actual moving
Check the new area to make sure it's large enough
Move cartons to the new location
Sort and label cartons
Check the amount of material to be moved
Inform and get approval of the supervisor involved
Stack cartons using the new system

Once Doyer has listed the elements involved in the operation, he is in a position to apply the PERT program.

HOW TO USE

The carton-moving example above can be used to illustrate the specific steps of the PERT method:

1. List everything that is to be done. The list in the previous example illustrates this step.

2. Put the jobs in sequence. Go over your list of job steps and put them in the sequence in which they must be done. In the foregoing list, for example, the first step would be to make sure that the material to store will fit into the new area.

3. Estimate time for each step. Express the time in minutes, hours, days, or as you will, and indicate time alongside each step on the sequence of operations you've listed. Your new list will look like this:

A. Check amount of material (.8 hours)
B. Check capacity of new areas (.4 hours)
C. Get truck (.2 hours)

D. Assemble employees (.1 hours)

E. Move material (5 hours)

F. Sort and label (2 hours)

G. Okay by supervisor (.5 hours)j

H. Stack (3 hours)

4. Make an arrow diagram. The PERT chart or "network" is a key tool, shows how the various parts of the job interrelate. To draw the chart, use an arrow to indicate each step in the operation. The lengths of the arrows don't matter, but their *directions* show you how a particular step relates to the rest of the job.

Construct the diagram by asking three questions of each element in the sequence:

- What immediately precedes this element?
- What immediately follows it?
- What other elements can be done at the same time?

Here's how a PERT chart for the carton-moving operation might look:

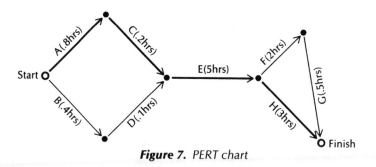

Figure 7. PERT chart

Note some of the things the chart tells you at a glance. First, Step E, the actual moving, can't take place until after Steps A through D are completed. Second, it shows the general scope of the operation. Third, it helps you determine the critical path.

The *critical path* is the total of the longest consecutive jobs. In the chart, the critical path is shown by the heavy line. Knowing the critical path, you're now in a position to do several things:

- ***Estimate the total time for the job.*** In our example, it would be nine hours.

- *Spot bottlenecks.* Every operation on the critical path is theoretically a bottleneck. Operations not on the critical path (these are called slack paths) may generally be done at the same time as those on the critical path. Since they take less time, it is the critical path that limits your schedule.

- *Expedite the schedule.* You have two alternatives, if you want to shorten your completion time: (1) have steps on the slack path performed as much as possible at the same time as those on the critical path; or (2) shorten critical path operations by making them "crash" activities, that is, by putting more men or equipment on the job, devising a more efficient method, and so on.

Used wisely, PERT can also help you keep costs down. You could, for example, devise two alternative charts representing two different ways of getting a job done. Comparing man-hours, possible overtime, and other cost elements, and stacking completion time of one method against the other, you can come up with figures that tell you whether a normal production or a "souped-up" schedule is more desirable from a dollar and delivery standpoint.

▷ 57
Prioritizing

CONCEPT

"Doing first things first," is clearly a practical necessity, and so the idea of priority grew naturally in business practice. Experts discoursing on executive routine repeatedly reminded, "Set your priorities." Peter Drucker points out that doing Chore X extremely well is a waste of time if it doesn't need doing at all.

Despite the good counsel to set priorities, few advice-givers explain exactly how this is to be done. "First things first" is a simple but ambiguous expression. How do you decide which is the first thing? In what ways must a situation change for one first thing to be replaced by another? Many executives understand the principle and instinctively do a good job of prioritizing their work. But some are handicapped by ignorance of the rules that make for maximum effectiveness.

ACTION OPPORTUNITIES

Everything that needs doing in your area of responsibility can benefit from knowledgeable priority setting, that is, deciding on how to order work and how to alter the order when circumstances change. Two major areas for consideration are your own workload and schedules, and the work produced by your department or workgroup.

EXAMPLE

Executive Harold Lamp has laid out the sequence of his major tasks:

1. *A letter to the company president about changes in his department's operation that require major adjustments in budgetary needs*
2. *A meeting of his subordinate managers to discuss a serious sag in morale in the division*
3. *Meeting with Jensen, the head of Research and Development, to discuss a program for bringing along his idea for a new product*

As Lamp hangs up his hat at the start of the day a call comes in from Jensen: "A friend of mine from Switzerland is passing through on a visit. He's a top man on the subject of your idea. He's willing to stop in for a discussion but he only has two hours starting from right now. Shall I arrange it?"

The low priority item immediately takes precedence for Harold Lamp. Even though the two other items seemed more urgent, the opportunity for consultation with the expert is too good to miss.

HOW TO USE

Setting meaningful priorities requires understanding the factors that determine them. The major ones are:

1. Money. The dollar outcome that depends on your order of performance is often the dominant factor. If missing a delivery deadline for Customer A brings a cash penalty, Customer A's order may well head your schedule. Occasionally, however, executives have been willing to take cash losses if other factors dominate.

2. Time. Time factors figure in a number of ways:

- One manager says, "Occasionally I have a big order from an important customer that bumps everything else. But if that would preempt our facilities and hold up several smaller orders, I would process the short jobs and hope I could get the big one out in a reasonable time. In other words, I'm willing to risk a possible complaint from a big customer, rather than upset a number of smaller customers for sure."

■ Another manager says, "If I can get short tasks taken care of easily, I like to get them out of the way for two reasons: first, to cut down on the number of items on my to do list, and second, to be able to concentrate on the longer jobs without the uneasiness of feeling that things are piling up."

3. Stops and starts. As every industrial engineer knows, stops and starts can be time wasters. From this fact arises two priority considerations:

■ *Finish up.* It may make for higher efficiency in the long run to stick with a lower-priority job and wrap it up than to stop it, turn to a higher-priority task, and then have to return to the interrupted task with probable losses due to having to get reorganized, picking up the mental threads, and so on.

■ *The human factor.* If subordinates are involved, you can be up against the natural dislike many people feel toward being interrupted (see the Zeigarnik Effect, page 97). If other factors like costs and time are not decisive, it may pay to permit the subordinate to conclude a procedure before going on to another one.

4. Facilities. The availability of equipment, space, and materials, may determine sequence. If an important meeting requires use of a conference room that is being used by a group that cannot be bumped, you may have to hold off, and turn to the next items on your agenda.

The manager of a mixing room in a plastics factory says, "When we're running black or dark pigments on our rolls, we hold off on the light or pastel colors until we finish the darks, then we can have a thorough clean-up and start with the transparents."

5. Goodwill/clout. This factor requires a "last-but-not-least" introduction. In the real world of business that mythic "best customer"— perhaps the largest organization, or the one who bills the most—can, like the 800-pound gorilla, have almost anything it wants. Other things being equal, that's the way it will be. Other qualities may exert the same kind of pressure:

■ A boss may deliver "a request you can't refuse." Other executives at higher levels in the organization may preempt your time or facilities because of status and authority.

■ A friend and colleague may need help to the point where you drop everything to assist.

■ Personal and humane considerations also can cause you to junk a sequence of priorities: An employee may have an accident, or there may be an emergency at home. An emotional plea from a supplier, customer, or colleague may sway your priority sense.

Another factor, which is difficult because it usually calls for guess-work, is weighing short-range versus long-range consequences. You may satisfy one person but in so doing draw complaints from another. Eventually the ill will of the second person can be costly, causing a damaged relationship, or a dollar loss. The important thing is to weigh long against short-term and make a considered decision. Your subjective judgment is frequently your final resource.

▷ 58
Quantification

CONCEPT

Roger Bacon said that knowledge was not scientific unless it used numbers. Sir Francis Galton, who launched the modern theory of statistics suggested, "Whenever you can, count." Numbers are an important tool in problem solving. Matters that seem vague and unmanageable come into focus whenever you can count and compare.

ACTION OPPORTUNITIES

For some problems quantification is built in, for example, "In order to break even, we have to produce and sell 1000 widgets a week." For others, efforts must be made to put factors into numbers or other systems of quantification. The more successful the effort, the better your chances of dealing with the situation.

EXAMPLES

1. You want to move some equipment from the west to the east coast. You phone Shipping and ask the manager for the best way to send it. "Are you talking ten pounds or 1000?" he asks. Quantity dictates the solution.

2. *A group of executives are assessing the three finalists for filling a vice-presidential job. Credentials and experience on paper have been noted, and each has interviewed the candidates. But the discussion of comparative merits gets out of hand. Finally the president says, "We must simplify matters. Let's agree on the five key qualifications for this job and rate each for the candidates on a scale of 0 to 10." Now they can clarify the murk of abstractions and generalities.*

HOW TO USE

To inject quantification into situations and problems:

1. Pinpoint the factors. You must be clear on exactly what you are assigning values to. For instance, abstractions sometimes used in rating personnel—attitude, effort, and creativity—are meaningful only if there is understanding and agreement as to what they mean. Using known examples like "Let's say that Tom represents a 6 in dependability, and Sandra a 10," sets a standard.

2. Assign values. There can be a complication in numerical rating. The factors may be unequal, when compared to each other. This may be overcome by "weighting." For instance, you want to evaluate the performance of an employee whose job involves three elements of differing importance. You assign 50 percent to Factor A, B and C are given 25 percent each. Now as your rate performance in each area, the weighting makes your total more meaningful.

3. Rating scales. In situations where numbers may not apply in a literal sense, they may be used as a relative scale, such as the popular 0 to 10. Also, other quantifying systems may be used. Our earliest experience in school exposed us to grades such as excellent, good, poor and unsatisfactory. Assessments such as high, low, and medium, or often, occasionally, and never are also common.

▷ 59
Taskforce Management

CONCEPT

The taskforce idea grew out of management's need to deploy its personnel outside regular organization slots. For example, a group is recruited from one or more departments across hierarchal lines to deal with a special problem or goal.

Since the members have both vertical and horizontal affiliations, some authorities see the taskforce as an example of matrix management. And since the taskforce leader's authority coexists with that of the regular supervisor's and double bossing is typical of matrix structure, the tag is not unsuitable. But theoretical limitations need not infringe on practical functioning. "A taskforce does whatever I want it to do," asserts one untrammeled executive.

Authorities disagree about the role of the group:

Paul Mali, in his *Management Handbook,** states that a taskforce is "an examining group with only the authority to recommend." He then specifies their two areas of relevance as "Special projects, such as cost reduction and waste control," and "Activity analysis, questioning the value of each activity in terms of the cost of maintaining the activity."

In *Your Role in Task Force Management,†* Thomas L. Quick sees a broader role: "The task force, as the name indicates, is formed to accomplish a task." However, "It is a temporary group with temporary authority and responsibility." And, "The true task force has operational responsibility for what it proposes."

Executives needn't get bogged down by the ambiguities of definition. A hammer by any other name will perform as well. A broader view of the taskforce idea widens its potential use.

ACTION OPPORTUNITIES

Any goal that management feels is best reached by putting together the talents of several people, regardless of their regular assignments, may be considered for taskforce treatment. The range may include problems or

---

* Mali, Paul (1981). *Management Handbook.* New York: Wiley.
† Quick, Thomas L. (1972). *Your Role in Task Force Management.* Garden City, NY: Doubleday.

targets in any function; Production, Research and Development, Administration, Sales, Purchasing, and so on. The main question: does the goal warrant the special treatment?

EXAMPLE

A business publishing company wants to add a newsletter for field salespeople to its line. Many companies seem eager to provide ongoing training for their sales personnel, suggesting a market for bulk sales. A study by Marketing suggests a strong demand. Everything from analyzing existing competition to devising samples illustrating editorial policy, format, and content is required. Costs, sales, and profitability must also be projected.

The executive director decides on a taskforce of appropriate makeup. He checks with department heads and then designates six people; three editor/writers, the assistant art director, the assistant to the vice-president of Sales, and a treasurer, the last two to participate if and when needed. The most senior editor, an effective and creative manager, is made taskforce leader.

The group operates part-time, meeting two mornings each week with occasional after-hours sessions. The three editor/writers do most of the digging and planning, the art director is started on formats and the representative of Sales and the treasurer are asked to attend meetings when their help is needed.

At the end of six months, a report including four dummy bi-weekly issues is submitted to the executive director, who thanks the group for its efforts, and terminates it. Six months later, top management has modified and finalized the program and plans are begun to put the new newsletter into production.

HOW TO USE

To get the most out of the taskforce idea, and to avoid the pitfalls, consider these points:

1. Taskforce, yes or no? Some companies develop a taskforce addiction and overuse the device, complicating regular operations. Others neglect it when it could help. Three tests can help you decide whether it's taskforce time:

- Is the goal sufficiently important to justify the dislocations and possible drawbacks of double loading personnel?
- Will denuded departments be able to operate satisfactorily?

- Is the taskforce superior to other possible solutions such as outside consultants or bringing qualified people into the company as temporaries who may subsequently be made permanent?

2. Sponsorship and control. The sponsoring executive should be clearly identified, and should retain contact with the group, supplying help and guidance as needed. The executive should also walk the fine line that respects autonomy but intervenes to prevent major errors in judgment or direction.

3. Enlist cooperation. Check with department heads to smooth the selection and scheduling of taskforce recruits. Cooperation can forestall argument that can taint both taskforce and regular operations.

4. Form a viable group. The makeup of the force is largely determined by the nature of the task. Everything from group size to individual selection should be decided with an eye on the kind of people required to perform as needed. Some selection factors are:

- *Size.* Avoid over or understaffing. Too many people may cause clutter and confusion. Too few may mean top-heavy workloads. Two guidelines: Use the smallest number of people possible, to minimize communications and supervisory complexities, and, assemble a group large enough to assure sufficient resources to attain objectives within the desired time frame.

- *Qualifications.* Group members must collectively possess the talents and skills the project requires. If the objective is a study of budgeting procedures, at least one person should have professional-level familiarity with budgeting. And members must be able to work as a team. Avoid "oil-and-water" personalities. Loners whose skills are essential may have to be insulated from others to avoid friction.

5. Roles. Taskforces benefit from having members able to fill key group roles:

- *The Leader.* This person is essential. He or she must accept the responsibility of command, discuss and solve problems, describe basic objectives, make assignments and assure performance, and act as liaison between the group and the sponsoring executive.

- *The Dynamo.* This is the pusher, the one who is aware of progress and deadlines. "Can do," is his or her slogan. This person may be the group leader, but not necessarily.

- *The Hardhead.* This type of person holds out for facts in place of assumptions, for full achievement instead of almosts.

- *The Analyst.* He or she probes below the surface, looks for causes, and is good at untangling messes and spotting the real problem.

- **The Dreamer.** Essential in a task that requires creative thinking, this person produces ten good ideas while others labor for one.
- **The Detailer.** This member has a head for figures and the patience to stick with them, double and triple checks.
- **The Team Player.** Where dedication and loyalty are especially valuable, he or she will take on work others won't do.
- **The Resource Person.** An individual of experience who can fill knowledge gaps need not be a member, but should be available.

The importance of these roles vary with the task: an Analyst might be a key for problem-solving, a Dynamo wasted in a low-pressure planning project. And individuals may fill more than one role.

6. Progress monitoring. The sponsoring executive and the taskforce leader must assess group performance, and be ready to deal with obstacles. Quality and quantity elements must be evaluated and major disagreements thrashed out to expedite completion.

7. Wrap-up. Terminate the taskforce effort cleanly. A draggy, chaotic end is bad for group morale and an argument against further taskforce utilization. Ideally, the finish calls for recognition and reward, formal or otherwise. Unrecognized success can be as destructive as failure. Suitable reward brightens the taskforce future.

⬡ **60**
Wastebasketry

CONCEPT

Wastebasket control is an essential element in written communication. Psychological as well as physical considerations influence your wastebasketing. Imagine the problems of the person who literally can't throw anything out, or the one who winces at each decision of whether to keep or dump a memo or letter. But those in the know avoid litter and loose ends and never suffer from in-box malaise.

ACTION OPPORTUNITY

It's waiting for you at your desk.

EXAMPLE

Here is a case that illustrates the wastebasket's symbolic importance.

J. F. Trumble has the three top titles in his company, and an office that cost $150,000 to furnish, not counting the original Calder and Kelly prints. Placed against his desk is an oversize round wastebasket which he has one of his secretaries fill with an overflow-quantity of scrap paper when he has visitors. "I want to be seen as a working executive," he says.

HOW TO USE

Effective wastebasketry requires three essentials:

1. Physical details. Size, shape, and location of your wastebasket should reflect not only functional requirements but also personal preferences. Obviously, your basket should be big enough for the daily dose you feed it. And it should be convenient to your hand rather than occupy a spot determined by where the night sweeper leaves it. For some, a small, flat-sided basket is best, particularly where it can be fastened to a wall bracket or desk panel inside the knee hole. Many shapes and sizes are available.

2. The crucial choice. Two types of material pose no problem:

■ *Natural rejects.* A mail-order ad for a product of no interest, and announcements of matters with which you are already familiar fall into this category.

■ *Obvious must-keeps.* Weekly production figures for which you maintain a file, and information needed at a later date must be retained. The chart on the next page can help you decide on the disposition of materials between the two extremes.

3. Avoiding key hazards. Three practices are inimical to effective wastebasketry:

■ *Accepting conventional wisdom.* "When in doubt, throw it out," is often poor guidance. Consider instead, "If you hesitate, procrastinate." It is better to defer judgment than to rush into an irreversible action.

■ *Making yourself vulnerable to spies.* For some it is a joke, and for others a real threat. No secret, confidential, or personal information should be deep-sixed without shredding or other obliteration process.

■ *Colleague duping.* A common malpractice is summed up in the question, "Should you use the other fellow's wastebasket?" You occasionally receive useless materials and are tempted to perform a double coup. Routing such matter to a colleague may possibly help him, but it surely helps you get rid of it. Before sending along a useless letter, brochure, catalogue, or publication to a coworker, clear it with your conscience.

For the Wastebasket	To Be Retained
1. *Use and discard.* A memo announcing a conference, for example, can be tossed out after you've noted the conference date on your desk calendar.	1. *Reports.* Key periodic reports that fit into a series you use for comparison, etc.
2. *Extra copies.* You may be sent several copies of printed material. Where you need only one for the record, the others may be discarded.	2. *Items with a future.* You'll hold correspondence that contains: a. queries that require reply b. information you need for an as yet unmade decision c. ideas on which you'll want to follow up
3. *Unnecessary bulk.* Voluminous material of which you need only a summary or portion can be abstracted.	
4. *Irrelevant material.* Circulars, form letters of no interest to you should seldom survive at desktop level.	3. *"Evidence."* Letters sent you "for the record"—terms of an agreement, for example—are file material.
5. *Recorded elsewhere.* Sales figures that are posted on a centralized permanent record may be noted and disposed of.	4. *Reference material.* Manuals, instruction booklets, etc., for equipment or procedures in your area.
6, 7, 8, etc. Add your own.	5. *Carbons of your own memos, letters, etc.* These help clarify the record in case of misunderstanding, or qualify you for "credit," if due.
	6, 7, 8, etc. Add your own.

▷ **61**
Work Simplification

CONCEPT

Work simplification is an approach by which supervisors and employees can improve their work methods. Developed by industrial engineer Allan H. Mogensen, it became popular in factories, offices, and service organizations, from hospitals to supermarkets. Work simplification (sometimes designated W/S) can produce, as a beneficial side effect, improved motivation and teamwork between employees and their supervisors.

W/S derives from early studies of work methods by Frederick Winslow Taylor, father of scientific management. His investigations were advanced by Frank and Lillian Gilbreth, and Mogensen, the next link in the chain, brought methods improvement know-how to the operating echelons.

In a typical case, industrial engineering specialists teach the simplified methods analysis and improvement technique to front-line supervisors, who then pass it along to their groups. The actual work analysis and improvement method consists of a five-step approach which focuses on specific work elements in order to pinpoint and eliminate wasted time or motion. The side benefits come from employee participation, their acceptance of work improvement goals, and their increased awareness of the need for efficiency.

Mogensen says, "Work simplification includes automatic methods for consultation with, and participation by supervisors and employees. Without this participation most methods improvement programs are only partially effective."

ACTION OPPORTUNITIES

Every job, and every operation involving a human factor is subject to improvement. Over the years thousands of companies, tens of thousands of managers, and hundreds of thousands of employees have used Mogensen's approach to:

- Help managers make supervisors and workers more aware of their work routines and their potential for improvement

- Create a common ground on which front-line managers can meet with subordinates to discuss individual and departmentaɩ procedures
- Give employees the chance to exercise their ingenuity and design their own procedures
- Boost productivity, and increase work comfort and convenience

EXAMPLES

1.   Tim Harris, a woodworking shop owner, realizes that as the operation has enlarged, work methods have gotten sloppy. Rejects and errors have increased and jobs take longer than they should, partly because of the less experienced workers he has been hiring. They don't catch on to the difference between doing a job and doing it efficiently. And telling an employee, "Do the job the way Ken does it," seldom produces results.

Harris hears about work simplification, does some reading, talks to a factory executive familiar with it, and brings in a W/S consultant to teach his four foremen the approach. They pass the technique along to employees and eventually performance improves.

2.   Margaret Ellis is handed the job of office manager when her predecessor suddenly quits. The reason for the departure is no secret. Ellis has watched her former boss try to improve work methods, but between a lack of talent for analysis, and resistance from the staff, a nervous breakdown seemed more likely than productivity improvement.

Margaret Ellis's new boss assigns her primary target: "Frances was a good worker but couldn't get cooperation. The department must become more effective." He suggests that she look into work simplification. "It can give you a fresh view of work systems and methods. And once you master the technique and teach it to your staff, you will be able to discuss work in an objective way that will pay off in better performance for the whole office."

The executive finds a W/S "graduate" in the engineering department of a neighboring plastics company, and Ellis starts the training that equips her to get the employee participation and results her boss anticipated.

HOW TO USE

An important preliminary: As in any case of change, the reason behind it should be explained, and employees given the chance to ask questions and participate in planning the program. Proper preparation emphasizes the importance of productivity, waste reduction, error elimination, and safety, not for efficiency's sake alone, but to keep the company competitive.

Here is Mogensen's five-step approach:

1. Select a job to improve. As a start, keep it simple. Have the employee pinpoint a specific part of an operation rather than a complicated procedure. Repetitive tasks are best because even a small improvement will be multiplied many times.

2. Specify the elements. Most tasks can be broken down into a sequence of movements. Here is how an assembly operation might look when analyzed:

- Arrange for delivery of parts A, B, and C to workbench.
- Transfer parts from delivery boxes to workbench containers.
- Hand assemble A and B.
- Assemble C to A and B using a power wrench.
- Inspect finished assembly.
- Put finished assembly in cartons for delivery to Shipping.

3. Challenge each detail. This is a major point in W/S. The employee tests each step by asking the key questions:

- What is its purpose?
- Why is it necessary?
- Where should it be done?
- Who should do it?
- How should it be done?

The "how" of each step can be further analyzed by these possibilities:

- ***Eliminate?*** Can a step be cut out, either wholly or in part? For example, in assembling parts A and B, the employee may have to reach too far to get to the containers. Could a gravity feed deliver the parts from the container to the point of assembly, and so minimize an arm movement?
- ***Combine?*** Can the assembler make the reach for parts A and B a two-hand operation, grasping both at the same time?
- ***Change sequence?*** One employee came up with the idea of having parts A, B, and C preinspected before assembly, to eliminate the inspection element at the time of assembly, and also, the rejection of an entire assembly because of one defective part. The supervisor agreed it was worth trying.

- *Simplify?* Particularly with complex procedures, it may be possible to replace hand operations with mechanical ones, use fixtures to hold work, chutes for moving materials, and so on.

4. Test the new method. A good idea may not hold up, a seemingly poor one may prove out. Be sure employees understand the need for the tests that do justice to the changed method.

5. Install the improvement. The payoff only comes when the improvement is incorporated into the operation. And your supervisors should monitor the new method to make sure no unanticipated complications arise.

One long-range benefit of W/S: Employees become change-oriented. They not only accept a need for improvement, but tend to look for opportunities to achieve it. Naturally, recognition for successful changes should show up in a company's reward system.

▷ 62
Zero Defects

CONCEPT

The quality-control approach called "zero defects" (ZD) caught the imagination and backing of managers on the alert for a new way to minimize quality headaches. The target of the approach was clear: complete elimination of defective operations, a reject rate of 0 percent.

Originated at the Martin Company's Orlando Division, ZD sought to improve quality performance by getting the cooperation of all employees. Director of quality James F. Halpin saw the program as one of motivation. "We superimposed it on our normal inspection process," he says. "We weren't just looking for errors but to prevent them." Martin's slogan became, "Do It Right The First Time."

As invariably happens with innovations, critics eventually raised their dissenting heads:

"ZD is mostly hoopla, an employee relations circus," they said. True, but they missed the point. It was precisely the employee angle that made ZD effective. Says production-wise Lester Bittel, instructor of management at James Madison University, "Zero Defects is a quality-control program with a new wrinkle, it motivates, instills every employee with the craftsman's pride in his work, puts quality on a personal basis. ZD techniques stimulate people to seek accuracy and completeness, to pay attention to detail and so reduce errors to zero." In few instances was that zero goal reached, but rarely was there a failure to achieve some improvement.

Another criticism states that ZD is an attempt to make up for poor engineering. Again, true. It is poor management to put the quality burden on people where improved equipment design or better procedures are possible. But this need not be either-or. Maximizing both the human and machine elements will give better results than a method that neglects either.

ACTION OPPORTUNITIES

Where quality is a major concern and there is a significant human factor involved in operations, the zero defects idea holds considerable promise. Companies both large—General Electric, Lockheed—and small, scores of companies with less than a hundred employees, benefited from ZD.

EXAMPLE

The manager of a keypunch section asked his boss if he could start a ZD program. Since the error rate definitely needed improvement, the boss agreed to go along.

The manager realized that benefits weren't likely from a band-aid approach. He worked out a program that included more careful recruiting of keypunch operators, more intensive training, and a better random sampling of the work. Then he began his program with a surprise Monday morning meeting of the entire department, a speech by his boss stressing the importance of perfect work, and a dramatization of the consequences of errors on customers and suppliers.

Over the next few weeks he met with groups—he had divided his 15 employees into five three-person teams—and got their ideas on how to reduce errors. Once a week, inspection results scored by each team were posted, with prizes for the first and second best. As a result of: (1) management's spotlighting the problem; (2) a unified goal for the entire workgroup, stimulating the sense of team play; (3) employees' increased awareness of the consequences of mistakes; and (4) the competition among the triads and chance at the status and prizes for the winners, errors started declining and eventually reached a level of less than 2 percent.

HOW TO USE

The example above illustrates the major elements of an effective zero defects approach. Here are some preliminary considerations:

1. Be aware of the limits as well as the promise of ZD. The critics were correct in pointing out that it is no miracle formula, but a way to get employees to back quality goals. All the nonhuman factors from materials to equipment and facilities also require analysis and improvement for quality goals to be met. A zero defects program should come from managers who research the subject, weigh pros and cons, then decide whether or not to go ahead.

To recap the points of an effective ZD program illustrated in the Example:

2. Start a program in an attention-getting way, such as, by a surprise meeting, a well-publicized "mystery" event that will offer challenge and the chance for prizes, or whatever means are appropriate for the level of sophistication and company spirit of the people involved.

3. See that supervisors and department heads, your front-line managers, actively aid and abet the program by keeping in close contact with their subordinates on quality matters.

4. As much as possible, have the people who perform the work participate in planning the program's implementation and operation. Assigning duties like tallying inspection results, for example, that will increase employee identification with it, is desirable.

5. Management should stand ready to help cope with problems or to add to effectiveness. Adjustments may be necessary. For example, one company that started with three-person teams eventually changed to individual scoring of inspection results because of frictions: "Nora isn't pulling her weight," "Tom wants to be our leader and we're not willing to accept that," and so on.

Many companies eventually incorporate their ZD programs wholly or in part into routine operations. Others phase out ZD, sometimes as a result of technical advances in the basic processes. Managements with major quality concerns find that remaining flexible and open to innovation is necessary to maintaining acceptable quality results.

PART THREE

LORE AND INSIGHTS

The art/science of management has a mixed history, generated by both theorists and practitioners. Some of the Ideas, like Accident Proneness and the Halo Effect are psychological. Others, like Machiavelli's Principles, offer insights that shed light on contemporary problems of corporate power. In this Part you can learn how the Hawthorne Experiment, a seminal study going back five decades, uncovered facts that completely changed our ways of thinking about people at work. At this late date the experts are still arguing about the findings, but you will be able to make your own appraisals and applications. The following Ideas appear in this Part:

*   *   *

▷ **63**
Accident Proneness

CONCEPT

Almost every analysis of workscene mishaps reveals a small number of repeaters, people who have more accidents than the average. How can we explain this fact? Investigation will rule out some obvious answers, for example, their work is more hazardous—often the reverse is true; or they suffer a physical weakness such as poor coordination, or occasional dizzy spells—this is seldom the case. Psychologists rather than medical experts seem to have the answer for this phenomenon. Dr. Gerald Gordon of the Du Pont Company reports:

> Our studies reveal a small group around whom injuries seem to cluster in disproportionate numbers. Obviously there is something more than hard luck plaguing a person whose career shows a long series of injuries. What's back of the trouble? The answer is that the accident maker is suffering from a form of mental illness . . . a victim of bottled-up emotions.

Once identified, individuals in this group can be helped to diminish the results of their self-destructiveness, with a decided improvement in your overall safety performance.

ACTION OPPORTUNITIES

Every company has a safety problem. Most departments develop safeguards specific for their operations, everything from making floors less slippery to using shatterproof goggles and automatic pressure-release valves to prevent blowouts. But after all these physical preventives are in place, the human element, especially the accident-prone fraction, can benefit from your attention.

EXAMPLE

Grace Farmer is hired to operate a decorating press in a leather products plant. She is bright and strong, and the job, although monotonous, is simple. Foreman Tim Blount gives her half a day of training and is pleased with his new employee. The second week, Farmer burns her hand on the heating element of her machine. The injury is minor and she is back on the *job next day. But three weeks later she stacks her work too high and a carton topples and strikes her shoulder. She is out two days before she can resume her duties.*

After three months Blount reviews his accident records and sees that Grace Farmer has had four lost-time injuries. He talks to her. She is distressed by the accidents and assures her boss that she really tries to be careful.

The foreman discusses the situation with a psychologist friend who agrees that Grace Farmer seems to be accident prone and asks whether she has home problems. Blount says she and her husband aren't getting along.

The friend says, "I don't want to play amateur psychologist—that's a joke—but it is possible that if you checked you might find that each accident follows an argument with her husband and the accidents reflect her emotional upset."

Blount ponders the problem and decides that since she is a good worker, he will take Grace off the press and make her an inspector. His solution makes accidents involving her less likely by cutting way down on the opportunities for self-injury.

HOW TO USE

Be sure to avoid, as Blount's friend did, playing psychologist. You can play it safe by observing these points:

1. Alternative causes. Don't be too quick to assume an individual is accident prone. People who show up on records as accident repeaters are not necessarily in the prone group. There are other reasons that can cause repeated accidents:

- Insufficient training, lack of awareness of job hazards
- Unsafe or faulty equipment
- Unsafe conditions, poor lighting, slippery floors, and so on
- Physical infirmities, including poor coordination, dizziness
- Carelessness? This is not likely for repeaters. The carelessness label can be a cover-up for a variety of sins (see "Carelessness" Diagnosis page 186), including accident proneness.

Only after these are ruled out should the accident-prone possibility be considered.

2. Work-procedure review. Monitor the work habits of repeaters, especially those relating to the accidents. Try to spot, preferably with subordinates assisting, unsafe procedures, facilities, materials.

3. Hazard elimination. You would do this for every job and area in your office or shop. But repeated accidents—tripping over exposed wires, falling down the stairway—call for inspection of obstacles, slick surfaces, blind turns, and, in machine operations, the whole range of preventives from guards to automatic controls.

4. Transfer? Can be a good corrective. For example: A manager says, "I transferred an assistant to the drafting room when it seemed to me pressure on him was precipitating errors and minor accidents. I treated it matter-of-factly, as I would any transfer. The difficulties disappeared."

But two cautions:

- If other group members see that a ticket to a more desirable job comes from a poor record, accidents will soar.
- Don't foist a problem employee on another manager. Leveling, giving a forthright explanation, shouldn't interfere with a reasonable transfer.

5. Professional help? A truly accident-prone individual has an emotional problem that might benefit from professional counseling. Dr. Harry Levinson, widely known for his work as director of the Division of Industrial Mental Health, Menninger Foundation, Topeka, Kansas, suggests that if your own managerial efforts fail to yield results, "Report the case, in confidence of course, to the plant nurse or company physician. If these aren't available, consult with the personnel manager." Most communities have sources of help, that is, psychiatrists, psychologists, and psychiatric social workers that may be recommended. The employee's own doctor is another possible recourse. Dr. Levinson advises that a referral should simply mean opening another door for help.

Safety continues to be a matter of minimizing hazards and enforcing safety rules. Your know-how can help protect repeaters from themselves, and your safety performance from their neurosis. But remember, true accident-prone, self-injuring behavior is unconscious and your actions must take this fact into account.

◊ 64
Bottom-Line Fallacies

CONCEPT

"Bottom line" is less a phrase than an invocation. The executive who says "Let's look at the bottom line" is seen as tough-minded and result-oriented, willing to face up to the acid test of performance. And this high regard is probably deserved.

The bottom line, on a profit-and-loss sheet, the volume turned out by a production group, or final totals in an election, is often the definitive indicator. But the most impressive bottom line may hide information at least as important as it reveals.

ACTION OPPORTUNITIES

Critical analysis may yield important insights on those occasions when the bottom line is misleading.

EXAMPLES

1. *"I can't figure out," says a manager examining his company's annual report, "how we've had such a poor year. Last year we had a huge profit."*

"It's the expresident," says a colleague. "Old J. P. cooked up the books so he could leave in a blaze of glory. The new man in the front office got stuck with a lot of covered-over losses, some misrepresentation of items, and exaggerated values."

2. *Jed Tarleton is a hard-driving sales manager. His region usually wins the interregional annual contest, and although other groups are coming up, he is determined to come out on top again. And he does. His sales volume beats the next closest region by 4 percent, less of a margin than that of previous years, but enough to walk off with the prize.*

One of the salesmen, who knows what has been going on, makes a list of the tactics Tarleton used to inflate the figures:

- *Made some deals with under-the-table rebates*
- *Got credit for poor-risk customers who subsequently defaulted*
- *Offered best-possible terms usually restricted to special customers — cutting deeply into profitability — to those who demanded a last extra sweetener to sign a contract*

- *Pressured salesmen to meet assigned quotas, no matter what*

Tarleton's short-range results were impressive, but his tactics were ultimately injurious.

HOW TO USE

Most bottom lines are above reproach. But it helps to know some of the ways in which a total may hide important facts:

- A major consequence may be the hidden costs to get the results.
- Individuals may have been pushed to the point of breakdown.
- Ethical principles may be sacrificed.
- Relationships may have been exploited, to their subsequent detriment.
- Future prospects may have been milked for a quick payoff, lessening ultimate benefit.
- Where ruthless competitive effort has produced winning results—as between divisions—future teamwork is likely to be impaired.

A desirable end may be achieved by means that eventually prove too costly. Philosophers have said so for years.

▷ 65
The "Carelessness" Diagnosis

CONCEPT

"The employee was careless." This is a common explanation for mishaps on the workscene. When expert professionals—psychologists and engineers—of the Scrap Iron & Steel Institute analyzed the "carelessness" diagnosis, they found it was a catchall to explain work failures used in lieu of a more precise finding. They also concluded that it was a dead end. The responses to "carelessness" are reproach and the threat of punishment, not particularly strong deterrents.

Digging deeper, the investigators learned that many specific faults that could be dealt with hide behind the "carelessness" designation. Here is a list of possible reasons for employee failure which are masked by the misuse of the catchall term. The employee:

- Didn't follow instructions
- Wasn't given proper instructions
- Didn't follow rules and regulations
- Violated safe work methods
- Failed to follow standard procedures
- Didn't pay attention to the work at hand
- Was distracted, lost concentration
- Failed to anticipate an action or movement
- Neglected to wear personal protection equipment
- Didn't think ahead and plan future actions
- Failed to foresee the consequences of his or her own acts
- Didn't take into account his or her own physical capabilities or limitations
- Lacked skills needed for the work
- Didn't know the limits of strength or other qualities of materials
- Misused tools or equipment
- Failed to look
- Didn't think
- Lacked a constructive attitude towards the work
- Wasn't properly supervised
- Repressed hostility
- Other

Unlike "carelessness," most of the items listed previously are susceptible to remedy.

ACTION OPPORTUNITIES

All work failures, mishaps, or errors diagnosed as "carelessness" should be subject to probing and clarification of cause as suggested by the Institute list.

EXAMPLES

1.   A new employee ends her first week on the job by messing up the printing of a special insert in a promotion booklet. Her supervisor tells his boss the employee is neglectful and doesn't seem to catch on to the work. The manager investigates further and learns that the supervisor failed to provide adequate instruction.

2.   Manager Paul Peele is once again upset by Henry, his star pro-grammer who, at least once a month, screws up badly. "He just doesn't seem to give a damn," he concludes, and once again tries to decide whether Henry's successes justify an occasional failure. But a colleague to whom he confides his problem suggests that Henry's lapses don't seem adequately explained by his being careless. Peele has a long talk with Henry who eventually blurts, "How come I'm senior here, I get handed the headache assignments and always lick them, and I'm treated just the same as the other programmers? And that includes my salary and bonus." Now the manager sees that Henry's resentment explains his foul-ups. His new diagnosis: Henry's failures reflect both frustration and wanting to get even. He starts developing remedies.

HOW TO USE

Don't consider "carelessness" an acceptable reason for unsatisfactory work. Any time that explanation comes to mind, use the Institute list as a basis for thinking about and rediagnosing the situation.

▷ 66
Cognitive Dissonance

CONCEPT

Behavioral psychologists, managers, and the public have been puzzled by a phenomenon that bears the label, "cognitive dissonance" (CD).

The *Dictionary of Psychology* defines the term as "an uncomfortable psychological state in which the individual experiences two incompatible beliefs or cognitions." Cognitive dissonance theory holds that individuals are made uncomfortable by the conflicting beliefs and try to reduce the discomfort.

Executives have found the concept helpful in explaining behavior, sometimes unexpected and strange, that shows up when employees are in mental conflict.

ACTION OPPORTUNITIES

The concept provides a psychological tool to help understand and deal with the complications that result when an individual suffers from dissonance.

- You yourself may suffer the effects of cognitive dissonance, and understanding the term can lessen the mental confusion.
- A colleague or subordinate may be upset by this kind of mental pressure and you may be able to assist in resolving it.

Instances of the reaction are fairly common on the workscene. Many situations in which two forces are in conflict can push a person into the CD response.

EXAMPLES

Here are three typical instances:

1. A publishing executive says: "I worked for the X Company for a number of years. Their human relations policy—some called it their inhuman relations policy—viewed employees as replaceable robots. Wages were the lowest around, and anyone who complained was invited to leave. When my boss told me to fire a subordinate who argued about a raise that I felt was justified, I got very upset."

The executive's dissonance was between his resentment of the unfair treatment of an employee and the need to be part of it. His first move to ease his dissatisfaction and tension was to complain to his wife and a few trusted colleagues about having to enforce an unfair decision. This helped to get part of the load off his chest. Next, he helped the subordinate find another job. The executive felt somewhat better, but the dissonance finally stopped only when he got himself another job and both elements of it disappeared.

2. Unlike the previous example, this one shows attempts to manipulate the factors mentally by a process called rationalization, resulting in behavior that may seem strange to others.

Manager Kevin Kidder has to fire Joe Harley, his subordinate and friend of many years. Kidder's boss has told him, "I know how you feel about Joe, but he hasn't been cutting it and it's costing too much to carry him. I'll O.K. a liberal separation arrangement. . . ."

Kevin Kidder is stuck between loyalty to a friend and the dollars-and-cents of the business world. There is a dissonance between his feelings for his friend and his company loyalty. But Kidder now goes through some mental moves to lessen the dissonance. He mitigates his sense of guilt by thinking, "Joe will be better off, the job was getting too much for him . . . he'll be able to get an easier job out west, where Madge has been wanting to move anyway." And, he concludes, Joe has exploited him, dropping in at all hours to discuss problems, and asking him to use his influence in the front office on his behalf. By tearing Joe down he makes him a less worthy friend, and so lessens the dissonance.

3. This case involves mitigation in a romantic situation. An assistant tells her boss about meeting a man she likes. "This could get serious," she says and they both smile. The couple date, and the assistant is really getting interested, when abruptly the gentleman caller fades away and the courtship is over. The assistant meets her boss in the ladies' room and the latter asks how Fred is. "I decided to ditch him," she says. "I discovered that deep down underneath he was pretty shallow," repeating the words of a famous wit, "and besides, he sure was a tightwad."

She is diminishing her disappointment by saying she didn't lose much, which is easier to bear than acknowledging the loss of an attractive hot-shot. This mitigation is the same method Kevin Kidder used to lessen his guilt at firing his friend Joe.

HOW TO USE

You have two areas of action:

1. With others, colleagues, subordinates, and possibly your boss:

■ Be aware of the cognitive dissonance possibility when you observe someone caught in a conflict of feelings. Some signs are agonizing over a decision, or exaggerated criticism against one or another party in a conflict.

■ Help them adjust the dissonance:

1. Try to spot the two "incompatible beliefs" mentioned in the definition. For instance, in the first Example they are the executive's self-respect versus being a representative of an

exploitive employer. In the second, executive Kevin Kidder is in conflict over his friendship for Joe Harley and his duty to fire him. The third Example involves the assistant's disappointment at losing a potential lover, and her self-esteem.

2. Let them sound off to you, and unload their feelings.
3. If possible, tactfully supply the mitigators that help the person to live with the situation. Your aim is to lessen the guilt or ease the upset. One executive tells a subordinate: "As J.F.K. said, it's not always a fair world, and this is your share of the unfair part. You may have to learn to live with it."

2. With yourself, follow the same course of action suggested for helping others:

- Try to pinpoint the incompatible beliefs.
- Don't bottle up the conflict. Release it, if you can, by talking to a confidante—a spouse, colleague, or boss.
- Think through the factors that can put the dissonance in acceptable balance, as mentioned above.
- Face up the the realities of the situation, distinguish between what you want to do, can do, and must do. If you are not satisfied with the results of your analysis, see whether there is some action that will get you out from under. This could include a discussion with your boss, a professional counselor or in serious situations possibly quitting at a time of your convenience.

▷ 67
Corporate Culture

CONCEPT

Why does one company do extraordinarily well, while a similar one wallows in mediocrity? Some investigators feel the answer lies in the "culture" of an organization. And culture derives from a company's values, beliefs and practices. In their book *Corporate Cultures,** Terrence Deal and Allan Kennedy list key aspects of the concept:

* Deal, Terrence & Kennedy, Allan. (1984). *Corporate Cultures.* Reading, MA: Addison-Wesley.

- **Business environment.** This covers the relation between the company and its marketplace, which in turn depends on what it sells, its competitors, technologies, and government relations.
- **Values.** These are the basic beliefs as to what rates high or low. A typical value prescribes successful conduct for employees: "If you do thus and so—make a big sale, solve a costly problem, come up with a new idea—you will be rewarded."
- **Heroes.** These are the exemplars of achievement. For example, General Electric's heroes include inventor Thomas Edison and Charles Steinmetz, its great innovative engineer. Organization heroes may be a top executive, an outstanding can-do performer, or an extremely popular individual at any level.
- **Rites and rituals.** Anthropologists speak of "reinforcing rituals," which strengthen the bonds between the individual and the group. For example, singing the national anthem is a rite observed in countries throughout the world. Deal and Kennedy mention corporate practices such as anniversary celebrations, picnics, parties, retirement dinners, and so on.
- **"Secret" network.** This is the subsurface communication by storytellers, spies, cliques, rumor mongers, and whisperers who form a "hidden hierarchy of power."

Edwin L. Baker, of McKinsey & Company, in the *Management Review,* describes how an organization may flourish, and then fade as its cultural vitality changes. Based on observations of over a dozen cases, Baker says that initially each company grew and flourished under the direction of its founder. Domination by one person gave employees an on-the-spot hero, and his or her values dominated. When the founder retired, informality gave way to formal rules and procedures, and the culture tended toward rigidity and less group identification by employees. Subsequently effectiveness, market share, and profitability shrank.

ACTION OPPORTUNITIES

The culture concept is one of the more imaginative views of business organization. It encourages analysis of the inner core, the hidden corners of company policy and beliefs. This process alone can stimulate review and raise the possibility of beneficial restructuring and new directions. Reappraisal that balances objective analysis and realistic conclusions could benefit and refurbish the organization.

EXAMPLE

In establishing their criteria for the successful company, Thomas J. Peters and Robert H. Waterman Jr., in In Search of Excellence,* *made observations that in their minds indicate vital cultures:*

- **Customer relations.** *The authors report a comment by a hospital executive regarding the quality of IBM's customer contacts: "IBM took the trouble to get to know us. They interviewed extensively up and down the line. They talked our language, no mumbo jumbo on computer innards. Their price was fully twenty-five percent higher, but they guaranteed reliability and service. Our decision, even with severe budget pressure, was really easy."*

- **Spirit-rousing.** *Japanese corporate culture exhibits a proclivity for meetings, singing of company songs, and chanting the corporate litany. American companies such as Tupperware, Mary Kay Cosmetics, and many others do likewise.*

- **Pride in company and product.** *A Procter & Gamble executive asserted to a class in a Stanford summer executive program, "My company does too make the best toilet paper, and just because the product is toilet paper or soap, for that matter, doesn't mean that we don't make it a damn sight better than anyone else."*

HOW TO USE

While the culturists succeed in conveying a fresh and provocative way of looking at a business organization, they are not convincing on a key point: While analysis may show that an effective organization has qualities X, Y, and Z, is it possible to duplicate the company's success by copying these qualities? Or are these qualities a byproduct of that thing called culture, which, like a tree, can only be made by divine forces?

Nevertheless, the field work by the investigators is impressive and two sets of findings may provide specific directions for your thought and action regarding corporate excellence.

Peters' and Waterman's research yielded eight attributes of successful companies:

1. A bias for action. Analysis and decision making aren't neglected but standard operating procedure is "do it, fix it, try it." Tough problems

---

* Peters, Thomas J. & Waterman, Robert H. (1982). *In Search of Excellence.* New York: Harper & Row.

call for massive action by task forces that hole up in a room for a week, develop an answer, and implement it.

2. Good customer contact. Successful companies learn from those they serve. They listen to needs and often translate them into new products or services. And good service is not an exception.

3. Autonomy and entrepreneurship. Good-culture companies foster many leaders and innovators throughout the organization. They give people a loose rein, freedom to be creative, and encourage practical risk taking.

4. Productivity through people. Rank and file are regarded as the root source of quality and productivity gains.

5. Hands on, value driven. Company people are encouraged to get the feel of things, visit the plant floor, customer stores, observe what is done and not done.

6. Know your business. Excellent performance strongly favors organizations that stick to the business they understand. The better the understanding, the better the business can become.

7. Streamline. Structures and systems tend toward the simple, and staffs are lean.

8. Balance between centralization and decentralization. Autonomy at lower levels and tight control in functions that benefit from system and precision, provide advantages and avoid disadvantages.

Edwin L. Baker, in his previously mentioned *Management Review* article, offers a set of qualities found in good cultures. They are: teamwork; honesty; innovation in customer service; pride in work; belief in high standards; and commitment to the company.

Baker also suggests that the good-culture organizations strive to adapt and push for growth despite new competition, regulations, and changing technologies. During growth, the strains of expansion are anticipated and dealt with.

The authors of *In Search of Excellence* add a new insight into what makes the strong-culture company effective: "Above all, the intensity itself, stemming from strongly held beliefs, marks these companies."

This is a key observation. If you take the factor of commitment to the organization, for example, you will find a major difference between the zeal of a person who is fully dedicated to his or her company and one who merely identifies with it. The difference in degree creates a difference in kind.

▷ 68
Fallacy of "If It Ain't Broke Don't Fix It"

CONCEPT

Washington, not unfamiliar with the boondoggle and make-work programs, is the surprising place of origin of the phrase "If it ain't broke, don't fix it." Meant to warn against unnecessary action, the advice may be the height of wisdom. It also may represent poor judgment and lack of foresight.

ACTION OPPORTUNITIES

This saying applies to situations where remedy, repair, or other constructive action is contemplated.

EXAMPLE

Head Librarian Tess Thomas tells her boss that half the bookshelves need repair or replacement. "The budget's tight," he responds. "Do you want new books, or to have some lazy guy with a hammer and saw take a week to do a day's work? Besides I was in the library yesterday and the shelves look fine to me. Why waste time and money?"

A second request is turned down and a day later, one of the librarians is knocked off a ladder by a shelf that topples over on him. "We were lucky," Tess Thomas tells her boss. "Jimmy got off with only a broken leg and bruises."

HOW TO USE

To distinguish between a proper application of "If it ain't broke," get answers to the following questions, which may refer to people as well as machines or equipment:

1. Does careful consideration suggest that there is nothing to gain by fixing? If so, accept the "If it ain't broke" dictum but schedule another check at a future date.

2. Do the warning symptoms suggest a need for action? If Yes, proceed with a repair or remedy, if No, proceed to the next question.

3. Has examination been made carefully enough to detect minor but significant problems? If No, reinspect, or call in a more expert expert. If Yes, ask question 4.

4. Is the diagnosis clear? If so, does it involve: (1) a physical malfunction; (2) timing that is off, out of phase, and so on; (3) elements that are worn down; or (4) other problems?

The fixing operation should suit the need, in terms of the people doing the repair and the repair they'll be doing.

5. Something may not be broken, but may still need cleaning, refurbishing, or maintenance procedures such as greasing, oiling, or replacement of work parts (e.g., a typewriter ribbon).

Preventive maintenance—in this you can include exercise and controlled diet for humans—is the single strongest contradiction to "ain't broke" thinking. And don't let the apparently unassailable logic of "If it ain't broke don't fix it" intimidate you. Both the tense of the verb and the meaning of "broke" are ambiguous. A thing need not be broken to warrant attention. Today's perfection may herald tomorrow's breakdown.

⟂ 69
Grapevine

CONCEPT

The grapevine is the name given to an informal, spontaneous, somewhat erratic but also revealing system of communication that flourishes in organizations. Along with gossip and rumor, it is also the medium for information clandestinely gathered, or spread in advance of management's own timetable. (See Rumor Handling, page 80.)

ACTION OPPORTUNITIES

It is advisable to be up on this network as an adjunct to the regular communications systems in your company. The grapevine may report occasional nonsense, but in some cases, not to know the grapevine headlines may hurt.

EXAMPLE

Elsie, who delivers the mail on your floor, plops a handful of envelopes on your desk and says, "I wonder who's going to get J. T.'s job." Since J. T. is your boss's boss you're startled and say, "I didn't know J. T. was leaving." Elsie says, "Oh, sure. He's been offered a big job at IBM." Later you corner your boss: "I hear that J. T. is leaving. Any truth to it?" Your boss closes his door and says, "Yes, but it won't be announced until after the annual meeting. I can't imagine how those rumors get around."

HOW TO USE

There are as many kinds of grapevines as there are varieties of grapes. Some churn out news as rapidly as a daily newspaper, others produce occasional scraps. Some are wild and undependable, others are usually factual and scoop the formal system. To benefit from this informal network:

1. Be aware of the grapevine in your organization. Develop some sense of its dimension, accuracy, and why it exists. The common answer to the last is that organization channels may be slow and incomplete because too many developments are considered "confidential" and "secret." Often they aren't, and simply reflect management's belief in the axiom, "knowledge is power," which it doesn't want to share.

2. Don't assume the grapevine is accurate and dependable. Even if its last three rumors proved out, the next three may be total distortions. Consider every item you are interested in as subject to verification.

3. Try to identify the grapeviners. They won't wear identification and there is no explaining why some people are purveyors and others aren't, but by their works you will know them. There are three types: "Originators," those who feed the news into the system; "Carriers," those who pass the word; and the "Distorters," who exaggerate and embellish.

4. Tap in. If a member of the system is known to you—the mail deliverer in the Example, for instance—he or she will probably continue to be an information source. Just show occasional interest to keep the flow coming. Remember, they enjoy their role. It gives them recognition, superiority—they know something others don't—and an offbeat activity to enrich their regular job.

5. Protect your sources. Using the system makes you a part of it but grapevines are only occasionally out of line, and you can censor your own contribution. However, on the occasion that a damaging item is circulating, as an ethical matter you should try to kill it. For example, information that is essentially character assassination, like a story of somebody's dishonesty or immoral behavior, requires your intervention. Your statement. "Even if that's true, you shouldn't be spreading it around," is a good beginning. Then, if you check and find that the story is untrue, the victim or the victim's boss should be told, and some effort made to refute the tale.

6. Should you ever be an originator? Some authorities state categorically that managers should never use the grapevine to disseminate information. But there may be circumstances when the simplest and quickest way to get word around—it should be something positive, of course—is to drop a word or two into the ear of a "carrier." For instance, you might tell an identified grapeviner, "I understand that Helen G. is leaving to join her husband overseas. Wouldn't it be nice to give her a big surprise send-off?" Then, if Helen's boss or associates are dragging their feet, your move has a good chance of sparking action.

▷ 70
The Halo Effect

CONCEPT

Industrial psychologists working in the field of testing developed an idea that has been a revelation to managers. The scientists discovered that strong positive or negative traits may cause a manager to become blind to other traits in a person's makeup. The consequence: a single trait influences judgment of the whole person. In effect, these individuals acquire a "halo" and are not seen as they truly are.

ACTION OPPORTUNITIES

You can use your knowledge of the halo effect when—

1. Interviewing prospective employees. In this key hiring step it is essential that judgments be acute and objective, not distorted by an unconscious bias.

2. Making assignments. An employee may handle a particular task well, such as one requiring considerable repetitive work. When given an assignment requiring independent thinking, however, the person may have difficulty.

3. Judging job performance. It's easy to be blinded by showy results. In terms of total volume, a salesman may be among the top three in his group. But how about his cancellation rate, or instances of customers complaining of misrepresentations of quality, early delivery, and so on?

EXAMPLES

1. *Paula Baylin, an account executive in a PR firm, is being bawled out by her boss: "Paula, your department's performance depends on your employee group. Yet you have hired individuals who don't have the ability to work on their own . . ."*

Paula's poor hiring judgments result from the halo effect. One interviewee, Ben Bradley, wore a three-piece Pierre Cardin suit and expressed himself in a highly articulate manner. He glossed over his work history, which involved several past job changes. Ben's glibness hid the fact that he was irresponsible and goofed off as much as possible.

2. *Ken Ryan has been transferred from another department. His new boss decides to test his competence and asks him to investigate and report on ways to accommodate more supplies in the storage area. Ken returns with an innovative idea to maximize use of the space.*

His boss then gives him another task: Find out why the staff hasn't responded to a request for ideas on productivity improvement. Ken is lost. His query memos are buried on employees' desks, when he talks to people directly he can't get straight answers. A week later he reports back, empty-handed and discouraged. The boss realizes that Ken is fine when dealing with tangibles, but working with people is not one of his strong points.

HOW TO USE

To avoid being blinded:

1. Keep the halo effect in mind when rating or evaluating people. Remember that an industrious person may not be cooperative, that someone who knows the job thoroughly may not be a hard worker, the eager-to-please individual may not be able to work independently on a tough assignment.

2. Judge employees one trait at a time. If you're rating cooperation and initiative, be careful not to let John's high rating on the former influence his score on the latter. Don't rate Jane as creative because she is glib.

3. Avoid putting similar traits close together. Follow a work performance trait like job skill with a personality trait like initiative. This way there will be less chance of one tainting the others.

The halo effect distorts perception, inflating a single trait out of proportion. Being aware of this can help in arriving at balanced judgments.

◊ 71
Hawthorne Experiments

CONCEPT

Any survey of management ideas must include the studies called the Hawthorne Experiments, an investigation started in the late 1920s and continuing for almost two decades. It proved to be a seminal effort that fundamentally transformed our thinking about productivity and the worker's role in it. Discussion as to findings and conclusions persists to this day and will doubtless continue into the future.

An appreciation of the impact of Hawthorne is best begun with an understanding of previous attitudes toward the worker. Typically, factory employees were called "hands." Some men were huskier and could undertake heavier work, and some were hungrier or more ambitious and might work harder. Mental capacity and individuality didn't count. Tom, Dick, and Harry, Tess, Dinah, and Harriet were just different names for the same thing. Hawthorne changed all that.

The Western Electric Company plant in Hawthorne, Illinois was known for its enlightened management. Employees had the latest pension plans, sickness and accident benefits, and recreation programs, but production wasn't up to expectations. Somebody thought lighting might have something to do with it.

Eventually Western Electric executives and management experts from Harvard University joined forces. They decided to study the effects of lighting on performance.

Two groups of operators were selected, Group One using the "normal" amount of light, and Group Two getting more light. Output from Group Two increased, which was expected. Unexpectedly, so did the production from Group One.

Then Group Two was given less light. Their output went up, and so did that of Group One. Two workers were put in a dark room, working by sense of touch, completely in the dark. Despite the handicap, increased output was maintained.

Next the researchers studied a group of six female assembly workers, checking their production under the following different conditions:

- An hourly wage rate was changed to piece work. Output rose.
- The women were given two five-minute rest periods. Output increased.
- Two ten-minute rest periods were given. Output continued to go up.
- The morning rest period was lengthened to fifteen minutes and the workers were served hot snacks. Production continued upward.
- The women were let off half an hour early. Output soared. They were let off a full hour earlier, and output stayed at the same high level.
- The women were put back to working that extra hour. Output shot up again, and remained at that high level even when weekly hours were cut from forty-eight to forty.

As a last test the original conditions were restored: The women went back to time work with no rest periods, no hot snacks, and a forty-eight hour week. Output hit an all-time high.

The scientists thought they had gone back to the original working conditions but apparently they were mistaken. Something was now present that hadn't been there before. There was a change in the people themselves.

The researchers concluded that they had uncovered a psychological factor that influenced productivity. Exactly what that factor was and how it operated wasn't clear, and to this day there is disagreement. Some speculations follow:

- The women felt differently about themselves and about their work. Just separating them and using them in an experiment had made them feel important. They were more than small cogs in a large machine.

- Their work had taken on meaning, more than just turning out units. They had become a team whose help the company needed.
- As a result of recognition and special feelings about their roles and the purpose of their work, they had become motivated to exert effort toward producing more and better.

Awareness of the psychological factor and its effect on job performance suggested another experiment to the researchers. Twenty-one thousand Western Electric workers were interviewed and asked how they felt about their jobs and the company, what complaints they had, if any, and so on.

But the interviewing process itself turned up unexpected findings. Interviewers found the workers tended to stray from the questions asked and talked about other things, such as their feelings, aspirations, and personal problems. After a while the interviewees were permitted to discuss whatever they wanted to.

Eventually the researchers concluded that there was a therapeutic benefit from the conversations. Mental stress seemed to ease after people expressed their feelings about their bosses, working conditions, and company management. And minimizing the distraction caused by upset made possible a return to normal performance. This finding opened up a new prospect: having managers or in some cases company-sponsored professionals talk with employees about problems that undercut their mental well-being and ability to perform. (See Counseling, page 4.)

Challenging insights emerged from the studies of the Western Electric-Harvard investigators. Perhaps the most important result was the awareness of the worker's individuality, and the potential for improved performance by policies and practices that would effect employee motivation.

ACTION OPPORTUNITIES

Insights gained from Hawthorne can help you maximize workgroup performance. The studies suggest that employee performance is influenced by attitudes, which managers can change for the better by proper motivational practices.

EXAMPLE

Think of instances when your subordinates performed well or poorly, not as a result of objective factors, but because of factors relating to their individual personality and feelings of the moment. Think about your own idiosyncratic reactions to things at the workplace. Recall your efforts to improve subordinates' performance, and the results you got. Interest, concentration, and effort influence individual performance, and a perceptive manager may be able to add the trigger ingredients.

HOW TO USE

The Hawthorne findings relate to a number of key management areas:

- **Personnel policy.** Reexamination of personnel policies may be in order to see whether restrictive rules or overcontrol has held people back as well as kept them in line.
- **Manager training and indoctrination.** Could your managers be made more aware of the potential gains that can come from encouraging participation in problem solving and idea production? The question is simplistic as asked, but is intended to raise possibilities that, when followed up, can reap substantial improvements in relationships between employee and employer, to their mutual benefit.
- **Departmental performance.** Companies may benefit by starting their managers on a study of the degree to which the positive and creative abilities of their employees are being used. This is a big job, but the efforts and hazards can be minor compared to benefits gained. If appropriate, the project might be kicked off with a review of the Hawthorne studies and their results.

The human relations school of management, created by Hawthorne, focuses on employee motivation and performance. If, in your case, present results are satisfactory, you are probably on the right track. If you are less than satisfied, you may be interested in studying the Hawthorne Experiments further. Descriptions of the program, along with a large body of commentary, follow it. Here is a helpful bibliography:

Management and the Worker, and *Counseling in an Organization,* by F. J. Roethliserger and W. J. Dickson, Harvard University Press; *Human Problems of an Industrial Civilization,* and *Social Problems of an Industrial Civilization,* by Elton Mayo, Harvard Business School; *Hawthorne Revisited,* by Henry Landsberger, Cornell University Press.

▷ **72**
Hidden Agenda

CONCEPT

The "hidden agenda" is a phenomenon observed in conversations and meetings: A subject is being discussed when suddenly the talk switches to an unrelated topic. This topic often represents a hidden agenda, usually self-serving for the person who broaches it, and may concern matters not welcome to the other person or the group. It may be preplanned or spontaneous, but either way it represents a digression.

By its nature, the hidden agenda is a two-edged sword. If the interruption is benign, even desirable, it becomes a useful communications technique. If it is undesirable, negative, or destructive, however, the form in which it is most notable, it then becomes a problem that requires remedial action.

ACTION OPPORTUNITIES

Your awareness of the hidden agenda practice may come into play when:

- You are a conference leader and find the discussion on a course neither expected nor desirable.
- You are conversing with a subordinate and are confronted by the injection of a subject that is premature, improper, or otherwise out of order.

EXAMPLES

1. The X Department is holding its regular management meeting to discuss the previous month's performance. Sally Riffler asks for the floor and unexpectedly says, "I recently got bawled out for not turning in an analysis of accidents in my area on time. I think you people should know that the reason for my delinquency was the slow service from our library. That outfit is poorly run and badly organized, and needs a complete overhaul . . ."

The chairperson interrupts. "Sally, you're out of order. The library situation may demand a review, but this isn't the place or the time. Please see me later . . ."

2. *Executive Dave Smith is discussing a ticklish situation with a subordinate whose feud with a colleague has resulted in serious delays in order processing. There is a pause in the conversation and the subordinate says, "I've been wanting to talk to you about something that has been bothering me. It's over a year since my last raise and as you know, the cost of living has been going up . . ." Smith says, "Let's set a date to go into that some time next week," and resumes the previous discussion. He doesn't show the annoyance he feels, and wonders at the other's poor judgment in introducing the salary increase matter so inappropriately.*

HOW TO USE

Familiarity with the hidden agenda phenomenon can add another facet to your sophistication in the communications area. Here are some pointers towards the benefits:

1. Recognize it when it happens. Don't assume that every digression is a case of a hidden agenda. Another possible explanation is a poor sense of logic or what is expected from the speaker, or that he or she has lost the point of the ongoing discussion. But don't confuse a hidden-agenda digression with a new line of thought that has suddenly come to the speaker, and is worth discussion.

2. Ask why. The reason behind the introduction of a hidden agenda subject may be important for you to know. For instance, as untimely as the subject of a salary increase may have been in the talk between Dave Smith and subordinate, it may reveal some interesting possibilities:

- The subordinate has been stewing because he has heard, correctly, that the supervisor with whom he has been feuding has recently gotten a salary increase. Even though Smith feels that the raise was deserved in one case and not in the other, he knows he will have to discuss the matter with the complaining subordinate.
- Is poor communications the reason? Hidden agendas flourish when contacts between the parties are unsatisfactory. Then individuals may feel forced to bring up a subject that otherwise isn't likely to arise. Dave Smith's contact with his subordinate may have other serious gaps which the latter is trying to fill.

3. Should you go along? Hidden agenda items are not necessarily unacceptable or a waste of time. Make a quick decision as to whether the subject deserves first priority or second. If it is the latter, you may want to say, "Let's talk about that just as soon as we complete the business at hand."

4. How about your own hidden agenda? One executive says, "I have two or three subjects on tap to inject into conversations. I find that the fact that they are unexpected gets them special attention." In considering the usefulness of this approach:

- First, ask yourself why it should be a hidden topic? Is it because it is unpopular or touchy? Then you may want to rethink the advisability of broaching it at all.
- Next, ask yourself, "Why not add it in advance to a prepared agenda?" One reason for not doing so is that the subject may not be welcome to the chairperson. In this case you must make the judgment as to whether you want to force the issue in this manner.
- Is there a bridge? A subject you might think of as a hidden item may become suitable to an ongoing conversation or discussion if you can relate it. For example, "While we're talking about deadlines, I think it's relevant to talk about an information bottleneck that has slowed me up, and perhaps troubled others, and that is the service from our library. Can we take some action that will accelerate our requests for information?"

As has been made clear, hidden agendas are not necessarily bad. Where they flourish, however, the implication is that ordinary communications channels may be clogged or not open to needs, particularly concerning subjects that have an emotional component. Occurrence of hidden agendas in the area of your responsibility may deserve some analysis. Beyond that, you may care to pass along your observations to others in the organization when they occur.

◊ 73
The Intuitive Manager

CONCEPT

"The phrase 'intuitive manager,'" asserts an executive, "is a contradiction in terms." He is suggesting that management demands rational thought, order, and decisions that can be explained logically.

There is a bias against intuition in business because it doesn't seem "businesslike." Nevertheless, it is often used, although artfully disguised.

It's allright for an executive to "have a hunch." Also, when one acts on a "gut feeling," the tough-sounding words usually sell whatever the feeling happens to be.

Our two kinds of thinking, intuitive and cognitive (meaning conscious rationality), both assume an objective reality. Intuition doesn't mean flouting the real and the practical. The dictionary definition makes that point clear. Intuition is defined as "the immediate knowing of something without the conscious use of reasoning." "Knowing" is the key word.

Whether intuition can be of professional value to you depends on the answers to three questions:

- Could intuition broaden and increase your total brainpower?
- Are your intuitive powers sufficiently developed to serve you dependably?
- How can intuition be used in your job, in decision-making for example?

ACTION OPPORTUNITIES

Better use of your intuition may open up new paths in creativity, problem solving and people contacts.

EXAMPLE
Despite the dictionary definition, many professionals aren't clear on what intuition is. There is a touchstone, however, that demonstrates what it is and how it works. Humor is the key.

An anecdote is told about Vince Lombardi, the tough, assertive coach of Notre Dame in its football heyday. After a long overtime session on the gridiron, he returned home late and very tired. He got into bed, waking his wife in the process. "God, your feet are cold," she said. "In bed," he responded, "you can call me Vince."

Even if you have heard the joke before, you probably laughed, and that reaction is intuitive. You know it's funny, and your response is immediate. But *why* is it funny? Your intuition doesn't know why, it only knows it is. It's your cognitive mind that must analyze why. And so after a while—a minute, perhaps ten—you figure out that the humor lies in the incongruity of the coach accepting his godhood as a matter of course.

Your intuition recognizes the joke at once, but your rational mind takes longer. Imagine a stand-up comic who had to depend on reactions from an audience who only thought cognitively. The laughter would pop off like a chain of damp firecrackers, one at a time, slowly and intermittently. Only intuition saves him from the hook.

Can the instant perceptions of intuition be used in business? How?

HOW TO USE

The following points can help you determine the value intuition might have for you:

1. Psychologists believe everyone is intuitive to some degree, but some people are more aware of their intuitive responses than others. You can verify your own capability in three ways:

■ *Check your experience.* Do you fairly often register intuitive perceptions about people or events? For instance, when interviewing a job applicant, do you get a feeling about his or her rightness for the job apart from consideration of credentials, qualifications, and so on?

■ *Check your problem solving.* Do solutions tend to pop into your head? (Sometimes described as "inspiration.")

■ *Check your creativity.* Do ideas come quickly and often?

2. Distinguish between clear intuitive thinking and that which is distorted by bias or other emotional factors. For example, Judith Farina, lecturer in psychology at the University of Connecticut at Stamford, says that excessive hopes or fears can influence intuition: "Once you start to manipulate your thoughts rather than allow them to come to you spontaneously, it's probably wishful thinking, not intuition."

3. How do you deal with the intuitions you get: ( ) Mistrust them? ( ) Set them aside? ( ) Act on them?

4. If you tend to accept and apply them, how successful are the outcomes? ( ) Poor; ( ) Not too bad; ( ) Good; ( ) Excellent.

5. If you hesitate to act on hunches and gut feelings, consider the findings of Dr. Weston H. Agor, author of *Intuitive Management.** He analyzed the experience of 2000 managers and found that those who trusted their intuitions tended to be among the most successful.

Many management authorities advocate the use of intuition, even if it doesn't always prove out. One executive says, "Managers worth their salt play hunches and their mistakes are minor compared to their successes."

* Agor, Weston H. (1984). *Intuitive Management.* Englewood Cliffs, NJ: Prentice Hall.

6. Put your intuition to the test. Keep a record of decisions and judgments you make on intuitive impulses. Write them down, along with their outcomes. If the overall result is favorable, you're on the right track, and perhaps should broaden your use of spontaneous thinking.

7. Strengthen your mind's intuitive activity. If impulses don't appear readily for you, seek them out. Try to get in touch with your mind at the level that produces hunches. Ask yourself, at appropriate times, for example, when facing decisions, "What is my gut feeling about the question?"

Remember that your cognitions and intuitions come out of the same brain. To some extent you can cross check one with the other. There is no reason not to weigh an intuitive solution to a problem by cognitive probing. For example, your hunch is to buy the building next to your plant that's come up for sale. The cognitive mind is great for anticipating investment consequences. Put it to work on the buy impulse.

▷ 74
Lifecycle of an Idea

CONCEPT

Like old soldiers, ideas never die, and although they may fade away, they seldom vanish completely. In this author's book *Mastery of Management,** I charted the latency, growth, and downturn of interest in ideas that grasp management's imagination, flourish in management seminars and practices, and then retire to a resting place as mysterious as the legendary graveyard of the elephants.

On the next page is a version of a chart developed to represent the fate of that long-lived darling of management favor, brainstorming.

ACTION OPPORTUNITIES

Understanding the phases of interest can keep managers *au courant* on the changing array of subjects that claim the professional practitioner's

* Uris, Auren (1968). *Mastery of Management.* New York: Dow Jones-Irwin.

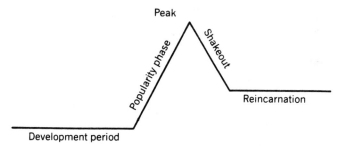

Figure 8. Lifecycle of an idea

attention. This knowledge can also help the manager probe for the practical value of an idea, and divorce it from its popular appeal. The two don't always go hand in hand.

EXAMPLES

1. *Brainstorming (see page 111) is a good example of a concept that won great favor, was practiced widely—in some organizations you couldn't open a meeting-room door without catching brainstormers in flagrante delicto—and then virtually disappeared from the management scene. And yet, the technique is still in use in companies where managers are aware of its unique benefits.*

2. *Zero defects is another idea that dominated seminar agendas for about five years, only to experience an apparent demise. Here too, astute managers who understand what it offers and why it works (see page 177 for coverage of this subject), continue to apply their version of the idea and report its advantages.*

HOW TO USE

You can put the lifecycle concept to work in two ways; first, for your own use. For example, one executive gets considerable professional pleasure, and, he maintains, profit, by digging into a repositories of management wisdom, such as texts, magazines, and old training programs. He disinters some vein of thought or practice and develops updated applications. "I find perfectly good ideas neglected, usually because they lack widespread acceptance. It is no secret that management is taken up with fads just as is the general public, and every other profession."

Second, lower-echelon managers and managers in training can be made more hardheaded in their thinking. Their responsiveness to fads can be put into perspective, while stimulating them to search for new ideas by analyzing and evaluating old, neglected ones.

◊ 75
Machiavelli's Power Principles

CONCEPT

Niccolo Machiavelli, the sixteenth century political theorist and adviser to kings and emperors, set forth principles aimed to help those in power to maintain and strengthen their leadership and control, an objective of today's executive. Machiavelli's rules for the nobles of Renaissance Italy are still relevant to the twentieth century managers, just as Newton's laws of gravity will always retain their validity. The basics of human nature are as timeless as physical laws, and the wider distribution of power and the intensity of competition makes the principles of even greater interest.

Niccolo Machiavelli's name is associated with cunning, duplicity, and distrust. This is unfortunate, because his thinking was not underhanded but forthright, not nihilistic but intended to reinforce the authority of accepted rulers. His concepts of power in *The Prince*, and *The Discourses*, intended for princes, are essential reading for today's top managers and their corporate domains. Commentators now see the Italian philosopher's ideas as a breakthrough from medievalism into a modern world of complexity and conflict. The realistic manager will respond to the power precepts of a man who would be one of the outstanding executive career consultants of our day. The rules selected are those that travel best from sixteenth century to the twentieth and beyond.

ACTION OPPORTUNITIES

Richard H. Buskirk, professor of business management at Southern Methodist University, in *Modern Management & Machiavelli,* * offers a neat

* Buskird, Richard H. (1974). *Modern Management & Machiavelli*. Paris: Cahners.

answer to the question, "What do a renaissance prince and a modern corporate president have in common?" He writes, "The ways of the modern corporation, with its rivalries in the marketplace and its internal power struggles, would have been instantly familiar to Niccolo Machiavelli—the man who saw through all sanctimonious rhetoric and pretense to the basic struggle of life and the underlying motivations of men.

"In the same way, the modern manager, whether he is on the way up or has reached the top, will recognize himself in Machiavelli's descriptions of men of authority and their methods of power."

EXAMPLE

Ben Boyle was caught between despair and rage. A promotion that he felt belonged to him had gone to a rival, and he knows why. It was a simple case of favoritism. The job went to Lester because he was a good friend of the CEO's. They played tennis together and went out with their wives as a foursome. Ben's colleague and well-wisher, Helen Flint, suggested that he quit. "That's what I would do. Seems to me your future here is shot." But Boyle, hardheaded realist that he was, understood the power system underlying his situation. "Colter got it because of H. R.. But H. R., as you've probably heard, is not long for his job. Give him a year, and when he's gone, my prospects will be darn good. I'm perfectly willing to play the game, be a good soldier and do my job, and get the call when Roy takes over the top spot. Roy and I have a kind of agreement. . . ."

Machiavelli would have approved of Boyle's understanding of the psychology and the realities of the situation.

HOW TO USE

Machiavelli's *The Prince,** in paperback with an introduction by editor Lester G. Crocker, in a translation he describes as "pure and vigorous prose," will prove worthwhile reading for many. Here are some excerpts of the principles selected for their relevance for today's wielders of power:

1. Whether to Be Liberal or Parsimonious. Although it is well to be considered liberal, it is impractical to be so. Liberality consumes endless resources and eats into the stability of the prince's rule. Taxes and other burdens must be levied upon citizens, making the prince odious to the

---

* Machiavelli, Niccolo (1972). *The Prince.* New York: Pocket Books.

people. Once resources are exhausted, he is scorned by all, including those he has benefited.

A wise prince will accept a reputation for parsimoniousness. By spending carefully, he can conduct his wars and other enterprises without burdening the people. He will be considered liberal by the many from whom he takes nothing and parsimonious only by the few to whom he gives nothing.

When spending the resources of others, it is good to be generous. When you dispense your own substance, be parsimonious. Spending other people's money enhances your reputation while spending one's own diminishes it.

2. Is It Better to Be Feared or Loved? A reputation for cruelty may arise from taking decisive action against individuals whose behavior may undermine the community. But a clear display of severity can be the truest clemency, for the execution of a limited number is preferable to damage to the many.

In a new situation, a prince may need to be merciless because a new organization is unstable and beset with many dangers. However, a leader should strive for humanity. He should not, out of his own fears, strike out in cruelty. Nor should be he unduly suspicious. However, over-confidence should not blind him to dangers. When it is necessary to choose between being loved or feared, choose the latter. It is much safer. One can be feared without being hated.

A knowledgeable prince will rely upon his own will and not upon the will of others, realizing that love comes from the free will of the citizen and that fear comes from the threat of punishment by the prince.

3. Should Princes Practice Integrity? Although integrity and good faith win praise, a sagacious prince understands that cunning is often preferable. Men carry on contests by law and animals by force; but law is often insufficient and force becomes necessary. Lasting results can be achieved only by a combination of animal and human natures. And animal natures differ. A fox can craftily avoid traps but it takes a lion to frighten away wolves.

Since men are by nature bad and untrustworthy, assuming they are good puts the prince at a disadvantage. . . . No one is perfect. While assuming a posture of humanity, charity and religion, a prince needs a versatile mind and readiness to move when the "winds of change and fortune" bid him . . . The end justifies the means.

4. Acquiring a Desirable Reputation. Grandeur and magnificence enhance the prince's stature in his subjects' eyes. Bold enterprises capture the imagination of the people and keep them busy and distracted from activities that might undermine the prince. It is also important to capitalize on opportunities to give dramatic reward or punishment in order that they may be talked about.

When contending parties are not so great that you need fear the victor, you should help him. Then he is obligated to you. However, one should never make common cause with a party more powerful than one's self, for then you are at his mercy. However, a prince must realize the necessity of taking risks, and accepting the least evil.

5. Avoiding Flatterers. Men will always be bad unless some necessity constrains them to be good. Therefore, no prince who is not himself wise can ever secure wise counsel, for his counselors will always seek their own interest, and not his.

A dilemma is found in seeking counsel. One needs to hear the truth and not adulation, but the act of seeking the truth tends to cause advisors to lose respect. The proper middle course is to use counselors who speak full truth, but only in areas where advice is needed. Then the prince should question them in a wide variety of subjects and finally, come to his own conclusions.

6. The Vagaries of Fortune. Life is like a great river, sometimes predictable, sometimes raging far beyond man's influence. However in still times man may build dams and dikes. About half of fortune and nature can be under man's control, but the rest is beyond any prince's influence.

It is not possible always to know what to do, and two princes following the same path will not necessarily end up with the same success or failure. There is no one way, then, to deal with nature. But on balance, impetuosity is preferable to caution and fortune should be commanded with audacity.

7. Seven Rules to Avoid Being Hated

- Do not deprive men of their property or women. Most people will stay content if you leave their families and property alone. It will then be necessary to deal only with the ambitious few.
- Seek a reputation of gravity and severity rather than softness. This will discourage conspiracies.
- Conspiracies against the prince are extremely difficult to coordinate and bring to success. Most fail. This is especially so if the prince has the good will of the people.
- Princes should seek to be identified with matters of grace and avoid those that involve blame.
- One must especially avoid the hatred of the powerful.
- One should equally take care not to offend one's servants.
- Shifting circumstances may dictate that at some time one should

develop favor with the military and at other times with the civilian population.

One executive said after reading *The Prince,* "I can't accept some of the ideas, but it helps to understand what the competition may be thinking and doing."

◊ 76
Organization Chart

CONCEPT

"The organization chart is the greatest tool for organization planning and development ever devised," says one expert. He's right.

Another says, "The organization chart is a fake, a deception, and can raise more questions than it answers." He's right.

Executives as well as the experts have varying experiences with and opinions of the organization chart, which is a visual tool, like a roadmap, designed to lessen the abstractness of company structure.

"Seeing is believing," say the chart makers, and from their lips it is paradox because what we see may be a total lie.

Nevertheless, some companies swear by their charts and keep them at hand. Those who feel self-conscious about the ambiguities that appear on paper keep the drawer locked.

On the positive side, the chart succeeds in putting down on paper the abstractions of structure, the units and their heads (from president on down), the authority, reporting relationships, and echelon levels. A sample chart is shown on the next page.

But the chart may also depict inaccuracies. Let's say the K position in the chart is Communications Director, a vague designation. Sometimes the vagueness is intentional. The holder of this title could be the publisher of the house organ, head of public relations, or administrator of a system of internal reports circulated among the company's policy makers. And although the chart clearly shows the director reporting directly to the company se etary, he or she might actually report to the comptroller, a grey eminence in the company.

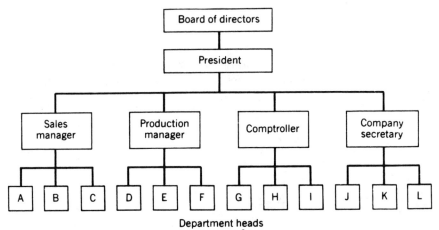

Figure 9. Organization chart

ACTION OPPORTUNITIES

The organization chart is an important idea distorted by misuse and expediency. Yet every manager can benefit from familiarity with the company's chart—for the record, to explain department relationships, and plan company operations, as well as to pinpoint contradictions and to conduct the analysis that will clarify company politics and power structure.

EXAMPLE

Executive Rod Cranby has just hired a bright assistant and wants to give him a good picture of the organization.

Cranby sits down with the newcomer, organization chart on the desk before them, and proceeds to go through the diagram, giving thumbnail descriptions of each department and its manager.

At one point the other asks, "I understood that Research and Development is involved in important projects on new products and the chart shows it as a separate department. But you said that the executive in charge reports to the head of Production and not to the president."

"That's true," Cranby says. "Top management feels that the Research and Development chief is smart but impractical, and the production chief helps keep him aware of the business realities."

"Then why," the assistant asks, "do you bother using a chart of

organization that can be so misleading?" The assistant is pleased with himself. He feels it's a sharp question.

Cranby replies, "The ambiguities of the chart can tell you as much about the company as the factual information. For example, you now have a realistic picture of the way Research and Development functions, one it might have taken months to discover otherwise."

HOW TO USE

Some executives blind themselves to the several uses of their company's chart. Some "do's and don'ts" can keep you out of that category:

1. Understand the basic paradox of the organization chart. The chart's faults are not inherent, but reflect the realities of company functioning. "Why does he use crutches?" a five-year old asks, seeing a neighbor who has broken his leg. "They get in the way of his walking." That is the contradiction of organization. While the company couldn't function without it, it sometimes hampers the activity it is meant to promote.

2. Understand the scorn of charts. "Wouldn't have one around," one executive asserts. Some of the reasons for this kind of feeling are:

■ "We're too small to bother. Our staff has the information where it does the most good, in their heads."

■ "We consider it confidential information." Maybe, but in some cases deviations from what the chart shows represent practices executives would rather not publicize.

■ "Company operations are disorganized and illogical, and the top people would rather not be reminded." Probably a new management will come in to right matters, chart and all.

■ One good reason for avoidance is that a company may be growing so fast that the chart would have to circulate like a daily newspaper to keep up. The top people would need charts constantly, however, both for checking present conditions and for future planning.

3. Understand some of the standard ambiguities:

■ Uniform boxes do not mean equal importance, status, or clout.

■ Dubious designations like "Vice-president, Personnel" may represent a variety of actual functions. The head of Personnel may be one of the most powerful policy makers on the executive staff, or be a figurehead whose main functions are record keeping and maintaining contacts with hiring sources—employment agencies, temporary agencies, and so on.

4. Don't be bullied by charts. Although many companies hide theirs and others say, "We don't believe in charts," some organizations use them as prods and bait to stimulate managers to greater effort toward advancement. The chart, for them, represents the ladder to the top. And don't let a chart with your name in one of the boxes give you more "understanding" than it should.

Analyze just what your position is as compared to what the chart says it is. Be hardheaded and analytical, using such measures as salary, reporting responsibility (both up and down), and the size and nature of your support staff and budget.

◊ 77
Overkill

CONCEPT

Overkill is an idea that has two faces; one harsh, the other benign. Usual usage suggests that overkill is a wasteful practice, for instance, sending a man to do a boy's job, or spending a million dollars in promotion to move half a million dollars' worth of merchandise.

The other aspect of the term promises highly desirable results, however. The sports world is a beneficiary of the overkill idea. You see it in training: A swimmer prepares for a 100-yard championship event by practicing the 125-yard distance. A runner wears heavy shoes so that his regular ones will make him feel light-footed in a race. A prize fighter will box with a fellow pugilist in the next heavier weight category to gain the edge with antagonists in his own class.

Industry is on to the concept. Zero defects is a program that aims high not necessarily to achieve 100 percent perfection, but to improve on previous results because of the extra effort made as people strain for the higher goal.

ACTION OPPORTUNITIES

The principle is a promising one for individual improvement. For example, a manager sees that an assistant has potential and trains him for challenges beyond present responsibilities. Training programs, formal and informal, can benefit from the extra edge gained by honing skills to a higher standard than may be required. Safety is another area that stands to gain. Measures beyond the merely adequate, for instance, "Let's get rid of every unsafe condition in the shop," can yield superior results.

EXAMPLE

A physicist on the science staff of a computer manufacturer is called on to make a presentation to Sales and Marketing personnel and customers. It's a frightening experience. "I had the worst case of stage fright on the planet," he tells his wife.

"Read a book on public speaking," she advises. "It will cut down on the shakes and sweaty palms next time."

"I'll do better than that," the harried scientist says. He takes a course in public speaking and works hard at preparing his practice talks. Although he still sweats a little and is anxious beforehand, he begins to enjoy facing a crowd and performs well—so well that his boss assigns him to outside speaking dates with trade and professional groups. He has gone far beyond the modest goal he yearned for—an end to shaky knees and dripping armpits. His public speaking skill is now an asset.

HOW TO USE

Set aside the pejorative connotation of the word overkill and it becomes a worthy principle. These points will help you win the benefits:

- **Keep an eye out for applications.** For instance, training, to boost skills well above adequacy levels; planning, that must deliver the goods beyond normal limits; setting goals and performance standards higher than necessary to increase the odds for favorable performance, are possibilities.
- **Use it for your own professional endeavors.** The scientist in the Example did this. Pass the idea along to subordinates to stimulate their aspirations.

■ *Benefit from the extra gain.* A manager who got fed up laboring over the writing of reports took instruction in writing, and soon became a contributor to trade journals, establishing himself as an expert in his field.

One executive says, "Overkill, in the broader sense, means going beyond the adequate and the necessary, expanding the horizons of the possible." An interesting turn of language uses a negative word to suggest a host of desirable ends.

▷ 78
Paternalism

CONCEPT

Paternalism started at least as far back as biblical days, when young people—strays, and orphans—were incorporated into family groups. In return they were expected to perform as family members, work willingly, and so on. The Industrial Revolution broadened the family to mean employers and the company. Corporate paternalism peaked in the 1920s, in part to compete with unions for the allegiance of workers. Ironically, unions themselves undertook a protective, parent-like stance to attract members.

"I'll treat you like a generous parent, you treat me like a devoted child," is the generic aspect of paternalism. In business it is assumed that if management is good to employees, they will work harder out of gratitude and loyalty. And of course it is a dominant factor in contemporary Japanese management.

Degrees of paternalism have ranged from a benign attitude reflected in free Christmas turkeys to elaborate benefit programs. In *The Legend of Henry Ford*, Keith Seward details the post World War I practices of the Ford Motor Company which "blended good sense with Ford whims and Puritan virtues."* Ford representatives made home visits to employees, supplying guidance in such matters as budgeting, savings, hygiene, and home management. The dark side was the talebearing of these visitors.

* Seward, Keith (1968). *Legend of Henry Ford.* New York: Antheneum.

They reported such matters as women taking in male boarders, use of liquor, and marital discord.

To contemporary managers, paternalism seems anachronistic, but it persists because it satisfies the emotional needs of some employers and employees. "Paternalism still thrives," reports one expert observer. "While it is more evident in small firms it may also crop up in giant corporations. The reason is, it originates in the psyche of individuals."

ACTION OPPORTUNITIES

Paternalism may appear on the contemporary workscene, for instance as a subtle element in mentoring. By recognizing it in both its benign (noninterfering) and undesirable (restrictive) forms, in yourself as well as in others, you may moderate behavior that could taint a working relationship.

EXAMPLE

Executive Cleo Moore is pleased with her assistant, bright, capable, willing Val Taunton. But one day Val makes an announcement: "I just talked to Bill Haynes and he tells me there is an opening in his department that would be a step up for me . . ."

Cleo is taken aback. "But you're doing so well here." Val says she feels she isn't learning as much as she'd like to about company operations. Moore blurts out, "But how can you leave after all I've done for you?"

"What have you done for me?" The forcefulness of the rejoinder surprises both of them. They are wise enough to detect the strong underlying resentment. "I've done my job and you've done yours," Val concludes.

Unconsciously, perhaps, Cleo Moore saw herself as a surrogate parent, with protective feelings and expectations that were out of line in a professional relationship. The shock of impending separation, therefore, became a strong blow.

HOW TO USE

Knowing the forms and feelings of paternalistic behavior can help you analyze and understand tendencies that otherwise might be inexplicable. The following points can sharpen your insights:

1. There is nothing wrong with paternalism per se. Although it may seem inappropriate and out of context in business, some of its aspects, such as helping a subordinate in their career development, can be eminently constructive. It may play a part in successful mentoring, and should not, therefore, be condemned out of hand. Some consequences, however, such as overdependence of the subordinate, and domination by the manager, are unacceptable.

2. In *Behavioral Strategies for Managers,* by George Strauss and Leonard R. Sayles, the authors make these criticisms:

- Paternalism may cause resentment rather than gratitude. It can imply that rewards are not earned but given as "gifts," and damage the subordinate's self-esteem. This fact explains "biting the hand that feeds," a bitter protest of the paternalistic philanthropist.
- Free handouts are eventually taken for granted, losing their novelty and any gratitude they may have engendered.
- When the paternalism is company-wide and everyone is equally benefited there is little motivational impact, and the tendency is to lapse into a get-by level of effort.
- Work is still seen as a punishment, made palatable by "reward" like salary and other benefits. This nullifies any attempt to make the work itself more rewarding.

3. In *Executive,* Dr. Harry Levinson suggests that there can be such a thing as a "bad-parent" model for an organization:

- "The management of a major heavy manufacturing organization believes that employees should want nothing from their jobs but their salaries." This is the tough parent in action.
- "Some companies are referred to by their employees as 'Mother (name of company).' It is an important psychological fact that companies that are called 'Mother' by their employees are benign and kindly and have either no union or a relatively nonmilitant union. In fact, some of the kindliness is an effort to head off unionization."

4. Here are three situations you should be prepared to handle in your own relationships:

- You perceive a colleague developing a paternalistic attitude toward a subordinate. If the colleague is not a particularly good friend, the wise course is to butt out. If he or she *is* a good friend, however you may broach the matter in a cautionary way, tentatively and unjudgmentally.
- You sense your boss is injecting paternalism into your relationship. Use symptom treatment. A confrontational approach might do considerable damage. It's up to you to prevent specific excesses, such

as overgenerosity and expectation of filial attitudes, by tactful disengagement.

■ You start feeling parental toward a subordinate. Try to limit the impulse to a reasonable level of interest and helpfulness. As the old cartographers used to write at the point on their maps where the known world ended, "past this point are monsters and whales."

◊ 79
Productivity Quest

CONCEPT

Productivity has been defined as the measure of how efficiently goods and services are produced. The pursuit of increased productivity, urged on by competition, pricing pressures, stockholder expectations of dividends, and survival, is management's most preoccupying goal. In *The Productivity Challenge*, Michael LeBoeuf of the University of New Orleans states that the rate of productivity growth has been slipping in the United States, and if the trend continues, the United States will be in fifth place by the end of this decade, behind France, West Germany, Japan, and Canada.* What's bad for America is bad for all of us. Conversely, by brightening the corner where you are you can also help your country. Action is called for.

ACTION OPPORTUNITIES

For managers interested in performance effectiveness, a fresh perspective can stimulate rethinking of a timeworn and complex subject. Seeing where the quest for productivity has taken us can serve as an effective entree.

EXAMPLES

1. One executive says, "Our workers are lazy." Others attribute inadequate productivity gains to their favorite scapegoat, from drug abuse to

* LeBoeuf, Michael (1982). *The Productivity Challenge*. New York: McGraw-Hill.

aging plant and equipment. You can surely make up your own negative example.

2. *Frederick Winslow Taylor, called the father of scientific management, studied the procedure of shoveling for the Bethlehem Steel Company in 1900. He learned that the optimum amount of material per shovelful was 21 pounds. He suggested using different shovels, a small one for ore and a large one for ashes. Workers' performance doubled and sometimes tripled.*

HOW TO USE

Noting the directions management has tried in the search for increased productivity broadens one's view of the problem. The following partial list shows the diversity of subject areas. It is in chronological order, but this is approximate because of overlaps and the differing periods of time for which ideas held sway.

In Search of the Productivity Grail

Scientific management.* Time and motion study, etc.
Mechanization
Improved working conditions. Better lighting, etc.
The human factor. After the Hawthorne* experiments
Morale.* "Improve morale and you boost output"
Leadership*
Motivation*
Automation
Participative management*
Job satisfaction*
Job redesign*
Management by objectives*
Brainstorming*
Computerization
Quality circles* (see Participative Management, page 152)
Robotics*
Corporate culture*

* The asterisked items can be found in the Index.

Note these aspects of the list:

- The differences in the nature of the subject area, from mechanization to the intricacies of corporate culture
- Back-and-forth shifts from human to technological factors
- Although some of the ideas are faddish, most are still given some credence today (See Lifecycle of an Idea, page 209.)

In pondering the productivity quest, here are some additional facts and ideas for your consideration:

1. The Wart Theory of Productivity Improvement. A dermatologist will confirm that almost anything can cure warts. Antibiotics? Yes. Iodine? Uh-huh. Distilled water. Affirmative. Rubbing a wart with a fresh-cut apple slice beneath a full moon? Definitely.

Similarly, almost anything can improve productivity. Emphasizing the *challenge* of an assignment can get it done better and faster. *Preventing machine break-down* keeps production figures up. *Improving layout* can boost output. The implication is plain: intelligent action often delivers results.

2. For many service organizations, the problem seems to be one of quality rather than quantity. Getting a service person in a department store or bank to be courteous, pleasant, and helpful to a customer seems removed from productivity considerations. Perhaps, strictly speaking. But if a bank teller performs 35 transactions per hour, that figure must reflect the quality factor. Certainly, 35 irritated, dissatisfied customers are not the same nor as "productive," as 35 that are pleased.

3. The "quality of help" excuse. "They're just bodies to us. They aren't interested in learning, or extending themselves." That's abdication.

4. "The human factor in our work is small." This view may make sense in equipment-paced output. And some expert observers agree that our biggest gains in productivity reflect technological advances like automation and robotics. But even then, the human factor, while not major in the mainline operation, might figure in overall management. Human factor contributions could include further technological development, future planning, and sales, which by increasing volume may permit lower per-unit costs, and so on.

Psychological obstacles translate into actual ones. But a way to encourage action is to view successful examples. A company history casts a bright light on the productivity picture.

The Lincoln Electric Company of Cleveland is a thriving organization whose productivity has confounded other companies. Sixty years ago they sold their arc-welders for $1,550. A comparable model recently sold at $996. Of course, improved productivity explains the price reduction. The question is, how do they do it?

The Lincoln approach is basically hardheaded. Workers themselves assert it: "You work for what you get." Pay is on a piece rate and there is no guaranteed minimum. Workers who are absent don't get paid. And if a machine goes down because of employee oversight, the repair is made on the employee's own time.

There is fast feedback. An employee in Shipping says, "At the end of each day your supervisor tells you how much you have produced and how much you have earned. On some days, when things are going well I've made as much as $100." In a recent year, employees earned an average of $44,000 in annual pay.

In the Lincoln system, called "incentive management," employees are self-motivated. There is considerable autonomy. A worker may rearrange workspace or change procedures. There is a reward system for suggestions, and bonuses are paid for teamwork and reliability. A company spokesman says, "We don't mind workers making a lot of money. The more they make, the more we make."

You would be right to question the matter of pressure. An official admits, "The system is not for everybody." Is there a high rate of burnout? Turnover figures contradict that possibility. They are unusually low.

Employees are encouraged to feel that they are part of the establishment, and to participate in some company decisions. To help maintain operations, the workgroup accepts flexibility in job assignments. An employee-elected advisory board gives management another interface with employees. Another morale builder is promotion from within. The company's financial operations are also the wonder of many visiting treasurers. Lincoln pays promptly in cash.

One caution: Lincoln is generous in extending invitations to those interested in studying the Lincoln approach. Some of these visitors have attempted to apply the system without success. Clearly, some of the factors in the Lincoln mix were not or could not be duplicated. But it isn't necessary to reproduce the whole system to gain advantages. Some of their operating policies and procedures are instructive in themselves.

William Baldwin, in *Forbes,* says, "In its iconoclastic way, Lincoln Electric remains one of the best-managed companies in the United States and is probably as good as anything across the Pacific." One executive's praise echoes the title of a recent movie; "Back to the Future." She says, "A return to the old verities may be the new wave." As has been said of the Japanese, it's not innovation but traditional organization and resolve that seems to do it.

▷ 80
Responsibility/Authority/Accountability

CONCEPT

Three interrelated concepts represent the executive's power base:

- **Responsibility.** An area of activity in the manager's charge
- **Authority.** The power management gives its managers to command the obedience and cooperation necessary to achieve desired goals
- **Accountability.** The manager's obligation to report on actions and results to a higher echelon

The relationship among these three is this: Management gives a manager a *responsibility*: "You are the head of the X Department." Along with the job goes sufficient *authority* to order and command the resources of the department. Management may call the manager to *account* by asking for reports and explanations as to how obligations have been fulfilled.

ACTION OPPORTUNITIES

Executives must understand each of the three elements and how they relate in order to assess their professional objectives and performance. This is essential for developing a practical perspective of their jobs.

EXAMPLE
There is trouble in the finishing division. Manager Bob Lee has just learned that an entire batch of radio chassis has been rejected because the group leader used the wrong finish. Lee gets to the scene of the trouble just as his boss, the vice-president, Production, does. He says angrily, "I told them to use the lacquer in the blue drums. How could they be so stupid!"

The boss shakes his head. "That's no excuse, Bob. Your responsibility doesn't end when you give an order, you have to see that it's carried out properly. You're still in charge, and that means you're accountable."

Bob Lee's situation as regards his subordinates and boss illustrates the interplay of responsibility, authority, and accountability.

HOW TO USE

Clear perceptions of the three terms can help you prevent errors in violating the bounds of your responsibility, overextending your authority, or realizing that no matter how powerful he or she is, an executive must submit to the judgment of superiors. Consider the following guidelines:

1. The basic element—responsibility. This is the given factor, on which the other two depend. Your responsibility determines your obligation to the company, the duties you must perform, and the actions you may and may not take. Usually, the job makes clear the arena of your activity. You are head of the X Department, Division, or Company. The functioning of the area and results produced depend on plans and their implementation approved by you.

The people you hire, and your entire employee roster, are responsible to you for their job performance and behavior. However, unlike employees, managers' responsibilities cover a broader area, as depicted by the chart:

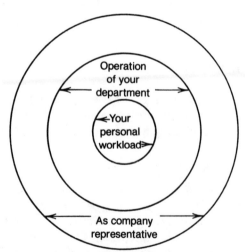

Figure 10. *The executive's total responsibility*

As the chart indicates, managers are responsible not only for: (1) their own job performance (that is, their administrative duties); but also, (2) the operation of their department; and (3) their acts as company representative. This last holds for the entire managerial hierarchy, down to the supervisory echelon.

2. Your authority. This is the power you have within the organization, commensurate with your job status, and necessary for its performance. It makes you the leader of the group, the assigner of tasks, the judge of results, the giver of rewards, and administrator of discipline. There are three danger points implicit in your position of power:

- *Authority gaps.* There may be gaps in your authority within your area of responsibility, theory to the contrary. For example, a department head hires an assistant to help with record keeping and other clerical matters. She has narrowed the field to three candidates when her boss steps in: "Gayle, I'd like to make the final selection," and makes a choice based on his personal preference. This means that Gayle will be responsible for the consequences of someone else's judgment, a breach in the logic of organizational command. This negative example illustrates a possible threat to, as well as the desirability of, the congruence of responsibility and authority.

- *Reversal of a decision by a higher echelon.* Even when justified, such undermining of authority can be a blow that though weathered, leaves a permanent scar for the manager vis a vis subordinates and colleagues.

- *Insubordination.* This means the contesting of a boss's authority by a subordinate. For example, Jess Hall tells his boss, "I'm not going to work overtime, no matter what you say." Perhaps the manager doesn't have the right to give the order, but if an order is rejected out of hand, the manager must assert authority, and either threaten or pronounce punishment. If the employee remains recalcitrant, the manager may seek backing from a higher authority. In case the order actually is beyond the manager's authority, it's up to the manager to accept that fact and try to save face by apologizing, "toughing it out," or whatever.

A practical modification often exists in the manager's authority. Note the diagram below:

Authority modified

Area of your full authority	→	You may act then report upward	→	You may not take action

As the preceding figure suggests, there are limits to power for most managers. Be aware of these in your own situation, seeking clarification if in doubt to avoid foot-in-mouth complications.

■ **Confused accountability link.** All employees are accountable for the performance of their jobs to their boss. But in the management group, accountability is sometimes fudged. The organization chart (See Organization Chart, page 215.) may show that Jim Jones is subordinate to and accountable to Executive X. But Executive Y, who wields power beyond his purported position, is actually Jones's boss. In this case the fault lies with the chart. The organizational realities dictate accountability, not their depiction on a sheet of paper.

The discrepancy between formal and informal accountability may extend to other relationships among the three power factors. These tend to vary from organization to organization. You must ascertain the specific "rules" that hold in your company and for your situation.

Your awareness makes possible the bending of the rules, and the possibility of practical changes that can affect your job. For example, you may seek to extend your responsibility, or the extent of your authority, beyond present limits.

(See also Delegation, page 120.)

▷ 81
Robotics

CONCEPT

Some executives see robots as the employees of the future. Others contend that as machines in human form they are a fad that will take only a limited place in the field of automatic machinery. Though the machine-as-humanoid piques the imagination, there is a lively argument between those who think the more human robots are, the better, and those like Steven J. Marcus in *The New York Times,* who avers that humanoid models would be grotesquely out of place in business.

Professor Warren Seering of MIT sees further humanizing of the robot as the wrong way for American industry to go. It results, he says, from the confusion between the "gee whiz" approach in which *people* are superceded, and a more practical one in which robotic systems replace other *machines.*

The Robot Institute of America provides a definition that distinguishes the robot from other man-made creations: "A robot is a reprogrammable, multifunctional manipulator designed to move material, parts, or specialized devices through variable programmed motions for the performance of a variety of tasks."

Joseph F. Engelberger, founder of an early robot-producing organization and author of *Robotics in Practice,** extends the Institute's definition: "One feature which a device must possess if it is to rank as a robot is the ability to operate automatically, on its own. This means that there must be inbuilt intelligence, or a programmable memory, or simply an arrangement of adjustable mechanisms that command manipulation."

Despite disagreements as to concept and ultimate direction, there is no doubt on two points. One is that there is strong interest in robots, and the other is the development of a lively, evolving robot industry. In the early 1980s a trade fair drew over 25,000 people to view robots and related equipment exhibited by more than 100 manufacturers, including Westinghouse, General Electric, Bendix, and IBM. But as one would expect in an advancing and competitive field, the financial journals have reported extensive shakeouts due to withdrawals and failure.

ACTION OPPORTUNITIES

For robots, the matter of application is central to the concept and its utility. It is also a matter of discussion and controversy. American Robot Inc. brought out a machine that is fast and accurate to within a one-thousandth of an inch. Promotional literature shows it putting a needle seven one-thousandths of an inch wide through a nine one-thousandths hole without touching the edges. But Victor Scheinman, vice-president of Automix, says that going for greater accuracy may mean missing the boat. "The robot of the future," he says, "may be less accurate than today's," but its lack of precision "will be compensated for by better sensors and more smarts."

A description of a state-of-the-art manufacturing plant further clarifies the direction of robotization. Japanese industrialist Shimpei Kato of Fujitsu Fanuc describes their new factory: "Robots have indeed replaced humans here. They work 24 hours a day, and they don't have to think. It

* Engelberger, Joseph F. (1980). *Robotics in Practice.* New York: AMACOM.

makes common sense. We only employ humans for research, maintenance, and supervisory work."

Robot proponents stress using robots in tasks which are destructively monotonous, dangerous, or debilitating.

EXAMPLE

A full-page advertisement by IBM featured a color photograph of a complicated articulated arm that illustrated its assembly capability. The copy reads:

> The robotic arm can locate a tiny hole and accurately insert a pin once or thousands of times. IBM robotic systems controlled by computers are doing precision work on complex or even hazardous tasks using special sensors and equipment in the "gripper." They are assembling complicated mechanisms, rejecting defective parts, testing complicated units and keeping inventories.
>
> IBM robotic systems can improve productivity, worker safety and product quality.

HOW TO USE

The interest an organization may have in robotics will depend on two immediate factors: engineering and cost. If robots can take over an operation wholly or in part, engineers, either your own or a supplier's, will develop proposals that spell out the possibilities. Some cost figures are persuasive. A recent calculation shows that the average labor cost is $15 per hour, while a comparative robot would cost $5 per hour.

Some uses have already stood the test of time. Welding, spray painting, assembly, and some types of inspection are widely roboticized. And robots have set foot in places no man has, or would want to. For example, the New York City Police Department uses a mobile unit to handle bombs. Remote controls direct it to the explosive device, which it then retrieves. The bottom of the sea and the moon have been explored by robotic stand-ins. But the history of robots is already long enough to suggest some limiting factors. The consequences to humans of the so-called "robot invasion" is a serious consideration for users.

George L. Whaley, visiting professor in the management sciences department at Florida A & M University, among others, has gazed into the future of the robot versus human controversy and inferred some of the complications. For example:

- The traditional argument against replacing workers by machines is being made: Unemployment will rise, "And this time it's really going to happen." But the opposition says that jobs lost will be offset by creation of jobs in the robot industry itself.

However, other points of impact are more certain:

- Some experts predict a broad change in human resources management in companies with major robot installations. Such basics as organizational structure, staffing, appraisal of human resources needs, compensation, training, and work climate could be affected.
- Because robots can perform onerous tasks, workers' jobs would change, possibly to be enriched and their status elevated, from machine operator to machine supervisor, for example.
- Planned and actual roboticization is likely to meet with worker suspicion and rejection, although enlisting their participation in evaluation and decision making could lessen resistance. At the very least, the situation calls for careful indoctrination and introduction of equipment. Benefits from the change, status, and pay improvement, for example, should be given early to hasten acceptance.
- Widespread use of robots might affect equal employment opportunity practices. When a company must choose between two equally qualified job candidates—one robot and one human—how will it decide? Should intelligent robots be considered "employees" under equal employment regulations?
- Will human frailties like absenteeism, emotional outbursts, and irresponsibility, which will contrast badly with robot behavior, be made inadmissible, and so, in effect roboticize human beings?
- Human career paths may both widen and constrict as increasingly intelligent robots come off the assembly line. A shrinking window of opportunity may make working in industry unattractive as compared to the jobs of poet, biologist, and jockey.

The fate of robots lies not so much with their manufacturers as with the computer industry. It is no trade secret that dozens of projects are underway, here and abroad, to create artificial intelligence and develop machines that each decade come closer to the thinking and even feeling potential of human beings. We must leave to tomorrow's wisdom the problems of the future. Meanwhile, the next decades hold out the traditional twin elements of innovation—danger and opportunity.

▷ 82
Scientific Management

CONCEPT

For today's manager, scientific management has the utility of a museum piece. It reminds us of our past, makes us more aware of the present, and encourages our thinking about the future. Frederick Winslow Taylor, the accredited father of scientific management, was a true genius who rocketed our industrial system from the nineteenth century into the twentieth by brilliant insights into new ways of working.

He saw about him a haphazard approach to labor in which people were handed rudimentary tools and cajoled and threatened, on pain of being fired, to produce. In a historic speech at Dartmouth College in 1911 he summed up his ideas of change:

*Let me repeat briefly these four principles of Scientific Management. . . .
They are the development of a science to replace the old rule-of-thumb
methods; the scientific selection and then the progressive teaching and development of the workmen; the bringing of the scientifically selected workmen and the science together; and then the almost equal division of the
work between the management and the men.*

The approach he espoused, also referred to as "Taylorism," gave birth to industrial engineering, with its advantages and the drawbacks that some quarters, particularly organized labor, saw as a technique for exploiting workers. Taylor's views, from today's standpoint, are seen as mixed. While he favored "the training and development of each individual . . . so that he can do . . . the highest class of work for which his abilities fit him," he thought the most satisfactory worker was one who was "as phlegmatic as an ox."

ACTION OPPORTUNITIES

In the executive's own work today, Taylorism still makes a contribution. The manager who tells himself, "I'd better get organized," reflects the essence of the engineer's way of thinking. And every office and shop to some degree and at some time seeks a better way. While the efficiency expert of the 1920s and 1930s has been removed from the scene for the sake of labor peace, the principles of time-and-motion study underlie most efforts to increase productivity and cut costs, especially of operations with a significant human element.

EXAMPLES

1.   In an automated and computerized world, hand operations may seem medieval, but Taylor's early studies made possible mechanization and the technologies that followed. A glimpse through the peephole of history demonstrates his approach:

In the 1880s Taylor was hired by the Midvale Steel Company to improve the cutting of metals. He selected the best machine and the best worker and proceeded to study every element of the operation; speeds, feeds, tools, materials, belting, shafting, and the worker's own movements. Eventually he came up with the best combination of the factors. Studies of this kind yielded improvements in some machine operations from 400 to 1800 percent.

2.   In a later study for the Bethlehem Steel Company in about 1900, his objective was to make shoveling "scientific." He selected three of the best shovelers and paid them extra wages for doing reliable work. Eventually he recommended ten different types of shovels, each appropriate for a given type of material. A load of twenty-one pounds proved optimum, with a small scoop for ore and a larger one for ashes. Production doubled and trebled.

HOW TO USE

Taylor planted seeds that were endlessly prolific. The scientific approach touched every industrial function and influenced new ones being born. The setting of standards and the concepts of inspection and control helped make operations more precise and products better. And industries that could not have existed without the discipline of the scientific method, such as autos, planes, marine engines, and so on, came into being.

Contemporaries and followers helped spread the wealth of ideas and technologies that moved the industrial juggernaut on its way. Abroad, the names of Joseph S. Lewis in England, Karol Adamiecki of Poland, and the brothers Andre and Eduard Michelin in France, became associated with scientific management, which was also in evidence in Germany and the Scandinavian countries. Switzerland imported in part and developed its own versions of Taylorism.

In the United States William H. Leffingwell applied the scientific approach, born in the factory, to the office. The Gilbreths, Frank and Lillian, spread the refinements of methods improvement in their development and consulting efforts. And Allan H. Mogensen developed techniques for training supervisors, and through them, rank-and-file employees, to apply improvement analysis to their own operations. (See Work Simplification, page 174.)

Some authorities feel that the wisest use we can make of scientific management theory is to realize it is obsolete. In *New Management Tools,* Margaret Butteriss and Karl Albrecht state:

> Frederick Taylor's 'scientific management,' well adapted to the simple industrial companies of the early century, has been stretched to the limits of its applicability. We now struggle with the costly and discouraging side effects of . . . 'production first and people second': declining productivity, dissatisfaction with work, hatred and hostility as the basis of a general union-management deadlock, loss of pride in workmanship and the near extinction of workers' organizational pride.

In the closing paragraph of the preface, Albrecht offers a hopeful new direction:

> You, the practicing manager, are the one who really establishes management theory and management method. . . . I know of no more significant challenge . . . than that of humanizing our business organizations and of mobilizing human effort in ways that are not only economically viable, but also rewarding and supportive for the citizens of our organizations.

◁ 83
Span of Control

CONCEPT

The theorists and practitioners concerned with organizational structure early examined the question: How many activities and/or people should managers have under their control? There was plenty of case history material around, depicting managers operating in happy productivity with well-rounded staffs, others driven to exhaustion or to the limit of their competence by overloading, and still others whose command activities were insufficient to fill their time productively.

Rules developed. Management authority Lester Bittel of James Madison University reminds us what they were: No manager should have the responsibility for more than six separate activities. The more specialized and complex the activities, the shorter the ideal span of control. The more uniform and simple the activities, the greater the span can be. Sometimes the span is defined by the number of people rather than by the activities. For example, it is not unusual for a department head to supervise thirty employees, provided they are engaged only in a few simple related activities. A middle manager might direct six departments through supervision of their leaders.

ACTION OPPORTUNITIES

The original span-of-control rules often don't suit contemporary management. For instance, the maximum rule, that is, no more than six activities in a manager's span, is no longer taken as gospel. The quality of the activities may be more important than their quantity.

It can be helpful to managers, however, to review their own spans and that of their subordinate managers. Both quantitative and qualitative factors are relevant. The determination that a manager is over or under loaded can be the start of significant improvement in performance.

EXAMPLE

A surge of company growth finds Joe Dunne managing four departments, since he is familiar with their operations. He accepts the burden willingly, seeing the load as a form of advancement, and makes heroic efforts to do the job. But the increments, like the proverbial straws that broke the camel's back, finally do him in. Without his awareness, he has been pushed to the point where his span exceeds his grasp.

"I guess," his boss says, noting the sagging performance, "Joe can't cut it." It's an unfair observation. The fault is the boss's, for creating an impossibly large area of responsibility.

HOW TO USE

Span of control is a factor in every manager's job. Often it is a combination of directing a personal staff and one or more subordinate managers. Occasional assessment is desirable. Consider these guidelines:

1. Watch out for underload. Insufficient responsibility can be as destructive as too much. Managers whose span of control is unnecessarily short may resort to make-work to keep busy, causing eventual damage to their motivation system, and wasting the benefits possible if they were challenged and exercising their skills. Those who keep after their bosses for extended assignments may be on to a good thing, if they don't overdo it.

2. Assess your span. List your responsibilities, people and departments reporting to you, and other assignments. One marketing executive's list looks like this:

Subordinates	Managers	Assignments
One assistant	Office manager	Monthly sales reports
One secretary	Head of mailroom	Next quarter's outlook and actions suggested
Two general clerical people	Head of printing	Promotional programs
	Head of promotion	Field-staff building and monitoring

Review your list, and assess the degree of satisfactoriness of each of the three headings. Is there anything you should add or subtract under each?

3. Forward planning. To further your own career as well as to advance the effectiveness of your department, analyze your present span to see whether modifying it, not only in quantity but also in quality, will help you. For example, consider trading an activity more relevant to your responsibility with another executive who will also benefit by taking over an equivalent area from you.

Span of control is usually flexible. Watch for opportunities to make worthwhile adjustments reflecting changes in your needs and that of the organization.

▷ 84
The Uncertainty Factor

CONCEPT

Some management procedures have as their first step, "getting the facts." Decision making, planning, and investigations of various kinds require this preliminary. However, it is often impossible to get *all* the facts. The most intensive probing may fail, either because necessary documents are missing, witnesses are unavailable, or future conditions are unpredictable. How do you proceed? "Take a calculated risk," is one answer. But what and how do you calculate?

ACTION OPPORTUNITIES

Every manager must make decisions and take actions despite incomplete information. A large gap may block action, but although you realize that unknowables increase the risk of failure, sometimes you must proceed anyway. Operating in the face of uncertainty is often unavoidable, but understanding the options can help you make better choices.

EXAMPLE

Wally Smith and his group have developed a new product due to start production in the spring. One of his staff members tells him that he has learned that a competitor is working in a similar direction.

"Maybe we'd better delay production," someone suggests, "until we see how they make out." Smith finally says, "We'll have to gamble. Let's review the whole project, fine-tune it as best we can, and hit the market on schedule." This sounds like a defensible decision, but the risk could be reduced. For instance, negative factors could be minimized. Smith could strengthen ties with selling outlets, and improve service and communications so that any selling difficulties that arise are dealt with early, and so on.

HOW TO USE

Handling uncertainty is a part of every manager's job. Understanding the process makes the odds more favorable. Here are some key points:

1. Accept uncertainty. This is achieved by:

- Being aware of it
- Realizing that you may have to act anyway

2. Make the odds more favorable. For instance, you may be able to improve you position by strengthening the known factors:

- **Seek expert opinion.** Individuals with relevant experience may be able to help you replan strategies.
- **Human resources.** Those who are involved in implementation of the action may be trained further, or individuals with superior skill added to the group.
- **Equipment and facilities.** You may be able to increase the potency of the physical factors; equipment, facilities, and so on.
- **Timing.** Reconsideration of this factor alone may help you strike while the iron is hot rather than unheated or cooled down.

3. Be aware of what you don't know. People sometimes say, "I'm taking a calculated risk," meaning that they have calculated the strengths of their position. But the risk can only be considered if the negative factors are taken into account, as well as the favorable ones.

"We can't delay any longer, we'll start the project in temporary quarters," a manager decides. Other negatives, like poor timing, people not fully trained, or tough competition may also threaten. Executives with a feeling for the pencil can take advantage of their special endowment and list the pros and cons to see where they stand.

4. Pretest. In addition to checking the elements of a project, you may undertake a trial run. For instance, an executive decides to adopt a new type of packaging. A marketing test is made, and he sets a high success level to justify going ahead. If only a get-by level is reached, the whole project may be junked.

A split test can further diminish uncertainty. Two different presentations are proposed for selling a new service. Proponents are vociferous in pushing their views. An executive says, "Let's use training methods A and B with ten salespeople each. Comparing the results can help us come up with an approach that incorporates the best of both."

(See Minimax Technique, page 149, and also, Quantification, page 166.)

▷ 85
The Winning Edge

CONCEPT

A simple statement of the winning edge idea: "All you need to win, either over a single competitor or a field of them, is a *slight advantage.*" You can see this principle at work at the racetrack, when a horse wins in a photo finish by a nose. A basketball team may defeat its opponent by a single point, but the feat goes into the winning column as solidly as if it had been by twenty or thirty points.

An early propounder of the idea was Professor Aaron Levenstein of City College of New York, who has helped prepare a generation of would-be managers for their profession. His familiarity with business practicalities led him to identify the concept as a guide for managers, who traditionally operate in competitive situations.

The principle gets support from a study of human capability. Dr. David Wechsler, in his *Range of Human Capacities,* asserts that, "Human variability, when compared to that of other phenomena in nature is extremely limited.* The differences which separate human beings from one another with respect to whatever trait or ability we may wish to compare, are far smaller than is ordinarily supposed."

Dr. Wechsler backs up his statement by comparing the general intelligence of the highest and lowest individuals in a group of 1000 people. How much "smarter" would you guess the top individual would be compared to the lowest? Ten times? Five? Surprisingly, the answer, even in this extreme case, was only two-and-one-half times. These figures depend on a comparison of extremes. In everyday executive life, individuals are more nearly matched.

ACTION OPPORTUNITIES

The slight edge can shape your thinking in large, small, or medium strivings, and in setting personal, departmental, or company goals. The recommendation isn't that you set objectives at a minimum, but that you view competition realistically. The margin of victory may be tiny, the fruits of victory huge. In a recent photo finish of a race of thoroughbreds,

---

* Wechsler, David. (1952). *Range of Human Capacities.* New York: Hafner.

the winner paid $35.20, coming in first not by a length, or even a part thereof, but a scant inch.

EXAMPLES

1. *In an interview a television executive was asked, "How do you explain your advancement against the tough competition?" His answer: "I was just a little better than the other fellow." Further conversation revealed that he didn't feel he had to be a world-beater, a slight advantage would put him ahead of his business competitors. He took pains to have that slight edge in areas that were meaningful for customers.*

2. *Bea Burgess wanted to head up a new department in her company. Trouble was, Sally Trent seemed way out front in the promotion race, and acted as though she had the job sewed up. Although the executive who would make the choice was neutral, colleagues took Trent's triumph as a foregone conclusion. But Burgess thought she had a chance, and in the months before the decision was made, she began a careful campaign to show the boss her strengths. She knew him well enough to identify the kinds of accomplishments that would impress him, for example he favored people who had ideas and showed initiative. She decided not to try to compete with Sally Trent in total performance, but to try to get an edge in an area that could have major impact.*

One day Bea Burgess got into a discussion with her boss about a problem with order processing and ended with the casual statement, "I'd like to look into that to see what can be done." A week later she handed him a report analyzing the delay and trouble spots and suggesting a number of specific improvements.

A while later she suggested to her boss the possibility of a new line of matched electric utensils aimed at the growing group of affluent professionals who are turning back to home food preparation. "Essentially," she said, "it's a matter of attractive design that we could produce with present facilities."

"Sounds interesting, look into it," her boss said. In two weeks she had a report with rough sketches and facts and figures of production and marketing possibilities spelled out.

The boss didn't have to be knocked unconscious to become aware of Burgess's clout. She got the promotion.

HOW TO USE

The principle of the winning edge holds promise, but the important element is implementation, that is, how cannily it is used. Five guidelines can help make it work on your behalf:

1. Focus on your adversary. The better you understand where your competition is, and the strengths and weaknesses you are up against, the more effectively you can make your next step.

2. Decide on the edge to strive for. The Bea Burgess example illustrates this point. For example, in a face-off with a competitor for an important customer, you may have to explore factors other than price, such as assured delivery, early delivery, a special benefit you can offer because of special equipment or personnel available to you.

3. Use your advantage. This is the implementation step. Exactly how you make your moves can be a decisive factor in the victory. To have an idea for a booth at a trade fair is fine. But when your exhibit is imaginative, clever, and well designed, you draw the crowds. Then be sure to have the trained people ready and able to pin down the contacts or make the sales that are now possible. People who are poorly qualified to tell your story—and they are all too common in this situation—will cost you rather than profit you.

4. Push for the payoff. This story may be apocryphal but it makes a point: Ed gets a red hot tip on a horse, it wins by a nose and he runs about shouting, "I won, I won." Then he tears up his winning ticket and goes home.

This final step is the wrap-up, the gleaning of the fruits of your triumph. Make sure you get the "prize money." Winning gives you a victory. Exploiting the victory gives you the benefits.

PART FOUR

SELF-HELP

At the center of the work universe is a presence whose values, attitudes, and capabilities help make the wheels turn. That entity is You. The goals you set for yourself, your mastery of the tools of your trade, and your executive savvy, are an important part of corporate achievement—and your own.

Your ability to manage time, to read Body Language, Chart Your Personal Efficiency, and wield the Executive Toolrack to good advantage are among the means for accomplishing more, more easily. And Enjoying Your Job is a worthy end in itself. The following Ideas appear in this Part:

★　　　★　　　★

▷ **86**
Body Language

CONCEPT

Body language is also called "nonverbal communication." The 1970s sparked interest in the idea that the human body is a communications instrument that complements speech. Unfortunately, popularizers of this notion gave the misleading impression that posture and gestures could be interpreted out of context. Articles and books featured illustrations demonstrating, for example, that crossed legs meant defensiveness, scratching one's nose was a statement of doubt or indecision. They could have that meaning, but several others as well.

Silent language deserves to be understood. The business world, attracted by the promise of better communication, embraced the subject avidly. Many management training programs incorporated sessions, and seminar-sponsoring organizations added it to their agendas. No question that an understanding of body language can be a meaningful adjunct to aural listening, and is a way to see through the occasional artificialities and dissembling possible with the spoken word. On occasions when it is crucial, you are in a stronger position to better understand other people than if you only hear them.

ACTION OPPORTUNITIES

You can refine your body language perceptions, get more of people's messages, and sometimes discover discrepancies between what is said and what is felt. Skill in this area provides an obvious advantage in interviewing, negotiation, argument and other confrontational situations. You can also be aware of your own occasional double talk, and learn how to prevent yourself from "saying" things in nonverbalese that contradicts what you express in words.

EXAMPLES

1. Helen Lang asks for a raise for the second time. She is angry about having to repeat the request. Her boss is sympathetic, admits she deserves an increase, but claims that Personnel, which has the last word, is opposed. Helen feels herself beginning to bristle. She feels her throat tightening, her face freeze in a mask of rage, and forces herself to cool down. She realizes that expressing her anger won't help. Instead, she says, "Let's make it easy for Mr. Herrold (the head of Personnel) to do the right thing. We'll go down to see him together, and convince him that it's only fair to give me the increase." In this case, Lang read her own body signals and used the message as a cue to switch tactics.

2. *Alice Getz asks a job candidate how he feels about working overtime, which is sometimes required. He says, "I don't mind," but along with the words he fidgets, frowns, and averts his eyes. Getz pursues the subject and learns that family demands would make overtime a hardship. "I'm glad you told me," she says. "I'll recommend you for another job without the overtime requirement."*

3. *Ben Gorden is telling his boss that his department will be unable to ship a special order by the deadline. The boss pushes back from the desk, stares at Ben, then looks out the window. Gorden interprets the behavior as anger, and decides to address that directly. "Greg, I know you're angry and I feel bad about it too. But we talked about this a week ago. Perhaps you've forgotten, but I told you we'd need better delivery from Supplies to complete on time. Call Smith right now and get him to deliver all the material by noon tomorrow, and we'll be able to ship."*

HOW TO USE

You are probably good at sensing body language but a refresher may help broaden your perceptions. The following points can add to your capabilities:

1. Keep in mind that body language expresses feeling. If you hold up two fingers to indicate how many lumps of sugar you take in your coffee, the meaning is explicit. But sign language aside, nonverbal communication is an expression of the emotions that augment the spoken word.

2. Skill at reading body language grows with the ability to refine your observations in matters of degree, to detect the nuances. If a body stance registers resentment, how strong is it? If a subordinate accepts an assignment, where would his or her enthusiasm register on a scale of 1 to 10?

3. Body language, like spoken language, is individualized, reflecting the person's emotional capacities and levels. One person's smile is another's laughter, a doleful expression on A's face is matched by B's tears.

4. Avoid snap readings. For instance, a manager has an appointment with a subordinate after lunch to discuss her poor performance. She comes in and sits down, shoulders hunched, knees pressed together. Meaning to be helpful, the manager says, "Grace, there's no need to be anxious or defensive . . ."

"Anxious!" Grace exclaims. "It's below zero outside. I just got in and I'm frozen."

The manager brings her some hot coffee, she relaxes, and the meeting proceeds in constructive fashion.

5. The chart that follows can remind you of some feelings that, in context, suggest a clear message. Note that for some terms there are no precise opposites, for example, anger and fear.

Typical "Vocabulary" Opposites

Attention: Head up, expression alert, body erect or forward	Inattention: Slack features, lackluster eyes, sagging body
Telling the truth: Features firm, lips normally compressed, eyes direct	Lying: No eye contact, uneasy manner, expression of discomfort
Pleasantness: Face relaxed, eyes bright, body relaxed	Anger: Eyes hard, lips compressed, body stiff
Hope: Head high, gaze bright, body erect	Despair: Slumped body, expression downcast, hands clasped
Resoluteness: Hands clenched, jaw thrust out, stance upright, gaze intent	Fear: Eyes staring, lips pale and trembling
Friendliness: Warm expression, relaxed manner, sense of reaching out, may touch	Hostility: Semicrouched posture, cold expression, eyes sharp, legs stiff

6. From the chart it is possible to develop a list of the several "tongues" of body language:

- *Facial expression.* A broad range, mirroring many feelings
- *Eyes.* The Chinese say the eyes can never lie, and while they themselves are immobile, the eyelids, brows, and skin around them give them expressiveness, including the possibility of tears
- *Cheeks.* Not too expressive for some people, but for others a clear mirror of anger or embarrassment when they turn red, or of depression, fear or anxiety when pale.
- *Hands.* Very expressive for most people, covering a range of emotions from hopelessness (hand wringing) to rage (clenched fists), from contemplation (finger steepling) to registering impatience by drumming, nose rubbing, head scratching, and other finger movements with meanings in their context
- *Legs.* Stiffness for aggressive feelings, slouched when sitting may mean tiredness or a disconsolate mood, actual dancing when happy

■ *Body posture.* Considerable variation here because of differences in prevailing postures of individuals, for example, some people are normally erect, others slouch, but emotions may be mirrored by degrees of stiffness, relaxation, and stance—for example, leaning forward or backward.

7. Finally, there is an aspect of body language that is seldom mentioned but which gives it an additional dimension. Psychologist William James expressed it in his insightful question, "Do people smile because they are happy, or are they happy because they smile?" He believed that emotional experience is the result of visceral changes resulting from emotion-provoking experience. He advanced a famous argument: That on meeting a bear in the woods we do not run because we are afraid, but are afraid because we run. Running stirs up a visceral reaction and this is the emotion we feel.

For managers, the theory suggests expressing in body language the feeling we want. And, as a matter of fact, we do it routinely. "Come in," an executive invites a visitor, "sit down in that chair, it's very comfortable . . ." He is putting the person at ease so that he will *feel* at ease. Similarly, a pep talk aims at stimulating the body into a posture that expresses determination and resolve, so that these feelings will help generate extra effort.

The wonder is that people don't speak and understand body language better. After all, it is a first language for us; we were brought up with it. But a refresher course can make better senders and receivers of us all.

▷ 87
Burnout

CONCEPT

In *Beyond Burnout,** authors Welch, Medeiros, and Tate define burnout as "a complex process which affects at least five major areas of human functioning: physical, intellectual, emotional, social and spiritual." The term "burnout" suggests managerial decrepitude resulting from work

* Welch, Medeiros, & Tate (1982). *Beyond Burnout.* Englewood Cliffs, NJ: Prentice-Hall.

pressures and a top-heavy workload. But burnout may result from deprivations as well as excesses. Rest and relaxation not taken can cost you. Coffee breaks, social chats and lunches with colleagues, and discussions of mutual avocational interests with the mail deliverer or chairman of the board, can make you less like an unoiled machine.

The concept is vivid, and the idea it represents is likely to nudge executives toward a worthwhile goal: their own mental and physical well-being.

ACTION OPPORTUNITIES

If you need encouragement to maintain your working and living fitness, the burnout idea can start the ball rolling. And you may want to get family members, friends, and colleagues on the bandwagon.

EXAMPLE

Ted Mooney wakes up Monday morning with two problems: the standard one of momentarily not knowing where he is, and the less common but even more frightening one of not knowing who he is. Gradually the murk thins. Someone is stirring, and sure enough it's his wife Ethel, so he must be Ted Mooney. The walls of the bedroom begin to come into focus.

"You'll miss the 7:50 if you don't hurry," Ethel says.

Not being on the 7:50 is, at the moment, his dream of heaven. He remembers going to bed and falling asleep the previous night, assisted by two pills. Later he awoke and tossed about, thinking of the next day's meeting with his boss to explain his region's failure to produce quota the second quarter in a row. Then he pondered what to do about Phil and Rex, his friends and a major cause of the department's poor showing. Talking to them hadn't helped. They agreed to everything he said but were unable to make the five calls a day they promised. And they shrugged off his suggestion that they change their presentations. "It's just a temporary slump," they assured him. He doubted it. He had taken two more pills and sleep had returned.

"Call me in sick," he tells Ethel.

HOW TO USE

The bright side of the burnout concept is that it can motivate managers toward positive goals of maximum well-being. Here are some recommendations to that end:

1. Get perspective. Accept as a principle of living that work doesn't come first. More power to those who say, "My work is my life." Many great people in the arts, sciences, and industry, have come out of those ranks. But for the average person, the richness of life lies in fulfillments off company premises. Think of all the things that may come before work and the job: family, personal happiness, health, peace of mind, pride, integrity. Putting your job in its proper place can lessen tension and prevent burnout.

2. Give your interests and activities the once-over. See whether you have a reasonably good distribution in the five areas the *Beyond Burnout* authors mention in their definition. Rate each for yourself on a scale of 1 to 10:

Physical   _____
Intellectual   _____
Emotional   _____
Social   _____
Spiritual   _____

A score of 7 or more for an area suggests you are reaping the benefits of the particular life area, 4 to 6 that you are gainfully occupied. Below 4 means a low interest. There's nothing wrong with that, unless there are gaps in your experience for which these might be rewarding fillers.

3. Turn your thinking directly to your job and/or career. In the context of burnout, the question isn't how successful you are, but to what extent you are satisfied and fulfilled in your work. Just making the distinction between success and satisfaction can help you water down the all-out drive for success that may cause burnout, and shine up the target of fulfillment in work. Fulfillment is perhaps no easier or harder to achieve than success, but it is less a measure by which you are judged, and so less demanding.

4. The Greek concept of a healthy mind in a healthy body isn't outdated. It's a good antiburnout goal for which you can devise your own action program, whether it's jogging and the theater, continuing education and tennis, or pursuing a literary interest and a lower golf score. Then you will go back to work refreshed and with less chance of even a slight burnout singe.

(See also Stress, page 89.)

▷ 88
Charting Personal Efficiency

CONCEPT

Industrial psychologist Normal R. F. Maier studied the working efficiency of a group of executives on a daily basis and charted his findings
in the following graph:

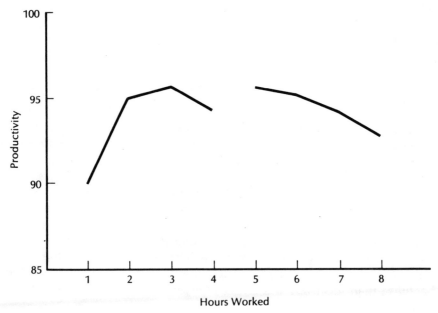

Figure 11. *Personal efficiency chart*

The curve represents the hourly rise and fall in efficiency of the
average individual. Your own personal energies may resemble those
charted, or may deviate somewhat. Check the following key points:

- **Warm-up period.** Note the rise after the morning start. Physiolo-
  gists explain the warm-up on a partially physical basis. Muscles
  must be limbered; changes in blood pressure and circulation take
  place.

- **Energy sag.** Fatigue is the usual explanation given for the lowering of efficiency in the course of the working period.
- **End spurt.** There is a tendency for efficiency to increase toward the end of the work period, usually for psychological reasons, to hasten completion. (See the Zeigarnik Effect, page 97.)

ACTION OPPORTUNITIES

The chart can be used to sharpen self-scheduling practices by managers at all levels, as a means of conserving personal energy and improving performance.

EXAMPLE

Executive Frank Tierney is dissatisfied with his work pace. He feels it drags, particularly in the morning. Examining the Maier chart, he sees his morning energy peak is about 11 A.M., with the low point at 9 A.M. Accordingly, he changes his routine. Instead of starting his day by tackling difficult tasks, he takes care of routine matters like going through the mail and writing short memos. He shifts the demanding items on his schedule to the hour or so before lunch.

HOW TO USE

To get a payoff from the Maier chart:

1. Chart your own energy peaks and valleys. Chart your ups and downs of daily efficiency by keeping a brief record, noting:

- The hours you feel peppiest
- The times fatigue catches up with you
- The periods you feel most at ease mentally
- The times you find it difficult to work

Tabulate the results over several days to pinpoint your strong and weak periods. Then:

2. Tailor your work schedule to your personal chart. For instance, save demanding jobs for high-energy periods. Fit routine tasks into low-energy periods. Fill in mental doldrums with the task that almost "do themselves." Tackle new projects or mentally taxing ones when your energy peaks are highest.

▷ **89**
"Edifice" Complex

CONCEPT

The "edifice" complex is an executive neurosis that feeds on power and status. Major symptoms are enlargement of the staff, cosmetic acquisitions of costly furniture and furnishings, and inflated quarters.

Bennett Cerf, the late publisher and TV personality, is given credit for the phrase, a takeoff on Oedipus complex, that started as a joke and ended up as a useful management idea. It is a cautionary concept, alerting executives to organizational elephantiasis stemming from ego rather than need. The victim of the disease has an irresistible urge to swell the dimensions of his or her empire, which he or she has distorted into a monument to greatness and achievement. The concept does have a positive side, however. Since expansion can be a necessary prelude to increased profitability, the edifice complex may be used as a monitoring idea by which to appraise growth plans.

ACTION OPPORTUNITIES

Managers who propose expanding their activities may be advocating a desirable improvement. But a second possibiity—a power grab—is less favorable. Here the good and bad are not always easy to separate. The evils of the edifice complex are the dark side of legitimate and desirable empire building, which may be appropriate for your contribution to company growth. This is not to suggest that when others are involved it's an edifice complex symptom, whereas in one's own case it's constructive expansion. The How to Use section ahead tells how to make the distinction between desirable and undesirable changes.

EXAMPLES

1.   Executive Marion Long discusses her department's need for more space and four more people with her boss. "I believe," she says, "in preparing for the future. And when our new customer service starts, we'll be all set."

Her boss knows two things about Long. First, she is very ambitious, and second, she thinks advancement in the company is like the gold rush, that is, you stake a claim to an area, then work it for all it's got. He tells her, "Marion, that new service hasn't been finalized. They're still checking costs and marketing."

"It can't hurt," she says, "to have a little extra capacity. And besides, we'll be prepared."

"Prepared," he says, "for something that is at least a year off, and may very well never happen. Besides, you're not using the people you've got as productively as possible." His answer, in short, is "No."

2. Len Grey's boss notes that Len has about 100 square feet of unused space in his department. "Why don't we put a copying machine in here and hire someone to run it," the boss suggests, "and start up that operation we've been discussing for special copying jobs?" Len Grey realizes it's a good idea. He should have been more assertive in pushing for its implementation as an extension of his responsibilities.

HOW TO USE

As has been suggested, managerial empire-building has both a negative and positive side. Here's how to eliminate the undesirable elements:

1. Recognize the ambiguity. No sharp line can be drawn between good and bad empire building. Although some of the symptoms of the unhealthy versus the robust activity are clear, don't be surprised to find you have to probe to make a satisfactory diagnosis. Both motivation and practicality are involved.

2. Burden of proof. Put the burden of proof on the would-be initiator by asking:

- "Why do you think it's worth doing? Exactly what do you have in mind?" If a ready answer is lacking, you're already ahead of the game by forcing subordinates to be realistic in their thinking.
- "What will the addition (of equipment, people, and so on) yield in terms of results?"
- "How do the projected results stack up against the cost?" Help the subordinate consider indirect expenditure along with direct, including everything from a stretch-out of managers' attention and effort to a blurring of the department's or company's priorities.

3. Get other opinions. Get the reactions and evaluations of others involved, particularly where the innovation might just as well become the province of another manager. This is desirable not only in order to provide a broader base for the final decision, but to minimize the possibility of foot dragging or even sabotage by those who may resent the change for one or another reason.

Some organizations encourage managers to actively seek expansion of their areas of responsibility. This policy, coupled with hard-headed and well-publicized methods of evaluation and reward, helps control the edifice complex.

▷ 90
Enjoying Your Job

CONCEPT

"I don't believe you're supposed to enjoy work," says one executive. He is not alone, and the belief goes far back in the history of our species. The distasteful association stems partly from Biblical strictures. In the book of Genesis the Lord tells Adam:

> Because thou hast eaten of the tree, in the sweat of thy face shalt thou eat bread, till thou return unto the ground.

There may seem to be little resemblance between the punished toilers of the earth pictured in the Bible and today's captains of industry. Yet executives sweat too, from the tension and physical exertion that their work demands. Happily, there is an opposed and more dominant view. "Work is a medicine of the soul," says the writer Grenville Kleiser. "It's more. It's your very life, without which you would amount to little."

Bertrand Russell asserted that people have an absolute need for fruitful activity: "Most of the idle rich suffer unspeakable boredom as the price of their freedom from drudgery. . . . Accordingly, the more intelligent rich work nearly as hard as if they were poor."

ACTION OPPORTUNITIES

Happiness on the job is a good in itself, and those who have the perspective and resolve can make job enjoyment a realistic goal. Most executives who have been interviewed on the subject reveal that professionally, they are doing what they want to do and that enjoyment is often come by naturally or by a small adjustment of attitude and priorities.

EXAMPLES

The following examples illustrate two different means by which enjoyment can be achieved:

1. Executive Carl Larsen and his wife return from their vacation in a Caribbean island paradise with Hilda complaining that Carl hadn't been able to relax for one minute. "I made more phone calls and sent off more telegrams for him than his secretary does in a week," she says. The Larsens get divorced a year later.

Larsen marries his secretary who apparently brings to their union a blueprint for a new Carl Larsen. As a result of getting himself an assistant, establishing a no-work-on-weekends rule, and being less of a Simon Legree with his staff—which has the effect of making them work harder—a draining job becomes an exciting game of many pleasures.

"Marion has been wonderful for Carl," his friends say, and she is.

2. "Mr. Larsen," Joe Britt says to his new boss, "this is my third night of overtime this week. I don't mind the work, and I'm sure you've seen that I'm a hard worker, but I have a wife and two kids, and we miss each other. I like my job, but . . ."

"Joe," Larsen responds, "bring in a temporary to help with the paperwork. I'm the last person who should ask you to kick your wife and kids in the teeth. You'll make a good executive some day." He doesn't say it, but he is thinking that Joe will do well because he has come to terms with his work.

HOW TO USE

"Thank God it's Monday," says one happy executive, not because things are unpleasant at home, but because they're so great at work.

A manager's job is more flexible than most, and can be patterned to give greater pleasure. The following suggestions may lead to worthwhile adjustments. You can get to the heart of the matter by a love-hate analysis, focusing on your own preferences, susceptibilities, and aversions. Fill out these two lists.

Your Love-Hate List

Things I Like about My Job: For example, working with people, planning and organizing your own work and/or your department's work, creating and innovating, lunching with colleagues, status, and so on, in your own words.

1. _____

2. _____

3. _____

4. _____

5. _____

Analysis: Review your entries. You probably noticed among the "for example" items leading into your list that the last two are conditions of work, while the others concern the work itself. As Frederick Herzberg and others contend, the deep satisfiers come from the work itself, while the "hygiene factors" prevent dissatisfaction. (See Herzberg's Motivator/ Hygiene Concept, page 26.)

Do your entries relate to the work itself or conditions of your work? A feeling of enterprise, meeting a challenge, and innovation can make Mondays the start of absorbing activity, and weekends a deserved period of relaxation instead of an escape from the grind. If conditions of work loom large, give them their due. If your review suggests the need for changes, look over your list and see how you can augment or extend the positive factors.

Things I Dislike about My Job: For example, relations with your superior, an aggravating commute, too many details, too much routine, too much pressure, no challenge, unsatisfactory staff, and no recognition.

1. _____

2. _____

3. _____

4. _____

5. _____

Analysis: Here again make the distinction between the work itself and your conditions of work. Are there too many, or key aspects of your actual work that rub you the wrong way? If so, are they something to talk to your boss about?

Job dissatisfaction may be caused by the equivalent of a pebble in the shoe; something insignificant may become a major nuisance, such as an undersized office or inadequate equipment. Especially important are factors that interfere with involvement in the work, such as a noncommunicative boss or poor staffing. Minimizing or eliminating such obstacles can clear the way. Such adjustments may not be simple, but take a fresh look at ways and means of making desirable changes. Your boss may be part of the problem, but may also be a source of help, or both.

In addition to the actions you may take as a result of your Love-Hate analysis, consider these additional possibilities:

1. **Increase the challenge of your job.** For example:

   ■ Seek to perform your job at higher levels of excellence.
   ■ Set yourself special projects, preferably something totally involving.
   ■ Be frontier-minded, seek the new, the leading edge of innovation in your business.

2. **Use your job for personal growth.** "I started this job when I was thirty-two and in the ten years since I've enlarged my vision of people, relationships, myself and my opportunities," says one executive. Every job is a growing experience. Try to make it more so.

3. **Make your job or career a personal monument.** The late Bennett Cerf, publisher and TV personality, created the phrase "edifice complex." Build one around your work, something of value and permanence you can be proud of, even if it will not endure the ages.

Boredom is the most obvious symptom of an unrewarding job. Executives have neither the time nor the self-indulgence to be bored. But a dull job can be revitalized by a fresh factor that adds zest to the workschedule. Accept joy on the job as the ultimate perk, pursue it as you would any other professional objective, and you may startle yourself and others with that happy sentiment, "Thank God it's Monday," an expression of anticipation, not relief.

▷ 91
Executive Dissent

CONCEPT

A top executive in a paper products company known for its advanced management approaches says, "In our system, dissent and protest have a natural place. The freedom to disagree, along with the privilege of being heard, is one of the great virtues of our way of doing things." Executive dissent is an idea whose time has come, bringing as it does a new vitality to corporate thought.

Expressions of dissatisfaction are not usually associated with managers. As part of the group that runs the company, it is assumed that they are more likely to receive complaints than generate them. But they may have cause:

- *Personal reasons.* An adverse salary decision, refusal of a requested privilege, disagreement with a performance assessment by a superior, protest at the rejection of an idea or proposal, are possible examples.
- *Principle.* A policy may be seen as being too strict or too lax, unfair to some groups, inadequate for the situation to which it applies, or its philosophical basis may be unacceptable. You may feel strongly enough to want to speak up.

ACTION OPPORTUNITIES

All managers can be affected by feelings of dissent, either in their own affairs or on behalf of subordinates, and sometimes they are the "management" to whom subordinates register their disagreements.

EXAMPLE

After a good deal of soul searching and sleeplessness, Roger Farr arranges a meeting with his boss in which he says: "Joe, I've been thinking over your final plans for the subdivision. If we go ahead on the basis you propose, it will violate everything this company stands for. Customers will lose on their investment, it will be bad for the surrounding community, and I'm not even touching on the question of legality. I believe we should shelve the project until we can come up with another plan."

The reasons for dissent may range from the trivial to the crucial. Somewhere along this continuum is a trigger point, a situation important enough and rousing enough to make a manager take exception to things as they are, and let his or her protest be known.

HOW TO USE

Here are guidelines for dealing with both sides of dissent, your own or from a subordinate manager:

1. Dissent need not be a dirty word. Some see it as as much a phenomenon of organizations as communication itself. Dan H. Fenn, Jr. and Daniel Yankelovich, in *The Harvard Business Review,* write:

> The military services, the Catholic Church, labor unions, professional athletics, and federal civil service —all have provided examples of dissent and even revolt. In such a climate, it would be foolhardy to cling to the hope that the corporation is immune.

Managements that develop concepts, attitudes, and procedures to harness rather than eliminate dissent, report that it becomes a vitalizing element.

A frequent obstacle to clear-headedness about disagreement is so-called "positive thinking." Positive thinking is fine until it is used as a club to crush negative thinking. Warning someone not to step into quicksand is a negative act with a positive outcome. And without criticism, improvement is often impossible.

2. Dissent as an organizational asset. One seasoned executive says, "Management often does not know best. And in the absence of questioning and criticism, decisions may be made without benefit of considered alternatives. I've found that ideas from unchallenged sources tend to be uninspired, repetitive, and second-rate."

Warren H. Schmidt, lecturer in behavioral science at UCLA, has noted some of the consequences of organizational disagreement, as follows:

- More heads become involved in handling issues, solving problems, and making decisions, with beneficial consequences.
- People are forced to question their assumptions and to search for new approaches.
- Better ideas are produced.

- Long-standing problems surface and are dealt with.
- People are forced to clarify their views.
- The tension stimulates interest and creativity.
- People have a chance to test their ideas and capabilities.

Schmidt's analysis suggests that organizations that question their assumptions—or permit them to be questioned—and subject ideas to criticism come up with fresh insights and breakthroughs that make for profitable innovation.

3. The psychology of confrontation. Whichever role you play in the meeting between dissenter and listener, it helps to focus on the interchange. Note these three factors:

- ***The dissenter.*** Not one but several emotions are likely for this person. They may include anger, defensiveness, and fear of consequences. Allies, adherents, and well-wishers may stand in the wings, to add a sense of mission to the mix.
- ***The listener.*** Insecurity may be triggered by what is seen as an attack, a threat to the manager's authority or judgment. Or anger and resentment may arise.
- ***The issue.*** The principle, policy, or action which is questioned may or may not be open to criticism. The dissent may be justified or unjustified. Often the face-off represents a conflict in values: the dissenter's against those of the higher authority. Then the adjudication cannot be made on the basis of right or wrong, but by the less clear-cut process of negotiation.

Realistically, the meeting is not of equals but between petitioner and judge, the initiative resting with the latter. Either as dissenter or listener, try to discern the attitude of the other person as a clue to your own approach.

4. The five responses. The meeting in which a dissenter faces the listener, usually a boss or other person in authority, may be settled by five different methods, adapted from the author's *Executive Dissent:*[*]

- ***Domination.*** Management assumes *it* is right and rejects the dissent. Usually this is done by justifying management's own viewpoint, and letting the person down easily or otherwise, depending on policy and feelings.
- ***Containment.*** The organization doesn't want to seem arbitrary, but still feels the dissent is undesirable. Rather than reject it, an attempt is made to water it down so that it can be easily dealt with. Typically,

---

[*] Uris, Auren (1978). *Executive Dissent.* New York: AMACOM.

this is done by mitigating, temporizing, and so on, by saying, for example, "It's only a slight difference in emphasis," "Essentially we're in agreement," or "If we had more time we might give your idea further consideration." The answer is still "no."

- **Capitulation.** One or the other party backs off. Usually, it is the dissenter that faces opposition strong enough to cause surrender. On the other hand, some people, like the proverbial 800-pound gorilla, can get anything they want. The engineering wizard, Charles Steinmetz, was a major force in the development of the General Electric Company in its early days. His criticism and arguments usually won the day. But the protester needn't be a genius or the president's relative. A better idea presented effectively can gain acceptance.
- **Compromise.** The protester's views are permitted to temper the policy, plan, decision, undertaking. This suggests that the listener is being fair to the dissenter, and responsible to itself. The result may be a strengthened hybrid.
- **Integrated solution.** The final judgment satisfies both parties fully, unlike a compromise, in which both lower their demands for the accommodation. (See The Integrated Solution, page 28.)

Executives who understand the constructive nature of dissent have a responsibility not only to accept it from their own subordinates, but to try to increase its acceptability in the organization. Dissent is an additional communication process which takes time and may arouse emotions. But it can have substantial benefits that touch on everything from the mental health of employees to improved creativity and initiative.

▷ **92**
Executive Job Engineering

CONCEPT

In *Practice of Management,** Peter Drucker says that to accept peak performance rather than happiness or satisfaction as an executive goal, "we have to go beyond Human Relations. By stressing human organization, we have to go beyond Scientific Management." And, "The first requirement for peak performance is the engineering of the individual

---

* Drucker, Peter (1954). *Practice of Management.* New York: Harper & Row.

job for maximum efficiency." In short, the job and the way you do it are the key. Acceptance of Drucker's idea can start managers on the road to superior performance.

Some executives hesitate to analyze their work content and methods, remembering the tale of the centipede who becomes unable to walk after trying to figure out how he does it. Contemporary businessese has a phrase that covers this phenomenon: paralysis by analysis. But for executives determined to realize their professional potential, analyzing what they do and how they do it is a prerequisite.

ACTION OPPORTUNITIES

Executives who are interested in self-improvement will find here the basis for reengineering their day-to-day job activity. The How-to-Use section will help you develop a performance profile in key areas, then interpret the results to evaluate and fine-tune as you wish.

EXAMPLE

Executive Sandra Lane has climbed the success ladder in her company and has just won her richest reward, the job of vice-president, Customer Relations. But even while exalting in her new status, anxiety poisons her triumph. She is not sure that she can cope with the new job's demands. She is aware of the Peter Principle, and suspects that she may be pressing hard against the ceiling of her capabilities. Even her old job had her staying late and working weekends. The new one will be no less demanding.

"Dealing with so many things stretches me thin," Lane tells herself. She is aware that her job consists of many facets, and that she does some things better than others. But like most executives, she has depended on pickup learning for her day-to-day "style." She starts reading books and articles on administration. Most are theoretical and abstract, but she does get a better view of her job and becomes more optimistic. "Practice makes perfect," she tells herself, but realizes that repeating the same wrong thing makes for nothing more than exhaustion. She wishes she could find a practical approach.

HOW TO USE

The following recommendations can help executives revamp their desk strategies and significantly improve their overall capabilities:

1. How are your basic skills? Rate your performance on each item below by placing a small circle around the dot in the appropriate column. The more accurate your answers, the more useful the profile that emerges. In the "contact" areas, items 6 through 9, rate objective results achieved as far as possible.

Your Executive Skills Profile

Skills	Rating		
	Low	Medium	High
1. Communications—written, face-to-face, phone	•	•	•
2. Planning—organizing strategies, tactics, tasks	•	•	•
3. Problem-solving—resolving operational obstacles	•	•	•
4. Decision making—choosing among possible actions	•	•	•
5. Detail handling—tying up loose ends	•	•	•
6. Upward contacts—with your boss, upper echelons	•	•	•
7. Peer contacts—with others at your level	•	•	•
8. Subordinate contacts—two-way, about the work, getting cooperation	•	•	•
9. Outside contacts—enlarging your professional world	•	•	•
10. Memory—your ability to recall facts, figures, faces	•	•	•
11. Speaking—in public, small and large groups	•	•	•
12. Writing—memos, letters, reports, for professional journals	•	•	•
13. Listening—to individuals, at group functions	•	•	•
14. Concentration—your ability to keep your mind focused	•	•	•
15. Negotiating—the ability to maneuver and persuade	•	•	•
16. Thinking—contemplating your work and its opportunities	•	•	•
17. Reading—profession-related magazines, books, newspapers	•	•	•
18. Routinizing work—forming constructive work habits	•	•	•

2. Develop your profile. Do this by connecting the dots as shown in the example:

Your Executive Skills Profile

	Rating		
Skills	Low	Medium	High
1. Communications—written, face-to-face, phone			
2. Planning—organizing strategies, tactics, tasks			
3. Problem-solving—resolving operational obstacles			
4. Decision making—choosing among possible actions			
5. Detail handling—tying up loose ends			
6. Upward contacts—with your boss, upper echelons			
7. Peer contacts—with others at your level			
8. Subordinate contacts—two-way, about the work, getting cooperation			
9. Outside contacts—enlarging your professional world			
10. Memory—your ability to recall facts, figures, faces			
11. Speaking—in public, small and large groups			
12. Writing—memos, letters, reports, for professional journals			
13. Listening—to individuals, at group functions			
14. Concentration—your ability to keep your mind focused			
15. Negotiating—the ability to maneuver and persuade			
16. Thinking—contemplating your work and its opportunities			
17. Reading—profession-related magazines, books, newspapers			
18. Routinizing work—forming constructive work habits			

3. Analyze your pattern. The interpretation of the profile above, that of a cooperating executive, is the next step in evaluating your own scoring.

■ *Overview.* To begin with, note that the eighteen skills fall into three categories: Management Procedures, Working Relationships, and Personal Skills. This division gives you an overview of how you are performing on three broad fronts. As the profile to the left suggests:

a. *Management procedures.* The executive shows a mixed result, but the three high items give this part of his performance a favorable tilt.

b. *Working relationships.* In this important area, the executive shows a uniform, passable performance.

c. *Personal skills.* These qualities that influence capability, are also mixed, but only two of the nine are high.

The recommendations that follow illustrate the remedial approaches that are available to him, and to you.

■ *Skills improvement.* Some managers may feel that the best step is to work on the weak spots. Perhaps. But consider the following:

a. *Skills rated high.* Skills scored at this level are the ones in which you have the strongest natural proficiency. There is a temptation to conclude: "Let well enough alone." But there is another reaction: "Since the highs represent natural strong points, a slight effort might make them outstanding." For example, you score high in communications skills. By concentrating on these skills, fine-tuning your writing ability, let's say, you may succeed at getting one or more articles published in a trade journal of your profession or industry, and become a "name" in your circles. This could advance your career in a number of ways.

b. *Skills rated medium.* These may be danger areas. For example, let's say your organization wants to enlarge its share of the market, and you and a peer are asked to submit plans of action. Your get-by level of performance may actually make you look bad against the other manager. It is thus advisable to examine your medium-rated skills to spot those which may one day prove a handicap.

c. *Skills rated low.* These may be the toughest to work on because they are the ones in which you may have the least natural proficiency. Improvement in these areas can mean an uphill battle, and you may have to go all out for a modest gain. But if improvement in the area is crucial to your needs, it will pay off.

4. Pinpointing your targets. Be systematic in going over your scores and selecting the skills that promise optimum results from your improvement efforts. The following questions can help:

- Quick kill? One manager worked in a company that was sponsoring a course on public speaking at night in its own meeting room. He registered fast. He couldn't lose.
- Which skills does your boss think would be your best improvement targets? (That's right, ask him.)
- Which skills do you use most?
- Which figure most in the operation of your department?
- Which are most important for your next career step?
- Which are most important for your long-range goals?

Workstyles don't just grow, they have to be nurtured. Just ask any high-performance executive.

▷ 93
Executive Toolrack

CONCEPT

"Man is a tool-using animal. . . . Without tools he is nothing, with tools he is all," says Thomas Carlyle. That statement doesn't apply to the bad old days of management practice. The early executives were content to work their way through their tasks with bare hands and brain. It was called "seat-of-the-pants" management. The contemporary executive, however, fits Carlyle's precept. A modern manager would no more think of making a crucial presentation without benefit of hand drawn, printed, or projected visuals than a carpenter would try to drive a nail without a hammer. Modern technology and a taste for innovation have brought an array of tools into the executive suite.

ACTION OPPORTUNITIES

Management tools can be used by managers at every echelon and for many purposes, from communication to work expediting.

EXAMPLE

Manager Len Vernon is the company's liaison with the building of a new annex in another state. He has been asked to supply progress reports to the president and other top executives. Along with his written reports he includes photographs, both from a distance and close-up, to show ongoing construction.

The camera, instant or otherwise, can illustrate phases of a machine taking shape in the engineering department, a new product developing in Research and Development, evidence of damage for which the company is filing an insurance claim, and so on. It can be a much used and dependable addition to the manager's toolkit.

HOW TO USE

A list of executive tools will help you check those you already use, and spot those that might be helpful. Any one of the following items could increase effectiveness in an important part of your work. As you scan the list, keep in mind your own operations and points at which one or another tool may be adapted.

1. Computer, either a personal, desktop, or terminal. There is no practical limit to the programs or applications to satisfy needs for information, calculation, visualization, record keeping, and so on.

2. Phone adaptations. You can have speaker phones that sit on the desk and require no handling, or conference hookups, automatic follow-up on busy signals, and timers on long-distance calls. Check your phone company. New services and equipment are constantly being made available.

3. Blackboards, easel charts, and the like. You can use these in your office as well as in the conference room, for problem solving, visualizing ideas, developing charts, and to illustrate problems or solutions. Some executives post information for subordinates on bulletin boards, and also use them for checklists, reminders, and data for ready reference.

4. Adding or calculating machines. (These are largely replacing the slide rule.) "I run up a column of figures a dozen times a day," says an executive to explain the presence of a calculator beside his desk. Whether it's a budget or a cost estimate, a machine will give you the data to fit into the overall picture.

5. Work tables. You can get them large, medium or small to use as a second desk, a clear work area, for quick huddles, blueprint examination, and so on.

6. Calendars. They come in a wide range of sizes, formats and applications. You can slip a thin plastic one in your pocket, hang a huge one on your wall, keep one with quick-flip pages on your desk for appointments and as a tickler file, or start off a new year with your secretary writing in key dates for appointments, and deadlines, one to twelve months ahead.

7. Timepieces. Wristwatches, which one day will sport a TV picture, already have alarm and stopwatch modes, among other features, including total accuracy. Don't forget desk and wall models.

8. Radio and TV. Broadcast media have news, weather, business reports, and music with charms to soothe a savage breast, or a relaxing executive.

9. Projectors. Slide or film projectors can be used as an adjunct to a conference, as training devices, and to screen industrial films and so on. And, of course, VCR's and video cassette players.

10. Dictating machines or recorders. The use of a recording device for dictation, sometimes in conjunction with a typing pool or word processing unit, is standard. Miniaturization makes them pocket size, for use in travel. And putting a phone conversation or phone conference on tape provides a useful verbatim record.

11. Cameras. Movie, candid, or instant development cameras can be used for getting visual evidence of a damaged shipment, the scene of an accident, and so on. One department head photographs a process at various stages as a training aid.

Your ingenuity in seeking uses for new tools and new uses for old ones—or even improvising some—can make a decided improvement in your executive operations.

▷ 94
Office as Tool

CONCEPT

Most managers would agree that an office must be functional. Some would add, "And attractive," to which others would respond, "That is a function, too." Viewing your entire office as a tool emphasizes its role as a facilitator of work, and can spark ideas for procedures and time-saving.

Interior designers and office-equipment manufacturers have joined forces to make both space and its furnishings productive. But you may have outgrown the thinking that led to what you have now. Like an old saw, your office might need sharpening.

ACTION OPPORTUNITIES

Offices come in all sizes and differ in their potential as work environments. One interior designer says, "Offices come in two sizes, too big and too small." But for many, the comment is beside the point. The trick is to make the most of what you have, while (perhaps) working toward getting something better. The office-as-tool idea can help all managers optimize their use of space.

EXAMPLE

"I want a promotion," Ray Fenton tells his wife, "not only for the money, status, and power. It is the one way I'll get out of that hole-in-the-wall I do my work in . . ."

Fenton may have a lot to complain about, and his list probably spotlights key points with which many executives could identify, covering everything from cramped quarters to being three floors away from his boss, with whom he must keep close liaison.

HOW TO USE

In thinking about possible improvements for your office as a work-facilitating environment, some guidelines:

1. Two types of offices. Offices fall into one of two categories, each of which suggests its own design needs:

- **The "living room" office.** Many executive offices are essentially living rooms with desks in them, and rightly so. The rationale is that the executives are at a high level and their work is essentially social and heavily communicative.
- **The executive workroom.** Tenants of the workroom office have responsibilities that require considerable administrative activity and fewer social contacts than those typical of tenants of the living room office.

2. Trappings of the living room workplace. The status of the executive may justify the phrase "executive suite," which it is in fact. It has its own bathroom facility, including a shower. And adjoining the main room may be one or even two satellites, one for meetings of boardroom size, and a sitting room for private informal conversations.

An executive vice-president of an international corporation has a crystal chandelier, Chippendale chairs, oriental rugs, and custom-made leather armchairs and couches. His counterpart in a smaller firm makes do with wall-to-wall carpeting, coffee table and sofa and chairs as a conversation pit, and prints instead of original oil paintings on the wall. In both cases the offices are planned so as not to look like working areas. The very absence of files, computer terminal and so on, signals to all who enter that here is an important executive, above such mundane things as paperwork, though this is often far from the case.

A special element is style. One Park Avenue advertising agency rewards its vice-presidents with their choice of decor. And so, on the executive floor a French Provincial drawing room furnished in white and gold stands next to an austere Japanese-style domain, next to an Early American living room with hooked rugs, shelves with pewter ware and maple bookcases.

3. The executive workroom. This room is work-oriented, and while it too may boast its own bathroom facility, its size is dictated by the occupants' actual needs as well as by their position on the organization chart. The regional sales manager of a major furniture company has a ten by ten nook in his firm's headquarters showroom. His job takes him out of the office a good part of the working day and he needs only a few tools and privacy for his indoor work.

In another case, the designer-partner of an office design and decorating firm has two-part quarters. The working area contains a drafting table and cabinets for blueprints, specifications, and supplies. The conference area is larger, and is equipped with a round table, chairs, and equipment for visuals and slide projection. When the executive, who frequently travels, is "in residence," the entire suite is his private office. When he's away, an overhead garage-type door rolls down, sealing off the workroom so that the staff has an additional conference facility.

4. Layout. This may require the attention of a layout specialist, who may go so far as to plot the executive's movements on a floor plan. Essentially, design should follow function. The workroom office is tailored to the job and workstyle of the executive. "An office should provide a setting to support and stimulate its occupant to maximum performance," asserts one specialist. In practical terms this may mean any combination of the following:

- A table instead of a desk
- A standup desk instead of the normal variety
- A telephone headset instead of a desktop phone, so that the executive can be on the phone and still be free to move around
- A bulletin board, easel chart, blackboard
- Projection equipment for visual materials, and so on
- Electronic equipment, from TV to computer

5. A special category. Equipment for communications needs:

- Face-to-face meetings? The executive will need seating for largest groups. One executive has a desk that converts into a conference table.
- Wired? In addition to state-of-the-art phones with conference and loudspeaker features, many executives need dictation facility, facsimile-by-wire, and so on.

6. Basics. Not to be overlooked are these basics to individual taste:

- *Lighting.* Sufficient without glare, wherever needed
- *Air conditioning.* Protection from heat, cold, airlessness
- *Noise control.* Insulation to keep out aural distraction
- *Color.* To suit the executive, from paneling to wallpaper
- *The executive desk.* The choices are broader than ever
- *Chairs.* "Executives who sit pretty last longer." The wisdom of an office furniture manufacturer, who should know. Comfort yourself.

▷ 95
Reading

CONCEPT

Executives as a group are avid readers, and with good reason: They have to be. Management is a profession of continual development, and practitioners must monitor the flow of business news, information, and comment or risk isolation by ignorance.

John B. Bennett and Ronald L. Weiher, in the *Harvard Business Review,* write, "In an average week, as many as 60 new books relevant to business may reach large university libraries. Along with the books come the current issues of some 900 serial publications relating to business, ranging from *The Wall Street Journal* and *Business Week* to such exotica as *Fertilizer Trends* and *Business in Nebraska.*

A recent Research Institute of America newsletter reports that the "boom in books about business and business people shows no sign of fading. We've talked with publishers, find most now regard those subjects as hot copy . . . For many of us in the private sector it means that public acceptance of business as an 'intellectual discipline' is growing."

Managers must read in their job—everything from memos and letters to lengthy reports. But it is the written word from outside that is the lifesaver needed to keep managers' heads above the knowledge flood.

ACTION OPPORTUNITIES

Reading is of two kinds, haphazard and organized. The first variety is better than none at all, but is inefficient and spotty. Executives have a lot to gain by regularizing their reading. Better coverage can be a significant professional assist.

There is another offbeat but substantial benefit from familiarity with the press of your industry and profession. It could make you not only a reader but a writer. Traditionally, business journal editors have courted practitioners in their subject area as potential contributors. If you know what is wanted and have a moderate writing flair, you may have the opportunity to produce articles that can get your ideas and name before an audience of your peers and build status and reputation.

EXAMPLES

1. Here is how one business newspaper advertises its worth:

The Wall Street Journal *minces no words. In a recent television promotion campaign, the message was that executives who read the* Journal *get to the top. Those who don't . . . are clearly in trouble.*

2. John Kaye has been put down in a meeting by a colleague. In an argument about a dissatisfied customer, Kaye contended that the customer was being unreasonable and should be told so. Harold London replied with an analysis of the problem and offered two solutions to get to the heart of the customer's objections. London carried the day, and it was no consolation to Kaye to be told by another conferee as they left the meeting, "He read all that in a piece on customer relations in the California Management Review. *Kaye found the statement interesting but not therapeutic, until next day, when he had his secretary order a subscription.*

HOW TO USE

If your reading is already systematic, see if an idea or two among those below might fine-tune it further.

Consider these key aspects of business reading:

1. Why? Those who feel the need for professional information, ideas, and opinions will make out better in their business reading than those who do it just to get on the bandwagon.

2. Why not? Even if you don't go along with *The Wall Street Journal* in its intimation of the unspeakable fate of nonreaders, check to see if any of these obstacles block your business reading:

■ *Not enough time.* This is valid, but perhaps systematizing your effort could get more return for time spent.

■ *Some of the material is inept or boring.* Don't waste time on the reading that's not paying off. There's enough topnotch material around. You can be choosy.

■ *Can't seem to find the good stuff.* Get help from your company or local library. A professional librarian can be a rich source of information and assistance in helping you hit paydirt.

3. What? Be clear on the three reading areas that impinge on managerial interest:

■ *Business.* There are a dozen outstanding publications, weeklies and monthlies, that deal with the "outside" aspects, like finances, acquisitions, mergers, reportage on the coming, going, and work methods of outstanding executives, competition, international trade, and so on. Contents are occasionally sweetened with articles in the management field.

■ *Management.* This is the inside-the-organization area, covering general management and administration, planning and strategy, marketing, the individual and the organization, interpersonal relations, control, production and operations, and management horizons (subjects such as corporate growth, policy, ethics, self-improvement).

■ *Professional.* Coverage is broad and publications number in the thousands. Almost every industry, business, craft, or specialty—woodworking, electrical engineering, and even fertilizer trends mentioned by Bennett and Weiher—can boast a trade press.

In addition, there are scores of business books, including novels in the business setting, and, as the Research Institute suggested, new titles are continually arriving at bookstores and libraries. Some become best sellers, a mark of their wide interest.

To screen what is available, or to track down specific publications, there are three standard reference sources: the *Business Periodicals Index* (BPI), and the "Business-Management" heading in *Books in Print* and *Paperbound Books in Print*.

4. How? You undoubtedly have your own personal reading style, and reading habits can be as distinctive as how you dress. But there are techniques that can get you more for your reading time:

■ *Mind set.* Philosopher John Locke, in "An Essay Concerning Human Understanding," wrote, "Reading furnishes our mind only with materials of knowledge; it is thinking makes what we read ours." Milton, in *Paradise Regained,* said somewhat the same thing, that we must bring "spirit and judgment" to what we read or we become "deep-versed in books and shallow in ourselves."

■ *Skimming.* Mitchell J. Posner, in *Executive Essentials,** gives some pointers on skimming technique:

Move your eyes in rapid broad sweeps, one line at a time.

Look for key words or phrases that convey the general ideas of the text.

Make notes, mental or written, of the paragraphs or pages your skimming tells you are worth returning to.

* Posner, Mitchell J. (1982). *Executive Essentials.* New York: Avon Books.

Posner also suggests these previewing tips: Read summaries; the eye-catchers, italicized and bold-face material, and chapter, sub-chapter, and section headings.

■ *Rapid reading.* An interest sparked by reports of great increases in reading speeds seized the business community some years ago. For the time-starved manager the appeal was almost irresistible, but drawbacks developed. For example, although speed could be improved, comprehension tended to suffer past a certain point. The payoff comes not from how fast you scan a page, but what you grasp. Another limiting factor is the nature of the material. Complexity or diffuseness slows comprehension and cuts down on speed as well.

5. When and Where? Reading time can be apportioned in two ways, regularly—for example, some managers incorporate their trade journal and business newspaper reading into their on-the-job reading periods—and opportunistically. These same executives would rather be caught barefoot in the office than reading a hardcover book, even one on a business subject. Hardcover reading is generally saved for home or travel.

For some, a solution to the time complaint is to set up a daily or weekly time and place, for example during deskside lunch, at home before retiring, and so on. Others find they can get through a lot of reading by filling in the interstices of their workschedules with a pile of prioritized material, the most important or interesting at the top.

6. And after. The value of reading depends on what comes of it, not only through mental enrichment, but in terms of action. Written notes of two kinds help maximize your investment in reading time:

■ *For filing.* Some of the facts, ideas, opinions or quotes that you want to retain might go into a file folder, a small box, or a desk-drawer compartment. Chronological filing may be the most trouble-free method, but use similar sized sheets to keep the file neat.

■ *For action.* Those notes that you want to use immediately—to show to a subordinate, to discuss with a colleague, or to send to someone "For Your Information" (FYI)—should be dispatched as soon as possible, to get them taken care of and out of the way.

Finally, to tie up a loose end from an earlier statement: If you want to get published, send what professional writers call a "query letter" to the editorial department of a publication that you think might be interested. Tell them your idea, explain who you are, and ask if they'd like to have you do the piece. If they're interested, they might agree and suggest a treatment or outline. Some publications are staff written, but even these might send a staff writer for an interview and credit and quote you.

▷ **96**
Self-Communication

CONCEPT

The executive's need for a closed-loop internal communication system is suggested in *Executive Excellence* (Alexander Hamilton Institute) by this author. After considering all other lines of communication (see Executive Communications Network, page 124), some key activities remain unincluded. On analysis, they prove to be the inputs and outputs *by* the executive *for* the executive him or herself.

The term self-communication identifies this vital, personal area. Like IBM's designation of the many procedures in the important activity now called "word processing," "self-communication" delineates executive procedures that might otherwise seem haphazard and unrelated, but once labeled, become a unified entity susceptible to improvement. The major areas:

- **Input for preserving information.** Everything from material you read and make notes about to a policy meeting you put on tape is included. How this input is made and kept available is a key to its usefulness.
- **Assigning yourself a task.** You jot a note on your deskpad: "Meet with Pat Smith to discuss the Adams order."
- **Internal dialogue.** Most executives are aware of the "conversational" aspect of making decisions. While few executives talk to themselves, evaluation of alternatives is generally a matter of you telling you the pros and cons of your options. It's an ongoing internal dialogue that ends when you decide.
- **Reminding yourself.** You put an entry on next Monday's deskpad page: "Send memo to Inventory Control about changed order points."
- **Idea production.** This aspect of self-communication can be one of your most crucial activities. You need an idea: "The warehouse mess is delaying service to customers. We've got to come up with a reorganization plan before the end of the month." You have just put yourself on notice to think through a problem by a specific date. You may meet with others for their input, but your own thinking—self-communication—will evaluate, refine, and finally resolve.

ACTION OPPORTUNITIES

Once you see self-communication as an identifiable branch of your communications network, you are in a better position to utilize it in the areas of:

- Systematizing your input of information and knowledge for your records
- Self-scheduling
- Prioritizing (see page 163)
- Using external aids for purposes of remembering
- Producing ideas

EXAMPLES

1.   Jed Sanders, at 65, is an effective manager but finds himself handicapped by increasing absent-mindedness. His doctor tells him its normal at his age, but he fumes at the nuisance and interference with his work. Eventually, he and his secretary arrange a system whereby appointments, deadlines, dates to start an action or project, make phone calls, or get off important letters are noted by him on a pad, slip of paper, or pocket tape recorder. These are all passed to the secretary, who arranges them chronologically on a "to do" form, a kind of sequential tickler file. The procedure reduces Sanders's forgetting to near zero.

Ticklers need no longer be manual files on paper. The computer offers a convenient assist. Some programs provide on-line real time help. For instance, along with storing in sequence the matters requiring executive attention, a beeping cue can remind you of a meeting in half-an-hour, along with a reminder of what to bring.

2.   Helga Andersen, head of Personnel for a medium-sized insurance company, begins to realize there is a communications weakness between top management and employees. She decides a house organ might bridge the gap, but what kind should it be? Her knowledge of company publications is too limited for her to proceed.

She digs into other companies' house organ experience, meets with editors of other organizations, and analyzes their publications. Eventually she visualizes the kind of house organ that would be most effective in her company, with its unique makeup of employees and their level of sophisti-

cation. It combines other people's ideas and her own, to print both personal and company-oriented features.

The self-communication principle she has followed is to use input to build up a subject area —by reading and conversing with experienced and expert individuals —which eventually becomes her mental resource: a mix of concepts, data, and experience which her creative mind now can use to produce ideas tailored to her specific needs.

HOW TO USE

The following guidelines can help you improve your self-communication skills and system:

1. Think of self-communication as you would any of the other channels, for example, upward to your boss, or downward to subordinates. Identify it, visualize your uses of it, and your strong points and weak points.

2. Use the tools and take the actions that can strengthen the system. For instance:

■ *Depend on memory supports.* Remembering can be done in various ways, from deskpad notes to tape recording, to dictating to a secretary. While the string-on-the-finger technique is fine for kids, executives develop other devices. One who wants to remember to take a special report home puts it in his coat pocket. Another attaches the report to the key he must use to lock up his office.

■ *The tickler file is standard.* Executives with a heavy load make sure this self-communication device is foolproofed by having it accessible at all times. At the ready on the desk, it must be checked every day. If you keep your things-to-do record arranged in sequence on a computer, the daily check must be regularized as an essential follow-up. Some executives put a subordinate in charge of the file, both to maintain it and to remind them when an action is due.

■ *Take advantage of your memory type.* Some people are visual minded, others remember better by ear. (If you have to write out a word to verify proper spelling, you are eye-minded. If you have to say it aloud before you can spell it, you tend to have an auditory memory.) Use the kinds of reminders that play up to your memory type.

■ *Converse with yourself.* "I give myself the best advice," an executive says. Some probing discloses the fact that he poses questions to himself, supplies answers, considers them critically, and eventually comes up with a satisfactory response. "And I'm not schizophrenic nor am I likely to be. I only do overtly what many people do subconsciously."

▷ 97
Self-Image Remodeling

CONCEPT

In *The Realworld Management Deskbook,** an iconoclastic view of management verities, this author presents a unique idea for executive self-betterment. The term "self-image remodeling" suggests that since the self-image guides behavior, you undertake to alter it to taste. The new image is one you design, adding or substituting the qualities that will make desirable differences.

The basis of the concept is this: The way people see themselves influences their behavior. This fact has been proved by studies in which school children who were told they were smart scored better than a similar group who saw themselves as second-rate.

Some management experts with whom self-image remodeling was discussed said, "It's just a tricky way of reinforcing one's confidence." That may be, but the use of your self-image can buttress you internally. You will be guided from within, an effective source.

ACTION OPPORTUNITIES

Executives seeking improvement in their professional capabilities and results may use this concept.

EXAMPLES

1. Gerda Rawls is due to see her boss for a merit-rating session. "I'm so bad in that type of confrontation," she tells her husband. But the night

* Uris, Auren (1984). *The Realworld Management Deskbook.* New York: Van Nostrand Reinhold.

before the meeting she undertakes a self-confrontation. "Listen here, Rawls," she tells herself, "You are bright, articulate and have been doing a good job. You should make out well." A critical change is taking place. She sees herself not as unsure and helpless, but as one who can deal with her boss satisfactorily.

2.   *Ralph Braden's office is always untidy, and he knows it. His secretary also knows it and tries valiantly to help, but confesses, "The best I can do is keep the piles from toppling." Braden admits glibly, "I'm a little disorganized." That's the way he sees himself, it's part of his self-image. He even gets perverse satisfaction from the admission, it seems to excuse the mess. Why expect neatness from a slob?*

One day he spends an hour hunting a file his boss calls for urgently. He finds it in his top drawer, where he had put it for safekeeping. He confronts himself: "Ralph, you're as capable of neatness as anybody. Messiness is a handicap." He and his secretary discuss a reorganization of the files and furniture. With the help of some musclemen from Maintenance he exchanges one small file for three large ones, and over the next few days all the stacks of documents, periodicals, and correspondence disappear into the drawers. He explains to his boss, "I discovered that deep down underneath I'm a neat person." The boss contributes a rubber plant and an Alexander Calder print to celebrate the new insight.

HOW TO USE

A person's self-image usually reflects feelings going back to childhood. And that image may persist despite education, experience, and acquired skills of high levels. Negative perceptions may persist in the face of success and the esteem of others: A capable executive may see himself as a neglected, put-upon child, and thus, needlessly limit his aspirations.

Remodeling a self-image may not be possible for everyone—some find it more difficult than others to outgrow the impressions and traumas of the past—but guides like these can help:

1. Bring your self-image into focus. We all have one, but it may be unclear or subliminal for some. It can be made to appear, however, by answering the question, "What kind of a person am I, really?"

The trouble is, some of us delude ourselves, and draw a highly favorable but inaccurate picture. Consider Scrooge. He thought of himself as a worthy member of the human race, going about his business successfully, free of the weaknesses of sentiment. Dickens helped him and us see the worthlessness of that image and the value of a warm-hearted and generous one.

An assist in sketching out your self-image is to make a list of qualities involved in your work, for example, ability to speak in public, persuasiveness, combativeness, judging people, working with subordinates, decision making, and the like. Then rate each on a scale of 1 to 10. From your scores will emerge a revealing self-portrait.

2. Be realistic. You are not after a self-image like Superman or Superwoman. A more reasonable goal would be to substitute desirable replacements for one or two qualities.

3. Look for a trigger—an imminent situation. For instance, the first of the two Examples concerned a critical interview with the boss, and the other, Braden's realization that he was suffering from a self-imposed chaos. In your own case, day-to-day pressures are likely to create crises better handled by a substitution of one or another quality of your image. It helps if your remodeling has application to a current situation.

4. Start with the simpler contradictions. If possible, focus on an aspect of your self-image that is farthest from the real you. For instance, there was a considerable spread between Gerda Rawls's original view of herself as timid and tongue-tied, and the self-confident, articulate, even persuasive person she actually could be. In your own case, such qualities as assertiveness, imaginativeness, ability to lead, and the self-assurance to stand up to a hot-shot colleague who is out to make you look bad, may replace qualities that suggest inadequacy.

5. Watch for the moment of truth. There is a point at which your remodeled self-image is put to the test. Be aware of it to firm up your resolve. The self-imposed tension should work on your behalf, which is typical when you mobilize your body's stress reaction for a trial.

Self-image remodeling works because you use reality to counter the obsolete and inappropriate aspects of your self-image. You won't become a different person, but you can change your behavior in desirable ways.

▷ 98
Self-Timestudy

CONCEPT

Some well-intentioned people writing on personal time control start by directing, "Make a self-timestudy. Keep a complete, accurate record of your time expenditures over a two-month period . . ." This is a monumental task, tossed off in a sentence. But a brief self-timestudy can yield useful information.

ACTION OPPORTUNITIES

This approach is for the executive who is interested in analyzing his or her work patterns, and converting the findings into time savings.

EXAMPLE

Executive Jane Blake, looking back at a week with too many matters put on hold, decides she has to find out where her time goes. "Maybe the load's too heavy," she muses, "or I'm not working efficiently." She reads up on time control. A few recommendations are helpful and she plans to apply them, but feels she needs more. She knows enough about industrial engineering to conclude that a timestudy of her work week might help. Her improvised approach lacks finesse, but not results. She is able to shuffle her routines around to her considerable benefit.

HOW TO USE

Three simple steps can give you the data and the means to optimize your time outlays. If possible, get your secretary or assistant to work with you, keeping track of your time expenditures and recording them.

1. Keep a record. Select a normal work week. If unexpected developments disarrange a day, restudy this same day during the following week. Note starting and stopping times of each activity, for example, "9:00 to 9:20, reading incoming correspondence; 9:21 to 9:45, talk to Smith about the new desk for my office."

Keep your record sheets close at hand. Make your notations as soon as possible after the task is finished. Don't overlook small items. A number of ten-minute jobs can account for a major chunk of working time. After you have kept the record for a week or its equivalent, and you feel it's representative of your schedule, proceed to the next step:

2. Analyze the data. Sort out your time expenditures. The chart on the following page suggests four general categories with a number of specifics under each. Add or subtract items according to your own time usage. Then total the subcategory expenditures, write them into the chart, and get a grand total for each column.

Contacts with subordinates	Time totals	Administrative matters	Time totals	Intracompany contacts	Time totals	Outside contacts	Time totals
Training and instruction Work assignment and discussion General personnel matters "Social" contacts Other		Correspondence Departmental progress review Planning Other		Meetings with boss Interviews and conferences Contacting other departments Other		Customers Suppliers Service firms Other	
Total: _____		Total: _____		Total: _____		Total: _____	

Figure 12. Time analysis form

First question to ask as you examine the figures: Are the time allocations desirably balanced among the four categories, that is, is there a logical balance between time totals and your priorities? Major totals for minor matters, minor totals for top priorities suggests reconsideration, possibly a change in procedures.

Am I devoting adequate time for communications with my staff, boss, and other executives? Low figures should be questioned.

Am I leaving sufficient time for planning creative long-range projects?

How about time devoted to the development of my staff, both as individuals and as a team?

Add your own.

3. Restructure time outlays. Your analysis can be used to revise your allocations and schedules. Rearranging a few key activities can make a major difference in efficiency:

■ *Eliminate time waste.* Perhaps unscheduled items, like interruptions, chew away the hours. Your "screen" may be at fault, either due to an easygoing secretary or your own failure to say, "Call me tomorrow," or, "Put it in writing."

■ *Another possibility.* Back and forth visits with subordinates lead to what timestudy engineers call "starts and stops." Perhaps group meetings can serve instead.

■ *Change the timing.* Can you benefit by switching some items from morning to afternoon, or vice versa? A daily progress check with assistants, for example, might go better the following morning, instead of at the end of the day, or the other way around.

- **Balance the pressure.** Shift low-priority and routine items to low-pressure hours of your workday. Your personal energy cycle may suggest changes. (See Charting Personal Efficiency, page 252.)

(See also Time Sense, page 294, and Time Scheduling, page 291.)

▷ **99**
Sensitivity Training

CONCEPT

The "human relations solution" in the last few decades seemed the way to go. Managers and their expert consultants felt that the problems of morale, job satisfaction, and productivity all come together in relationships on the job, especially between managers and subordinates. If managers' interpersonal skills could only be raised to a high enough level, the drags on individual and group effort could be eliminated, and the 50 percent efficiency at which employees were said to work could be raised to the point where creativity and productivity would go off the chart.

Although the goal could be readily stated, the stopper always came to this: Managers lacked the sensivity, not only to others, but to their own feelings, to deal effectively with personal interaction on the job.

Into this vacuum came a startling new idea, developed by the outstanding industrial psychologists Kurt Lewin, Kenneth D. Benne, Leland Bradford, Ronald Lippitt, and Alfred J. Marrow, among others. It was an educating technique known as "sensitivity training" (ST), "laboratory training," or "T-group training," and its aim was nothing less than to provide a benign and protected setting in which people in small groups could experiment and experience interactions that would reveal inner feelings, their own and others, so these could be examined, analyzed, discussed, and if necessary, "repaired," that is, decontaminated of counter-productive attitudes and feelings.

It was the National Training Laboratory (NTL), directed by Leland Bradford, that eventually became the center of the movement, exciting the hopes of management that at last science would solve the interpersonal problems of the workscene that they had previously only been able to describe.

The sensitivity training procedure itself is relatively simple. As described in *Behind the Executive Mask** by Dr. Alfred J. Marrow, a psychologist/business man whose company, Harwood Manufacturing Corporation, became a showcase for T-group success, the procedure is as follows:

A laboratory training course runs from four days to four weeks, although two weeks is most common. The T-group of about ten participants is the basic unit. No two members of the same company are permitted in a group, to bar any extraneous pressures, and participants have chosen to attend, some by suggestion of their company.

A typical enrollment for NTL at its facility at Bethel, Maine, numbered between 150 and 200. The start is an orientation session in which the attendees are given their schedules. Explanations and directives are kept to a minimum. Next, each participant turns up in a small meeting room with nine or ten others. One of the group is on the NTL staff, but at the beginning he or she is not identified. The reason is that the unstructured-group aspect is important to the process.

With no agenda, no leader, and no clear purpose, the members usually begin by asking, "Why are we here?" With no one to give ready answers, the participants are especially sensitive to one another's behavior, and to their own insensitivities and distortions. Their interest in fellow trainees is also heightened.

Interviews with ST graduates provide specific experiences:

In one group a can-do executive—head of personnel of a large midwestern paper products company—decided to take over. After half an hour of seeming aimlessness had passed, he confidently stepped up to the blackboard and wrote the heading, "Why We Are Here." Then he added: (1) We will work out an agenda. (2) We will elect officers.

He never got to 3. "Sit down!" a member called, and was echoed by a second voice. The would-be leader slunk back to his seat. Apparently the group was not of a mind to hand over its agenda or fate to a usurper. Later it was realized that the behavior of both the would-be leader and his critics reflected the freedom of the laboratory setting. None of the group members would have behaved this way back at the office.

A little later the group organized itself to the point of dispensing with the schoolroom setup of chairs facing the front of the room, and sat in a circle on the floor, where, after a while, the following conversation took place:

---

* Marrow, Alfred J. (1964). *Behind the Executive Mask*. New York: AMACOM.

Participant A (to B): There's something about you I don't like.

Participant B: Well, what is it?

A: I'm not sure . . . something about your size . . . yes, that's it . . . you seem so big, powerful . . . I'm afraid we might get into a fight . . .

At this point the staff member, a psychologist who had kept his participation to a minimum, started the group to probing the confrontation just enacted. Participant A became aware for the first time that he reacted negatively to burly, heavy-set men. With this insight he was able to understand why he avoided (or worked poorly with) men who seemed to be threateningly aggressive. And Participant B also developed a new insight. He learned how his appearance might affect other people, why they might become uneasy or defensive in dealing with him. He can't change his appearance, he decides, but he could tone down his approach to people. The group also benefits from the others' learning.

ACTION OPPORTUNITIES

Although some sensitivity-training activity persists, its major contribution lies in the past. Various dissatisfactions, which will be described shortly, weaned management from its original interest. Nevertheless, the importance of the movement is extreme. It became a high-water mark in efforts to cut through the knot that constricts human relationships on the job, especially those tainted by the inadequacies of managers' interpersonal skills. And it sought to do this by going to the root of the problem, the psyche of managers themselves.

Many T-group "graduates" extol sensitivity training as one of the great learning experiences of their lives. That it proved an incomplete solution to business needs doesn't detract from its personal benefits. This is an instance in which there is much to be learned from what some say is a "glorious failure." One executive refers to ST as "management's Camelot."

EXAMPLE

After reading the foregoing, you can probably devise your own examples, based on first-hand professional experience. But here is a simple instance that can be used to highlight the problem that sensitivity training aims to deal with:

*"You have to be more aware of your subordinate's feelings," an execu-
tive tells a rookie manager. "The new girl was ready to quit because she
said you made her feel stupid when she had trouble catching on to the
work procedure."*

The subordinate splutters, "But all I said was . . ."

"Did you feel she was stupid?"

"Well, no. Just a bit slow . . ."

The manager and the employee are in trouble because:

- *The manager isn't aware of his own feelings.*
- *He isn't aware of the feelings of others.*
- *He isn't aware of what he does that arouses resentment.*

HOW TO USE

The diminished popularity of ST makes it less likely that you can expose
yourself to its procedures. But that need not end interest in the process.
There is a great deal to be learned by understanding why, despite its effectiveness, it faded as a training method and proved only of limited value as a
remedy for interpersonal difficulties on the job. Note these points:

1. Although a high percentage of participants had favorable ST experience, there were individual failures. Some people reacted negatively
to the self-exposure aspect of the laboratory climate. And some were
not flexible enough to accept the demonstrations of their weaknesses of
values, attitudes, or behavior. These reactions ranged from clamming up,
and in effect being present but not participating, to actually leaving the
premises.

2. From psychoanalytically-oriented people came the criticism that
ST didn't take into account unconscious motivation as a shaper of behavior, to which psychoanalysis addresses itself. This opinion seemed at
times to be self-serving, as adherents of ST stated that in some cases
participants who had failed to benefit from therapy fared better in their
ST group than in one-on-one treatment.

3. More serious was the realization that even though ST did deliver
unquestionable benefits through insights into oneself and others, the
"new person" that showed up on the job—and indeed, at home after the
T-group experience—was out of tune with the unchanged situation. For
example:

Kate Gurney, a fiftyish assistant high-school principal, told a T-group
buddy, "I can hardly wait to get back to work. On Monday we have our

weekly staff meeting, with its dull dull discussions. When the molasses starts oozing, I'll let it go on for a while and then I'll stand up and holler, 'B——t!'" While her fantasy was a heart-warming display of a newly liberated spirit, imagine the destructive consequences of her behavior.

4. The staff at Bethel was fully aware of the problem of meshing new attitudes with an established climate. And efforts were made to help participants make the transition.

The final exercise of all the T-groups addressed itself to what was called "the shock of reentry." The objective was to prepare participants for the reception back home.

Simple role-playing situations were set up in which the graduate and boss, or in some cases spouse, confronted one another. People played in pairs, each individual taking turns with both roles. In one case the device was unsettling. A graduate, confronted by a boss who began to quiz him in a baiting fashion, suddenly burst out into a shouting rage. The initiates who witnessed the incident realized what had happened: The man, whose feelings had been loosened by his training experience, finally let go his long-repressed rage against his boss.

Despite the efforts of the ST professionals, in many cases the benefits of the training didn't help at work. In the world of the blind apparently the one-eyed man becomes an outcast.

Happily, the rigidities of the workplace have somewhat softened, as a result of enlightenments in society at large, and a higher level of management sophistication that has come with the advancing decades. Today's managers, by and large, are more adept than their predecessors, have become more aware—in part due to the ST concept—of the nature of the problems and some of the ways to deal with them interpersonally.

It should also be mentioned that despite its lessening influence on the workscene, the sensitivity training idea has been seminal. Under different names and auspices—encounter groups, personal growth groups, the human potential movement, Esalen, EST—the sensitivity training seed has sprouted widely. It was a particularly effective tool for helping the two great liberation surges, of blacks and women, make advances against entrenched attitudes. In communities, and on campuses, groups confronted themselves and each other to achieve better understanding.

▷ 100
Time Scheduling

CONCEPT

The executive job is prone to shifts of direction. An unexpected crisis or a change in priorities may send the day's agenda into the wastebasket. At least a tentative sequence of tasks should be kept in mind, however. A flexible approach is the obvious essential. You must be ready to set aside one task for a more important one, or to drop everything for an emergency. How you manage your task sequences is a major key to personal effectiveness.

ACTION OPPORTUNITIES

Managers must control time instead of vice versa. But remember, your particular use of time is bound to be unique, reflecting your individual needs and ways of adjustment.

EXAMPLE

George Harmin is distressed by the feeling that he is floundering in his job. Before he became a manager, time passed in the same routine, day after day. But along with higher status, more pay, and broader responsibility came a mix of activities that had him skipping about, trying to touch all bases, but often left with loose ends and partially completed tasks.

His boss, Jeff Rader, finally caught on to his problem. "George," he said at lunch one day, "I have bad news and good news for you. The bad is that you're the most overworked manager on my staff. The good is that you don't have to be. You must learn how to control your time. Our library is jammed with books on time management. Read one or two. Just thinking about it can make a difference."

HOW TO USE

The basic "rules" of time management are simple. As you go through the nine listed below, ask yourself three key questions that will help you

relate each rule to your own situation. Your objectives are better understanding and time saving.

"Does this apply to me?"

"How does it apply?"

"Can I use it to change my awareness or practices?"

1. The executive job is essentially nonroutine. While all executives
have recurring tasks—for example, they must cope with the in-box
regularly—many responsibilities are one-shot, are unexpected, or are
emergencies requiring immediate attention.

2. Consider troubleshooting standard parts of your job. You can't let
yourself become upset by interruptions or emergencies. In addition to
your own headaches, you often inherit those of subordinates. Helping
your staff members become independent can be a big time-saver.

3. Single time expenditures tend to be short. A study of executive
time shows that seldom do executives spend more than twenty minutes
on a single task. This fact partly accounts for "executive homework," the
many items in the executive briefcase that require hours of undivided
attention. On the job you can seldom tie yourself down for such long
periods.

4. Habits can save time. Repetitive tasks may be scheduled at the
same time of the day, so that they become habitual. Psychologists make
the point that habits are of two kinds:

- *Adaptive.* These are useful. For example, you check the mail
first thing in the morning because it often contains orders or requests
that influence the day's sequence of business.

- *Nonadaptive.* These are illogical and time-wasting. For instance,
an executive checks his mail first thing. But this delivery only contains
routine items. The second delivery usually has the communications
that require follow-up, which means he could save time by tackling
the in-box after the second arrival. Nonadaptive habits are often
adaptive habits that no longer serve a useful purpose. For example, an
executive reaches for a pencil in his vest pocket only to recall he no
longer wears a vest. Adopting habits that save instead of waste time
means eliminating nonadaptive habits and developing adaptive ones.

5. Watch out for time killers. A pet project, an intriguing but low-
priority problem, or the persuasiveness of an attention-seeking subordinate, may waste time. Spot and sidestep such diversions.

6. Find time for long-range projects. Thomas Watson's admonition to
his managers, "Think," is not misplaced. Thinking appears all too seldom in
executive activity. Yet planning, problem solving, and applying creativity

to objectives are often important. Indeed these are the payoff elements in your job. If such long-range matters are missing from your schedule, do what is necessary to include them, through delegation, a part-time or full-time assistant, and so on.

7. Use deadlines and subgoals. These not only keep you time oriented, but also add challenge and self-competition. Deadlines are sometimes built into a task, for instance, your boss may ask, "Let me know by 3 P.M. whether we'll be able to meet the Johnson request." Sometimes you can add your own: "Let's finish the report so that we can get it into the last mail pickup." Subgoals not only give you a time target, but also help you keep track of progress.

8. Do two things at once. There's a popular idea around that it can't be done, although a political figure was once damned by the accusation that he couldn't "walk and chew gum" at the same time. More complicated activities than that can be paired. The following illustration is no less apt for being in jest: An executive: (1) sits in his bathtub; (2) under a sunlamp; (3) reading a fistful of reports.

Here are some suggestions for getting a double payoff from your time:

■ *Design dual-purpose activities.* A manager screening resumes for a secretarial job watches for a highly qualified applicant who might serve as an executive secretary.

■ *Link activities that might be done simultaneously.* A manager supervises a subordinate who is preparing a report, catches up on his own mail, and discusses plans for the week with his assistant.

■ *Combine tasks that can be done at the same time.* A common time-saving practice is to bunch telephone calls or dictation.

Finally, distinguish between quantity and quality of time. Your effectiveness is not measured in hours spent, but by how you spend the hours. Time devoted to routines that could be done as easily by a subordinate are profitless. One inspired idea developed in a few minutes can make your company rich.

(See also Time Sense, page 294; Self-Timestudy, page 283, and Charting Personal Efficiency, page 252.)

◊ 101
Time Sense

CONCEPT

Some shortages come and go, but time shortage for executives is never-ending. Time control, accordingly, is a much covered subject in management literature. After decades of attention, books, articles, and seminars continue to be popular. One factor is often neglected, even though it is central to time saving, and that is the executive's own awareness of the passage of time.

ACTION OPPORTUNITIES

All citizens of the world of work operate under time pressure—hour by hour, minute by minute. By sharpening their awareness of these pressures, executives can heighten their sense of time and strengthen their ability to control it.

EXAMPLE

A and B are two executives with contrasting styles:

A. That he works under pressure is immediately obvious. He is always rushed, always late, seldom meets deadlines, and the end of the day finds him exhausted and wondering how he will ever meet the next day's obligations.

B. His workload is no smaller, and his capabilities no stronger than A's, but he always seems on top of his job, and finishes his daily stint comparatively fresh and ready for tomorrow's demands.

You won't be surprised to learn that B has a well-developed sense of time and its work content, while A labors in a kind of fog, churning away as well as he can at each task as it comes to hand.

HOW TO USE

Time perceptions are highly subjective. Yours can be shaped by the following precepts, which will help you develop a useful view of the time factors in your job:

1. Be a clock watcher. Check for the correct time during the day to know where you are. This will help you estimate time passage, expenditures, and progress through your schedule.

2. Keep a "task chain" in your mind. What will you do next, and after that? Is there a chore you can fit into the short span between a meeting with your boss and dictation? Before starting a task do you, perhaps unconsciously, answer questions like these:

- "Is this the highest priority?"
- "Is it the most convenient?" (One executive holds off going through old records—a hot, dusty job—till day's end, because he can then go home and wash up without a feeling of discomfort interfering with subsequent work.)
- "Can I get preparations started for a job I'll be tackling later on?" (Delegating the preliminaries to a subordinate is a frequently used means of saving executive time.)
- "Are my tasks scheduled at the optimum time of my energy cycle?" (See Charting Personal Efficiency, page 252.)

3. Watch out when time drags. This may be a signal of time waste and should prompt you to rearrange your task sequence and tackle a demanding task that will put you under pressure.

4. Take occasional breaks. A few minutes' relaxation can be like coming up for air, providing a refreshing change of pace.

5. Watch out when you feel rushed. You may be swinging along at peak efficiency, but it may also mean you are being pushed along by a task that doesn't deserve the all-out treatment you are giving it. Recheck your priorities.

6. Keep the end of the day in view. Knowing that you have just one more hour to go may suggest a rearrangement of tasks, so that those that can't wait get taken care of, and others are carried over to tomorrow's agenda.

(See also, Time Scheduling, page 291, and Self-Timestudy, page 283.)

Index